ROUTLEDGE LIBRARY EDITIONS: THE HISTORY OF SOCIAL WELFARE

Volume 4

LABOUR AND THE POOR IN ENGLAND AND WALES 1849–1851

LABOUR AND THE POOR IN ENGLAND AND WALES 1849–1851

The Letters to *The Morning Chronicle* from the Correspondents in the Manufacturing and Mining Districts, the Towns of Liverpool and Birmingham, and the Rural Districts

Volume II
Northumberland and Durham, Staffordshire, the Midlands

Edited, with an Introduction by
J. GINSWICK

LONDON AND NEW YORK

First published in 1983 by Frank Cass and Company Limited

This edition first published in 2017
by Routledge
2 Park Square, Milton Park, Abingdon, Oxon OX14 4RN

and by Routledge
711 Third Avenue, New York, NY 10017

Routledge is an imprint of the Taylor & Francis Group, an informa business

© 1983 J. Ginswick

All rights reserved. No part of this book may be reprinted or reproduced or utilised in any form or by any electronic, mechanical, or other means, now known or hereafter invented, including photocopying and recording, or in any information storage or retrieval system, without permission in writing from the publishers.

Trademark notice: Product or corporate names may be trademarks or registered trademarks, and are used only for identification and explanation without intent to infringe.

British Library Cataloguing in Publication Data
A catalogue record for this book is available from the British Library

ISBN: 978-1-138-20330-3 (Set)
ISBN: 978-1-315-45977-6 (Set) (ebk)
ISBN: 978-1-138-20740-0 (Volume 4) (hbk)
ISBN: 978-1-138-20750-9 (Volume 4) (pbk)
ISBN: 978-1-315-46213-4 (Volume 4) (ebk)

Publisher's Note
The publisher has gone to great lengths to ensure the quality of this reprint but points out that some imperfections in the original copies may be apparent.

Disclaimer
The publisher has made every effort to trace copyright holders and would welcome correspondence from those they have been unable to trace.

LABOUR AND THE POOR IN ENGLAND AND WALES 1849-1851

The Letters to *The Morning Chronicle* from the Correspondents in the Manufacturing and Mining Districts, the Towns of Liverpool and Birmingham, and the Rural Districts

Volume II

Northumberland and Durham, Staffordshire, the Midlands

Edited, with an Introduction by

J. GINSWICK

FRANK CASS

First published 1983 in Great Britain by
FRANK CASS AND COMPANY LIMITED
Gainsborough House, 11 Gainsborough Road,
London, E11 1RS, England

and in the United States of America by
FRANK CASS AND COMPANY LIMITED
% Biblio Distribution Centre,
81 Adams Drive, P.O. Box 327, Totowa, N.J. 07511

Introduction and supplementary material
copyright © 1983 J. Ginswick

British Library Cataloguing in Publication Data

Labour and the poor in England and Wales, 1849–1851.
  Vol. 2: Northumberland and Durham, Staffordshire, the Midlands
  1. Poor—England   2. Labor and laboring classes—England
  I. Ginswick, J.   II. Morning Chronicle
  305.5'69'0941   HV4086

ISBN 0 7146 2960 X (cased)
ISBN 0 7146 4039 5 (paperback)

All rights reserved. No part of this publication may be reproduced, stored in a retrieval system, or transmitted in any form, or by any means, electronic, mechanical, photocopying, recording, or otherwise, without the prior permission of Frank Cass and Company Limited.

Typeset by Input Typesetting Ltd
Printed and bound in Great Britain by
Robert Hartnoll Ltd. Bodmin, Cornwall

To H.L.B.
to whom so many owe so much
and I perhaps most

Contents

List of Illustrations ix
Preface xi

I NORTHUMBERLAND AND DURHAM   1

A general view of the Northumberland and Durham coalfield – duration of supplies – structure of the strata – accidents – background of coal trade – the strike of 1844 – a description of the coal country – a coal-pit – the underground features – daily life and toil of a miner – a colliery village – housing – accidents in coal mines – relations between employers and colliers – the educational, moral and intellectual state of the district – the family in the mining districts – the amusements of the miner – the superstitions of the mining population – regulation of output – evictions in a colliery village – miscellania – transportation of the coal to the market.   3

II STAFFORDSHIRE   81

The South Staffordshire Collieries: Introduction – the working of the collieries – the organisation of the mines – the daily life of the Staffordshire miner – ventilation in the mines – the Staffordshire collieries at night – housing – the educational, moral, and sanitary state of the population – the ironworkers of South Staffordshire – the truck system.   83

The Potteries: Introduction – the industrial process and wages – housing in the Potteries – the water supply – the coal-pits in the Pottery district – social condition of the population – the manufacture of boys' marbles – the Potters' Joint Stock Emigration and Savings Fund.   111

Newcastle-under-Lyme   136

III THE MIDLANDS 139

Nottingham: Introduction – housing in Nottingham – the water supply – the state of education and morality – the lace industry of Nottingham – statistical background of the lace industry – the lace-making process – the hosiery trade in Nottingham – its rise and progress – wages in the hosiery trade – location of the hosiery industry – the organisation of the knitting-frame trade – the domestic workshop – female labour – allotments for workers. 141

Derby: Introduction – silk manufacture in Derby – silk glove and hose-makers – a lace factory – "mending" – broad silk weaving – Strutt's cotton mill at Belper. 173

Leicester: Introduction – the sanitary condition of Leicester – industry in Leicester – fancy work 188

Index 201

Illustrations

Following page 84

1. An explosion in a coal mine
2. Interior of a coal mine in Northumberland
3. Various positions assumed by hewers in digging at the coal
4. Holing coal
5. Flint-grinding
6. A potter's wheel: the thrower, ball-maker and wheel turner at work

Following page 116

7. Putting manufactured articles into saggars
8. Placing the saggars in the biscuit-kiln
9. Printing blue-ware
10. Transferring the print
11. View in a lace-dressing room
12. Specimen of machine lace
13. Specimen of run lace
14. Lace-runners or embroiderers at work
15. Throwing or spinning by hand

Nos. 5-15 are taken from the *Penny Magazine*, Supplements for February, March, April and May 1943.

Preface

In the years between October 1849 and October 1851, a London newspaper, *The Morning Chronicle*, published a survey of the condition of the labouring and working classes in England and Wales under the general title of *Labour and the Poor in the Metropolitan, Rural, and Manufacturing Districts of England and Wales*. The country was divided into six broad areas – The Manufacturing Districts, The Rural Districts, The Mining and Manufacturing Districts of South Wales, The Mining Districts of North Wales, The Metropolitan Districts, and the towns of Liverpool and Birmingham – and the investigation into them was undertaken by specially appointed highly gifted professional journalists who brought their findings to the public in language at once clear and graphic and made a profound impression. Since then a number of social inquiries have been undertaken and more efficient techniques of investigation have been developed; but, even so, the *Morning Chronicle* survey of an emerging class must still be considered among the best.

Angus Bethune Reach, a young Scotsman from Inverness and on the staff of *The Morning Chronicle*, wrote on the Manufacturing Districts. His findings have now been brought together for the first time and published in the first two volumes. Volume I covers the northern textile districts of Lancashire, Yorkshire, and Cheshire. Volume II contains the reports on the Northumberland and Durham coalfield, the South Staffordshire collieries, the Potteries, and the lace, silk and hosiery districts of Nottingham, Derby, and Leicester.

I

NORTHUMBERLAND AND DURHAM

Northumberland and Durham

A General View of the Coalfields

In the north-eastern corner of England lies the great carboniferous deposit which supplied in 1845 eleven-twelfths of the entire mass of coal burned in the grates and furnaces of the kingdom. The boundaries of the great northern coalfield are mapped out with some distinctness to the north and west, but their southern limits are vague and unsettled, and the eastern frontier of the mineral region lies deep within the German Ocean. Speaking in general terms, the Northumberland and Durham coalfield is bounded to the north and south by the Coquet and the Tees. The Coquet is a Northumbrian stream, rising amid the southern slopes of the Cheviots and joining the ocean some twenty miles north of Tynemouth. The Tees separates Durham from Yorkshire. Between these rivers run the Tyne and the Wear, draining the broadest and richest portions of the coalfield, and on their banks lie scattered the oldest, deepest and most extensive pits. Like almost all coal deposits, the strata forming the Newcastle field "dip" to a common bottom, somewhat in the manner of a basin, and of this basin, the centre, and therefore the deepest point, lies near the sea coast hard by Sunderland.

Here are situated the deepest mines, one of which, that of Monkwearmouth, is the most profound excavation in the world, sinking more than 1,500 feet beneath the level of the sea. The centre of the coal basin being thus near the centre of the ocean, and the line of coast running a pretty accurate transverse, it follows that, so far as we know, the land and sea divide into two pretty equal portions the great northern coalfield. Twenty miles westward from Tynemouth, the lower strata of course forming the under edge of the basin, begin to rise up into day; and it is probable that twenty miles eastwards of Tynemouth, the other extremities of these strata heave themselves upwards to the bottom of the ocean. The landward portion of the coalfield thus forms a sort of half oval, attaining its greatest breadth not far from the spot where the Tyne intersects its inland boundary. The length of the Newcastle field, or at all events the workable portion of it, is about 44 miles, and the greatest breadth about 20.

A glance at a geological map will show a great slice of the shires of Northumberland and Durham within which the coal strata extend. This slice includes about one third of the seaward face of the second. From its northern extremity at the mouth of the Coquet, the coalfield strikes gradually inland, running at an acute angle with the coast. From its southern angle, about Barnard Castle on the Tees, the precious mineral runs seaward, most at right angles to the coast line, being hereabout more or less overlapped by vast layers of magnesian limestone – beneath which it is now demonstrated that the coal extends to an unknown distance to the southward. Following the landward boundaries of the basin topographically, they may be described as commencing on the Coquet, and passing southwardly and westwardly in the vicinity of the Northumbrian towns of Acklington, Morpeth, Prestwich, Callerton, Heddon-Ovingham, Mickley and Newlands. Here the Tyne divides Northumberland from Durham; and passing into the latter county, we find the coal line stretching past Heyleyfield, Wolsingham, and Redburn to Barnard Castle where it forms an angle and runs in an undulating line, past Bishop Middleham and Castle Eden to the sea.

Coal strata, indeed, extend to the southward of this last stretch of boundary, but the workable part of the field lies north of it. The reader will thus perceive that the northern coalfield is an irregular, but (on the whole) oval space – the greatest portion of it to the west of high water mark, and that portion watered by two great rivers, bounded by two less important streams, and containing the smaller shipping stations of Amble and Blythe, and the greater shipping depots of Shields and Newcastle on the Tyne, Sunderland upon the Wear, Hartlepool and Stockton.

I have said that the coal strata dip in a basin-like shape, and that the centre of this basin, and therefore the centre of this coalfield lies near Sunderland. It will follow as a general rule that the deepest pits have been sunk upon the sea coast of Durham. Following the shore from the northern to the southern extremity of the field, the depth to which pits have been sunk so as to command good seams is as follows: In Northumberland the Coquet pits average 80 fathoms, the Cowpen pits 100, the Hartley 80, and the Whitby 60. In Durham at South Shields, coal is brought from a depth of 200 fathoms, at Monkwearmouth from a depth of 263 fathoms, at Marton Winning from 220, and at Castle Eden from 150 fathoms. Several of the southern and eastern collieries are situated upon the overlapping strata of magnesian limestone, which here intrudes into the coalfield. It was long thought that where the limestone began, the successful search for coals would end. This was the favourite scientific theory of which Professors Sedgwick and Buckland were the chief expounders. Practical miners, however, have demonstrated the fact to be otherwise. At Hetton 156 feet, at Monkwearmouth 200 feet, and at Haswell 280 feet of solid limestone were pierced through before the adventurers arrived at coal seams extensive enough to be profitably worked.

The basin-shaped strata of coal are divided from each other by great layers of sandstone and bituminous clay. On a rough calculation, there may be about eighty distinct beds of coal, one lying beneath the other, and all of them as a general rule, dipping in a similar direction. Out of about 1,700 feet penetrated, it is calculated that the various layers of coal make up an aggregate bed of 24 feet in depth. The different strata are of all degrees of thickness, from more than six feet to less than six inches.

Of course the very thin strata count practically for nothing; they cannot be worked. Of the principal layers, that called the High Main, from which the original Wallsend coals were dug, is about six feet in thickness. The Low Main is about six and a half feet; the Bensham seam is four feet; and the Coalyard seam three feet.

These layers of coal must not be supposed to extend to uniform sheets across the whole field. Great convulsions of the earth have broken and scattered them – flung them at one point and ground them down at another. Indeed, it often happens that with the change of level the quality of the coals changes also. Thus in the valley of the Tyne, a particular seam, called the Low Main, furnishes a species of coal used for furnace purposes, having a splinty fracture, little bitumen, yielding a rapid although not a lasting heat, and depositing a quantity of white ashes. This is the class of mineral called steam coal; but the vein which furnishes it, in pressing south, acquires another quality, takes another name, and under the titles of Hetton's, Lambton, Stewart's etc, commands the highest price as a household coal in the London market. As a general rule, the deeper a seam runs, the higher becomes the quality of the coals. In spite of this however, it often happens that a seam running still lower furnishes an inferior species of mineral. So far as the nature and the quality of the coals, the production of the Newcastle field can be topographically arranged. I have reason to believe that the following classification can be relied on. The main seams of the Tyne, the Wear, and the Tees, and the Hetton seam of the second river, furnish the coals best adapted for household purposes. The best gas and coke coals come from the mines to the south-west of Newcastle, in the vicinity of Durham and Chester-le-Street. The Northumberland coals, as well as the Low Main of the valley of the Wear, are those best suited for steam purposes.

Duration of Supplies

The probable duration of the supplies afforded by the coalfield of Northumberland and Durham is perhaps, to us, not a very practical, but it is a very interesting, question and a communication professing to give a general prefatory view of the coal trade would hardly be complete without some reference to it. In 1829 and 1830 two parliamentary committees sat upon the coal trade, and calculations as to the probable duration of the supply from the Durham and Northumberland field was laid before each. Dr. Buckland was one of the intimators. He admitted that his calculations were "vague and conjectural", and he founded them upon a basis which has since been practically demonstrated to be erroneous. Dr. Buckland believed that beneath the masses of limestone which formed the old south-eastern boundaries of the basin no coal would be found, and he fixed the probable duration of the supply to the northward and westward at about 400 years; taking the quantity of the mines to be annually brought to the surface at the amount dug up during the year previous to his calculations. Other and more practical estimates fixed a far longer date to the era at which the Northumbrian and Durham mines will become unworkable. Mr. Buddle estimated the average thickness of all the coal seams in Durham at twenty-five feet eight inches, and of all those in Northumberland at twenty-one feet—the calculation, taking it in connection with the comparative extent of each field, giving an average thickness of twenty-four feet over the whole coal basin. But of the twenty-four feet, a considerable proportion is made up of beds only a few inches or perhaps a foot or two thick and therefore practically unavailable. Mr. Hugh Taylor, a gentleman of vast practical experience, estimated the depth of coal over the whole field as eight feet of available mine—a calculation which, taking the vend of 1829, would give us 1727 years ere we shall have exhausted the Great Northern field.

Later calculations have somewhat shortened the period, because they are founded upon the supposition of an increasing vend. An estimate, drawn up on high practical authority, computes the extent of the coal area in 924 square miles. The mean thickness of the mineral is taken at eighteen feet. To make allowance for what are called "denudations"—that is, spots where strata have broken entirely off—three feet are allowed, leaving the net thickness fifteen feet. But still further reductions have to be made for minor obstacles such as "dykes" and "troubles", by which the level of a seam is suddenly changed and also for the impossibility, in all cases, of working out the entire mass of coal. For these drawbacks, the estimator gives up one third of his calculated available thickness, leaving finally a depth of ten feet of coal extending over a superficies of 924 square miles. The produce would be about 9,107,000,000 tons of coal. From this there being subtracted 1,517,900,000 tons as already excavated, the results would be about 7,590,000,000 tons which at the consumption of 1837 would give us a supply for 1,480 years. Let the precise period, however, be what it may, the majority of calculators estimate the time during which the yield of coals in the Newcastle field is likely to last is over one thousand years.

Structure of the Strata

I have mentioned various irregularities in the lie of the strata. These are known to miners as "faults", "troubles", "hitches" and "dykes". Sometimes a vein of stone suddenly intersects the seam. Sometimes it breaks off short, and then continues at a different level either above or below. Two principal dykes, or sudden breakings off and changes of level, intersect the northern coalfield, both of them running in a general easterly direction. The Great Dyke flings the seams principally worked near Newcastle and North Shields, including Wallsend, perpendicularly down to an extra depth of 130 fathoms; so that two collieries may be working the same seam within a quarter of a mile of each other, but at a difference in depth of from 90 fathoms to 130 fathoms perpendicularly. The low level extends on the northern side of the dyke. The other principal phenomenon of the seam is the Hemerth dyke south of which the main seams suddenly rise 25 fathoms. These dykes are considered to be on the whole advantageous rather than otherwise to the miner. Sometimes, indeed, the great convulsive movements of the earth, of which they are the tokens, have sunk masses of coal to an impracticable depth, but they have as often upheaved seams to within a working distance of the surface. The Great Dyke has been useful in preventing the Wallsend seam from "cropping out", that is, appearing at the surface, in which case masses of coal now available would have been long ago wasted by the action of the elements.

The operations of the pitmen are of course frequently impeded by springs of water, which were it not for the systems of pumps continually kept at work would gradually fill up and "drown" the mine. In some pits the amount of water present is trifling. Throughout the extensive workings of the Gosforth Colliery embracing dozens of miles of underground galleries, only a few gallons per minute distil. Other pits are very watery. Mention was made before a parliamentary committee of a mine, the weight of water lifted from which was just eighteen times that of the coals. At Friars Goose Colliery, 1,000 gallons per minute are pumped out, or above 6,000 tons per day—the weight of coals extracted being from 250 to 300 tons per day; and when the Haswell pit was being sunk beneath the magnesian limestone, the engine pump drew from the earth no less than 27,600 tons of water daily. These springs if arising from beneath a certain depth, are uniformly salt. Where the impregnating matter lies is a mystery, as no indication of rock salt has ever been discovered near a coalfield. In some mines however the water which trickles far down amid the coal seams is three times as salt as the sea. This is the case in the St. Lawrence Colliery. At several of the pits, the saline springs are so copious that salt works have been established in the vicinity. At Birtle Colliery, near Chester-le-Street a runnel of salt water was discovered in 1794, producing about 1,100 gallons per hour. At Lambton Colliery, at the south, and at Walker Colliery, close to the Tyne, salt works are also in operation.

The temperature of coal mines rises in proportion to the depth—the deepest parts being of course the hottest. Much necessarily depends upon the efficiency of the ventilating apparatus; but the following statement of temperatures in and about the Jarrow Pit gives an idea of the general average proportions of atmospheric heat at different depths:

At the surface	46 degrees
At the bottom of the shaft, 146 fathoms	61 degrees
Returned air after having traversed the workings	75 degrees
Engine boiler house, 700 yards from the shaft	144 degrees

All coal pits are ventilated upon the simple principle of creating a draught of air, by means of a great furnace kept constantly blazing near the bottom of one of the shafts. The details of the contrivances in use I shall state, when, after having, as I am now striving to do, given the reader a general idea of what the coal district and the coal trade are, I come to describe in all their minutiae, the appliances and the working of a pit.

In sinking a coal mine, the object of the engineer is not, as might be at first supposed, to come up the seam at its highest elevation. On the contrary, he digs his shaft where he has reason to believe that the bed dips most deeply. Having reached the coals, he then works upwards, and gains the advantage of inclines, down which his laden waggons run to the bottom of the shaft. The old manner of working a seam, and that still practised in Scotland, is called the "long-wall system"—in which the miner digs almost the whole mass of coals and supporting the roof of the hollow thus formed with wooden props, so long as he is digging in it, and then when his portion of the seam is exhausted, withdrawing the props, and leaving the undermined soil to collapse behind him. The manner of working adopted in the Newcastle and Durham field, is the withdrawal of the mineral in passages crossing each other at right angles, and between which square masses of coal (called pillars) are left. The seam is thus honeycombed, and when the process is complete throughout its whole extent, the miner retraces his steps, and cuts away as much of the pillars as he can with safety to himself, leaving the roof to fall in, and the exhausted part of the mine to become a series of crumbling caverns, often filled with stagnant masses of firedamp.

Accidents

The accidents in mines produced by atmospheric causes, are usually most numerous in warm weather, because the temperature of the air of the pit being then more equable, the difficulty of causing a column of fresh air to descend is very much increased. Out of seventy accidents, causing the loss of nearly a thousand lives, there have occurred—

In the winter months	8 explosions
In the spring months	13 explosions
In the summer months	20 explosions
In the autumn months	30 explosions
Total	71 explosions

In all deep mines, and more especially in working at a distance from the shaft, the Davy lamp is uniformly used. It will, however, astonish many persons to learn that during the eighteen years previous to 1816 when the safety-lamp was introduced, the loss of life in the counties of Northumberland and Durham by explosion was 447, whereas during the 18 years subsequent to 1816, the amount of life lost in the same way was 538—the difference being accounted for by the working of many "fiery collieries", previously inaccessible; by the neglect and carelessness of the workmen themselves in the management of their lamps; and by the too frequent relaxation of ventilation measures that were previously rigidly carried into effect.

With respect to accidents of all kinds in collieries, I transcribe a table given among the results of one of the parliamentary inquiries into the subject, detailing the number of fatal accidents during the year 1838, and applying to 55 mining districts:

By falling down shafts	63
Breaking of ropes	1
During the time of ascending and descending shafts	10
Drowned	22
Fall of stones and coals	97
Various injuries in coal-pits	43
Explosions of gas	88
Explosions of gunpowder	4
By traffic and waggons	21
Total	349

For the purposes of ascending and descending into mines, wire-ropes are now coming into general use, and an ingenious invention, which I shall afterwards describe with the fulness which its importance deserves, has lately been patented, the object being to prevent loss of life in case of breakage of the rope drawing the buckets up the shaft.

As a general rule the mines in the coal district of Northumberland and Durham are worked by lessees, either companies or individuals, who rent the royalty, including everything beneath the surface, from the proprietors. The lessees have generally the power to vacate the colliery by giving a year's notice. They were bound to leave the pit in an open and tenantable state, and they are liable for all damage done to the surface in the course of working. The principal coal-pits worked by and for behoof of their owner, are those belonging to the Marquess of Londonderry and the Earl of Durham. The engagements made with pit-hands are always by the month, with an occasional stipulation for a certain number of days' work, greater or less, according to the season and the state of the market. The Miners' Union in the Newcastle district was almost totally overthrown by the great strike of 1844, which exercised a very important influence on the trade.

Background of the Coal Trade

The rise and extent of the great traffic in question, the amount of capital which it uses, and of labour which it employs, I shall now statistically sketch. As early as the thirteenth century, a royal charter enabled the "good men" of Newcastle to raise and dispose of coals, and the revenue of the town, principally derived from the sale of the mineral, soon amounted to £200 a year. In the course of the next century, vain efforts were made to put coal-burning down, on account of such fires lading the air with noxious vapours; and prohibitory duties were placed upon the export of the mineral to all continental ports, save Calais, then of course an English garrison town. The coal-pits, however, continued to increase and flourish; and as the ancient forests were consumed, "fears" pretty well grounded began to be entertained that "sea-cole will be good merchandise even in the Cities of London." In the reign of Elizabeth the price of coals in London was 9s per chaldron of six bolls. This was a monopoly price—for the right of working coals in the North was then possessed by an incorporated guild of "hostmen", whose proceedings caused frequent parliamentary interference. At this time the duty on exported coal was 5s per chaldron. In 1515 the coal trade employed 400 sail of ships, one half of which carried the mineral to the Thames; and as early as the reign of James I the coal duty of the town of Newcastle produced to the corporation a revenue of £10,000 per annum. In the time of Charles the First, coals for the first time became the almost universal fuel of London; and one of the most unpopular acts of the king was granting a new monopoly in the article. The selling price in London under this charter was 17s per chaldron in summer and 19s in winter. There were now employed in the collier trade 2,000 seamen, being not quite a fourth of the whole number in the kingdom. The trade suffered cruelly in the wars of the Commonwealth; and it was not until the Restoration that Sunderland became an important place. In 1676, the coal shipping of the Tyne was estimated at about 80,000 tons, of which a considerable proportion was foreign-built. Waggons and waggon-ways, the rude form of railroads, had already come into operation both above and below ground; and the right of way from the pit to the "staith", or wooden wharf, where the coals were shipped was rented at the dear rate of £20 per annum per rood. During the rise of the trade it was harrassed by duties perpetually fluctuating, and by monopolies which by increasing the price, diminished the consumption.

At the beginning of the last century coals sold in London for 18s 6d per chaldron, and the masters of the Trinity House estimated that 600 ships, able to carry on an average 80 Newcastle chaldrons, were necessary for the conveyance of the mineral between the Tyne and the Thames. There were at this period about 1,600 "keel" or barge men employed on the former river. In 1714 the first rude steam-engine north of the Tyne began to work, and within a few years the new machines were in common use for pumping water from the seams. The mines now began to grow individually great and important. Some employed from 600 to 700 carts and from 300 to 400 pitmen. The engines were gradually improved, and the piston rods gradually lengthened; and in 1764 the coast trade from the Tyne was 20,000 chaldrons, and the foreign trade 40,000. In this year, 3,727 vessels coal-laden cleared from the river, and 99 steam-engines on the Newcomen principle were at work throughout the valleys of the Tyne and Wear. In 1772, no less than 5,585 ships carrying 330,200 tons of coal left the former river. The wages of seamen at this period for the London voyage was £3 10s.

The beginning of the present century witnessed some of the greatest fluctuations which have occurred in the trade, with reference to both masters and workmen. In 1804 there was a mania for coal-digging, and a general scramble for workmen. Previously to that time it had been usual to bind pitmen for the twelvemonth, and to give them two or three guineas as binding or bounty money, at the season at which the annual engagement took place. In 1804, the binding money rose to twelve or fourteen guineas on the Tyne and to eighteen guineas on the Wear. Drink flowed abundantly on all sides, and the pit districts were the scene of one vast orgy— the regular wages being raised at the same time, upwards of 40 per cent. The consequence was a speedy overflow of labour. Workmen of all kinds flocked to obtain employment in the pits, and gradually the wages settled down to their former level. No binding money whatever is now paid. In 1810 the Durham water sale collieries employed 7,011 men, and the land sale collieries 382 men. The keelmen on the Wear amounted to 750 and the masters, trimmers, and fillers to 507; and the same classes of individuals employed by the Durham collieries in the Tyne were reckoned at more than 2,000. In 1816, the introduction of the safety lamp led, as I have stated, to the renewed working of many "fiery" pits, formerly considered unapproachable; and in 1826 the pitmen's union was founded. The progress of the trade will appear from the following statement of chaldrons exported from the Tyne and the Wear.

NEWCASTLE

In 1810 there were exported 649,552 chaldrons
In 1820 there were exported 801,309 chaldrons
In 1828 there were exported 784,407 chaldrons

SUNDERLAND

In 1810 there were exported 372,622 chaldrons
In 1820 there were exported 430,397 chaldrons
In 1828 there were exported 532,508 chaldrons

In the next year Newcastle was the second port in the kingdom, reckoning 967 ships of 202,379 tons; while Sunderland had 624 ships of 107,628 tons. In 1832 occurred one of the great pitmen's strikes the consequence of which was the introduction of a vast quantity of hitherto rural labour into the trade.

To this era a number of good authorities look back as the point subsequent to which the amount of labour in the trade became permanently too great for the demand, and the quantity of coal raised too great to allow of the profits formerly made by the traffic. In 1844 a second great and ineffectual turn-out took place, the yet existing effects of which are still displayed in the dissolved colliers' union. The number of collieries and of colliers, in the counties of Northumberland and Durham, as reported to the Coal-trade Office at Newcastle in 1844, was as follows. In the valley of the Tyne, including the Blyth pits, there were 66 collieries, employing 16,515 hands; on the Wear there were 31 collieries, employing 13,172 hands; and on the Tees 22 collieries employing 4,211 hands.

The engineering progress of the coal trade went hand-in-hand with its commercial advancement. The early wooden waggon-ways followed the natural undulations of the country. The waggons had wooden wheels studded with nails, and accidents were constantly occurring from their breaking away down the steep hills, up which they were dragged with great difficulty and labour. Cast iron rails were introduced in 1767, and some ten years later metal tramways were employed underground. Coals were first pulled to the surface by horse machines called "gins", and the drainage was effected by chain pumps, wrought by horses or water-power, and sometimes by strings of buckets working on the principle which may now be seen in dredging machines. By 1720, engines for draining, wrought by steam, had come into common use. It was about the middle of the last century that coals began to be screened, so as to divide the smaller sort from the more valuable lumps. Hewers' wages at this period ranged from 1s 6d to 1s 10d a day; they now vary from 3s to 4s. The hewer, as the reader will afterwards understand, is always paid by the piece, and about a hundred years ago the recompense for hewing was about 1d per peck of coal worked. The putter, who then conveyed the coal to the bottom of the shaft, made about 10d per day – the wages of little boys working as "trappers" at the present time.

The pits, until the application of steam, were mere surface scratches, compared with the depth to which they now extend; sixty fathoms was the utmost depth then attained. Ventilation was then neither understood nor attended to, and accidents by explosion were of constant occurrence. In 1732 furnaces for the promotion of a ventilating draught were first kindled in the Fatfield Colliery; and in 1756 the first air tube was erected at North Biddick. Women were occasionally, but not commonly, employed under ground; but they laboured in great numbers at the pit heaps, and at the staiths, emptying the waggons into the keels. The standard price for such work was from 1d to 1½d per ton. The first application of steam to pumping purposes was after a most curious roundabout fashion. The steam-engine first pumped water into a cistern; this running out turned a water-wheel; and the revolving water-wheel drew up the brimming buckets from the pits. The genius of Watt put an end to this rude contrivance, and about 1796 the first steam-engine in the modern sense of the term was erected on the Northumbrian bank of the Tyne, below Newcastle.

With deep pits contrivances for ventilation became a necessity, and means were found of splitting the descending current of air so as to fling it simultaneously into different levels and corridors, instead of the old practice of sending one current through the whole mine. In some pits, about the beginning of the present century, the air travelled thirty, forty and fifty miles before it rose again to mingle with the atmosphere. The consequence was that this current of air was almost unbreathable long before it had completed its circuit. Instances have indeed been known of the main current having arrived at the "up cast" shaft, so loaded with inflammable gas that it fired when brought into contact with the furnace blazing there. Many improvements were from time to time made in the ropes by which the communication between the top and the bottom of the shaft is kept up. Gunpowder was introduced for blasting, and, the main passages having been sufficiently enlarged, horses were let down to draw the trains of tubs to the shafts. From the year 1780 the improvements in mining engineering were constant. Cast-iron tramways were introduced underground; shafts were divided into compartments by wooden or iron tubbing; and the build and rig of keels were so much improved as to enable them to make five instead of three tides per week to the most distant collieries. Inclined planes were also put into requisition, along which the full wagons running down drew, by their own weight, the empty ones up.

About 1813 or 1814 the first rude locomotives were used to convey the coal from the pit to the staith. This invention produced a revolution in the trade, causing great fields of inland coal to be worked which had hitherto been neglected, owing to the difficulty of transport. In 1825 a coal railway was opened from Stockton to Whitton park colliery and now vast quantities of coal are carried to Shields by the Stanhope and Tyne and the Branding Junction Railways. About twenty years ago the corves or baskets in which the coals had been formerly carried, gave place to square tubs, fitted with wheels, and carrying from six to eight hundred-weight. The wire-rope invention came into notice in the same year, and shortly thereafter the pitmen began to be conveyed up and down the shafts in baskets, instead of dangling in a loop, after the old fashion.

The first parliamentary inquiry into the coal trade which has taken place in comparatively recent times was that of 1800. It was principally directed to the subject of combinations in trade to keep up the price of coals. These combinations in their modern shape, originated in 1771, and the committee recommended stringent measures for their repression. Before this committee it was stated that a pitman's wages had increased 50 per cent within the last ten years.

In 1829 another parliamentary inquiry was instituted. The trade was then open, the "regulation" or combination of coalowners having broken up in the previous year. Before this committee it was stated that the waste from screening, and the consequent rejection of the small coal, amounted to no less than one-fourth of the whole products of a mine. Among the facts elicited by this inquiry were the following—that the capital then employed in the Tyne collieries, independent of shipping amounted to 1½ million of money; and it was reckoned that the collieries then open were capable of producing twice the quantity of coals required. The number of men employed in the trade directly or indirectly, was stated as follows:

	Tyne	Wear
Above ground	3463	2300
Below ground	8491	6700
	11954	9000
In round numbers		21000
Employed on board colliers (men and boys)		15000
As keelmen, boatmen, trimmers etc		2000
In London and on the coast		7500

Total of men and boys employed by
the Newcastle and Durham coalfield—45500

The consumption of coal in England and Wales was estimated at 3½ million tons yearly for manufacturing purposes, and 5½ million for household purposes. These are the inland-dug coals. The additional quantity carried coastwise was estimated at 3 million of tons, making a grand total of 12 million of tons.

In the year 1830 another parliamentary inquiry took place, but as it chiefly related to the commercial and monetary affairs of the trade, I pass it over, as I do a subsequent investigation which was instituted in 1836, and in which the committee again reported against the policy of permitting combinations for limiting the sale, and of course raising the price of coals.

In the June of 1839 a local committee was formed at South Shields for the purpose of investigating the causes of and the remedies for accidents in collieries. Just before this body commenced their investigation an explosion had destroyed 52 lives in the South Hilda pit, near Shields. The committee ascertained that, within the last twenty years, no fewer than 620 miners had been killed in the districts of the Tyne and Wear by the ignition of inflammable gases. The committee described the general effect of an explosion in a northern coal-pit. They detailed its consequences as deranging and disfiguring every avenue, extinguishing every light, and blowing to pieces by the concussion, the doors and traps requisite for the general ventilation of the mine. The consequence often was that the survivors of the explosion, even when well acquainted with the topography of the works, could not make their way out of the pit shaft in time to escape the baneful "after-damp" or azotic acid gas which, almost as soon as the thunder of the explosion is stilled, comes rolling forth, and speedily fills great districts of the mine. This committee ascertained that the number of fatal explosive gases generated in coal-mines is three—light carburetted hydrogen, heavy carburetted hydrogen, and sulphuretted hydrogen. These gases explode at the flame of a lamp, or by contact with a metal heated to a red heat. Carbonic acid gas is commonly generated by explosion. It abounds in old and deserted workings. Lights will not burn in it. The miners call it "stythe", "choke damp", and "black damp" and a single breath of it, in an undiluted state, kills.

For the prevention of explosive accidents in mines, regular and scientific ventilation is what the committee strongly recommended. No lamp has ever been or can ever be constructed which is ever safe in an explosive atmosphere. The committee considered that, generally speaking, the ventilating currents were not large enough, and did not move fast enough through the mines; and the remedy suggested was an increase in the number of shafts. The committee further recommended the erection of an instrument, in all mines, for measuring the speed of the ventilating current; and cited without actually adopting, Mr George Stephenson's opinion, that the ventilation of mines ought to be put under parliamentary regulation. They strongly deprecate the present system of leaving the ventilation of colliers "to chance and the unassisted efforts of individuals".

In 1840, the commission for inquiring into the condition of women and children in mines commenced its labours. The investigation was followed by the legislative enactment for the regulation of mines and collieries now in force. Under this act no woman, on any pretence whatever, can be employed underground in any manner whatever. No boy can be employed until he has completed his tenth year, and no apprenticeship can last for a longer period than eight years. No person can have the charge of shaft machinery under the age of fifteen years; and no payment of wages made in a public house is valid. These are the main provisions of the act, which does not, as in the cases of factories, prescribe the length of the working day.

The Strike of 1844

I have repeatedly mentioned the great strike of 1844. It commenced on the 5th of April of that year, on which day nearly the whole of the underground workers in Northumberland and Durham ceased to labour. It was the fourth great industrial disturbance which took place in the district since 1826. The strike had been long debated, and was deliberately resolved on. At first it was believed that the turn-out would be general over the kingdom, but a meeting of delegates was held in March, at Glasgow, at which it was decided that no such movement should take place. Delegates representing 23,357 miners voted for the general strike, but delegates representing 28,042 miners were of a contrary opinion. As however it was represented that the organisation of the Durham and Northumberland pitmen was complete, it was resolved that in that section of the kingdom, underground labours should be suspended on the 5th of April; but that the other districts should not be called upon to contribute to the expenses of the turnout. The demands of the colliers were principally as follows: They sought for payments every week; for six-monthly engagements sure; to be guaranteed five days per week at 3s per day; to be paid by weight; hewers not to be called on to put; day's work to be limited to eight hours at 3s. In case of accident they required to be paid 10s a week, with medical attendance. In case of death, 5s per week to widow or children for 12 months, and £5 for burial. The terms of the owners were chiefly as follows. They would give no guarantee for work or wages; term of engagement to be for twelve months, terminable on either side at a month's notice; pay once a fortnight; and hewers to put or do any work required.

On the commencement of the strike great bodies of special constables were sworn in; but the conduct of the people, except in a few exceptional instances, was perfectly peaceable. Little or no injury was done to person or property. Every day great meetings were held, and exciting speeches delivered. Many conferences with the masters failed to bring about any amicable result. A religious feeling came to be strangely mixed up with the movement. The Ranters' chapels were crowded, and the success of the strike was prayed for from the pulpit. The people went to chapel and held prayer-meetings, as they said to "get their faith strengthened". The local preachers were frequently their fellow-workmen. These were often persons gifted with a rude energy and picturesque fluency of language, and their influence was almost unbounded. The men sustained themselves during the strike by various expedients. There were some who had saved money, in anticipation of it, and all began with a fortnight's wages in hand. When these were spent, and the short credit which the small shops could afford to give was exhausted, the pawnbrokers for a time supplied the funds, and in many cases the wedding rings of the wives were the last valuables parted with. The next resource was found in the benefit clubs which were broken up. But contributions from the other coal districts came in sparingly and slowly, and the condition of the colliers at length became desperate. Meantime the coalowners were moving heaven and earth to obtain labour. Men were sent for from Staffordshire, Derbyshire and Wales, and great numbers were taken from other species of work and sent into the pits. Hardly one colliery was entirely stopped even for a short time. The number of hewers generally employed in the districts of Tyne, Wear, and Tees is 6,000. On the first of June, the third month of the strike, 1,386 hewers were at work; on the 15th 2,656 were at work; and on the 6th of July 3,975 were in the pits. From the beginning of June the combination melted rapidly away. The influx of strangers intimidated even the most resolute, and towards the end of July there was a rush for employment – the strike was at an end, and the union utterly prostrate and overthrown.

The principal move of the union, previous to the strike, was to impose a restriction upon labour, by which each hewer bound himself to earn as little as possible above 3s a day. The average amount of earnings before the restriction was 3s 9½d per day, so that the men submitted to a voluntary loss of about 9½d per day. Although the union, as I have said, is shattered, there are pits where the men still restrict their labour. These cases may now, however, be said to be exceptional.

The consequence of the strike was disastrous to coalowners and coal-workers. The former lost upwards of £200,000 by the four months of partial cessation of labour. The number of the latter was greatly increased by the immigration from other coal districts. Before the strike it was calculated that there were 30 per cent more labourers in the market than the numbers requisite to perform the work; and since the resumption of labour, strangers in many cases occupy the places in the cottages and the pit of old hewers, and have been forced to seek employment in the new ironworks springing up upon the moors of Durham, Northumberland and Yorkshire.

A Description of the Coal Country

The traveller who enters the coal country from the manufacturing districts will be struck by the complete change of features presented to him. I have in the opening letter of this series sketched the first glances which a railway passenger catches of the cotton country. Let me try in a few rapid words, to describe the prima facie aspect of the great northern coal region. At first, the visitor will be struck by the comparative paucity of towns. The tendency of textile industry is always to the accumulation of human dwellings. The tall chimneys love to rise in clusters, and every few miles along the line of rail the train passes within gunshot of groups of huge factories, strung together by closely built rows of mean cottages. But in the coal district the case is different. In traversing that undulating region, the spectator will cast his eyes over vast ranges of country, of peculiarly soft and wavy outline, dotted with those buildings and scaffold apparatus which denote that beneath each of them a mine shaft sinks into the earth, but totally unmarked by that luxuriant crop of towns which the power-loom has called into being. The collier population is scattered because the pits are scattered. Millowners may be next door neighbours; but when we recollect that underground corridors of a mine may extend miles and miles from the bottom of the shaft, it is evident that the coal adventurers must give each other ample elbow-room. A "pit-row" of cottages, therefore situated near each shaft, affords accommodation for the population whose daily duty calls them to descend it. Far and near, on slope and hollow, their usually dumpy chimneys hardly peering above black piles of small coal and massive scaffoldings, are to be seen the erections characteristic of the region, and telling of the swart labour carried on hundreds of fathoms beneath our feet.

The country shows little of life upon its surface. The soil is cold and clayey and trees and hedges, if not stunted, are not luxuriant. The visitor will not fail to observe the net of small, rude, black railways, powdered with coal dust, which overlays the whole country – each line stretching away in the direction of a pit-heap, and dotted here and there with a convoy of coal waggons – drawn sometimes by horses, sometimes by steam power – speeding from the pit to the shipping place, at some "staith" which runs into the waters of the Tyne, the Wear, or the Tees. The gushes of steam from the engine-house, and the smoke from furnaces burning in the pit and at the surface, tell us that the mines are in full work beneath, while the stranger will observe a characteristic feature in the hill of small coal which surrounds each work, and the scores of tons which are blazing away unregarded – the oxygen of the air acting upon certain gases, distilled from the crumbling, earthy-looking mineral, and thus causing its spontaneous combustion. This catastrophe is rather encouraged than checked by the coal-owners seeing that, with the exception of comparatively rare cases, small coal is of little value, and that it is very desirable to keep down the size of the pit heap.

A Coal-Pit

Following a road, very often ankle-deep in coal mud, passing strings of carts laden with mineral and driven by men with well-besmirched faces, we come to the rising ground, formed in the first instance of the contents of the shaft, added to by the small-coal accumulations of years and always known as the "pit-heap". Scattered round this upon the waste ground at the bottom are frequently clusters of mean houses, stables, store-keeping places and such-like. The eye at once catches the grimy bulk of the engine house, with its hot steam gushes and clank of working mechanism. On the summit of the heap there rise those massive pieces of scaffolding which I have already alluded to. Look to their highest points, and you will observe two wheels, of some eight feet in diameter, set vertically, and round which run ropes or chains, one rising as the other sinks. These are the cords to which we have presently to trust ourselves in descending into the bowels of the earth. We proceed to notice things more minutely, as, by means generally of a slippery ladder, we mount to the summit of the heap. We usually find that it is partially roofed in. An irregularly-built covering stretches, at divers levels, above us, supported by posts and pillars. There is a great bustle and shouting and hurrying to and fro of full and empty tubs of coal, running upon small iron wheels. Looking over a stout railing upon a lower level beneath, we see great screens of oblong iron gratings, stretching at obtuse angles downwards from the stonepaved flooring on which we stand; while beneath them again, upon a rude uneven railway, stand a row of waggons. Everywhere upon the lower levels, are masses of small coal and coal dust, in which men are shovelling and digging assiduously—some filling carts, some distributing equally the constantly accumulating heap. In corners, horses and carts stand upon the straw littered earth.

As we watched the proceedings from the upper platform, we see strong hardy fellows, with great flannel jackets and leathern defences for the thighs, hurrying the wheeled square tubs, along the clattering pavement to the brink. Here the tub tilts over, being only kept from going bodily down, by a strong wooden rail against which it falls, upsetting, however, with the shock its cargo into one of the sloping screens beneath, through which the dust and small coal disappear, while the "knobbly" bits slide down into the wagons prepared to receive them. Nothing can be more admirable than the dexterity and strength with which the "banksman" trundles his tubs along the platform, dashes their contents out in an instant, rights them again with a sudden jerk, and then by a dexterous twist sends them spinning back in the direction whence they came.

We follow, and perhaps start back from two dark and oblong pits like black graves, yawning in the strong wooden floor which extends at this part of the platform. We are, in fact, standing over the mouth of the shaft, which of course, is circular in shape, but which is always divided by strong wooden partitions, reaching from the top to the bottom, into square or oblong compartments of smaller or greater size (according to circumstances I shall speedily explain), and down which the "cage" containing the tubs slides, steadied by grooved passages to the bottom of the mine. When we first catch sight of the openings the tubs are probably passing each other half way down the shaft—one set coming up full, the other going down empty. The two ropes of course are spinning past us—one rising from, the other descending, the black abyss. By the edge of what will be the ascending shaft in the next trip, stands one of the banksmen in his flannel dress, close to the empty tubs which it will be his duty to deposit in the cage as soon as a colleague has extricated the full ones. At the edge of the non-ascending compartment stands another man, dressed in the usual flannel costume, holding in his hand a piece of iron like a pump-handle, connected with which is a simple apparatus for steadying the different stages of the cage as it arrives at the pit mouth, and thus enabling it conveniently to deliver its two or three tiers of coal-laden tubs. Close behind him is a little wooden office or counting room, with a weighing apparatus, over which the coal tubs are run, and which tells the clerk outside the exact weight of each, a matter which he at once registers.

But there is another process hereabouts. You see upon the wall of the office ranges of pegs or nails, with chalked initials beneath each; and hanging from each are a greater or a smaller number of pieces of strong cord attached to little wooden labels, upon each of which are deeply carved letters corresponding with the chalked initials. A dirty-faced, shrill-voiced boy is darting about; and watching his motions, you suddenly see him pounce upon a tub, untie one of the little pieces of cord from one of its corners—and then, watching the opportunity, just as the tub is being weighed, he shrieks out the intial and the name for which they stand—thus, "J. S. John Smith". This is the name of the hewer who has filled the tub, and the clerk close to the register of its weight, books the weight of hewn coals to the credit of the labourer who has wrought them.

While we are watching the process, the wheels at the top of the great structure of beams and ladders begin to move slowly. The ascending cage is close to the bank of the pit; the alarm bell which has notified the fact to the engineer, has tingled among the machinery, and with his hand upon the slowly moving lever, he carefully watches the moment to shut the steam off. It has arrived. Up to the ledge of the gulf with a clatter and a surge comes the cage. It has a strong iron-bound floor, and iron rails, forming as it were the skeleton of a box. This cage stops with its bottom exactly on a level with the edge of the platform; and the banksman, whose business it is, suddenly seizes the tub which it contains, and lugs it out with a wrench, his colleagues substituting an empty one; while the third by a movement of his lever permits the second tier of the cage with a second tub to ascend the ledge of the aperture. Upon the top of the coals in his second tub there perhaps lies a little piece of rope. This is "a token" that men are coming up as the next cargo, and the lever man usually apprises the engineer, with whom he can immediately communicate, of the fact. Presently, if you are attentive, you observe a hammer rise from a block of iron, apparently without a hand, and strike two blows. The lever which moved it has been worked at the bottom of the mine, and sometimes the strokes simultaneously resound in the engine room and at the mouth of the pit. They form the signal that the men are ready to rise. Three blows in some collieries, and one in others, announce that the cargo is coals. The engineer, upon noting the double stroke, does his spiriting gently. The rope begins to move as easily as if a careful hand stirred it— the top cage slowly sinks into the darkness—then the engine gradually puts on its speed, and in a second or two the living freight is careering up through the strata of the earth. Before they make their appearance we shall describe the old and rude method, still practised in some of the remote parts of the country, of ascending and descending mines.

At one time the shafts were generally open, and undivided by the wooden partitions which now separate them into square boarded compartments. The coals were then raised, not in tubs placed in cages, but simply in "corves" or round baskets, shaped like pots and with a pot handle, which was attached to the hook in which the chain terminated. The men, however, seldom went down or came up in these corves—there being a risk of their grazing as they passed each other swinging in the darkness of the shaft. To ascend or descend, the pitmen simply stuck a hook in a link of the chain, and formed a loop. Into this two men inserted their right thighs, grasping the chain with their right hands, and armed with small sticks held in the left hand for the purpose of steadying the motion by keeping the end of the rods as much as possible in contact with the walls of the shaft. When men were on the chain no corf was allowed to be attached to the other extremity. Two was the regular number who could be accommodated on the loop; but three, four and five frequently went down or came up, clinging to each other and to the chain. Signals by blows were not then in use. The regular formula of communication between the top and the bottom was as follows:

The man at the bottom sung out "Hi! ho!"
To which the banksman responded, "Hillo!"
The first speaker then shouted, "Men going to ride!"
The banksman replied, "Men ride away!" and gave notice to the engineer.

Meantime the people below had hooked themselves on, and when all were ready they shouted up, "Tee ware!" Immediately the engine moved, and off they went.

The coal-pits in the north have generally excellent machinery for ascending and descending the shaft; but the Staffordshire pits are notoriously deficient in this respect. During the year from 1st January, 1848, to the 31st of December, there were killed in Staffordshire no less than 37 men by breakage of ropes and chains, while in all the Durham and Northumberland pits, the number so destroyed was only six. In Staffordshire common chains were generally made use of. In the north, wire ropes spun flat are becoming very common, although hemp has still its advocates. A not uncommon accident, occasioned almost invariably by pure negligence, is that of men being drawn, not only out of the pit, but right over the wheel and pulley, through the engine not being stopped in time. This catastrophe involves almost certain death, as the men are generally precipitated down the shaft, in which their coffins have often to be sent below as it would be impossible otherwise to remove the shattered fragments of mortality.

But meantime the cage has reached the surface, freighted with near half a dozen hewers and putters—a cluster of black smirched faces, grimy hands holding on to the chains, and flannel jackets, with here and there faint streaks of a shade somewhat resembling the original colour of the stuff. They speedily disengage themselves from the cage, and go blinking along in the sudden glare of the daylight. There are two classes of them—men and lads. All wear flannel jackets and coarse warm waistcoating. Some have wooden and tin canteens swung over their shoulders, and canvas bags protruding from their pockets. The headdress is generally a greasy cap. The men mostly carry small straight pick-axes, and wear sometimes trousers and sometimes breeches and stockings. These are the hewers and the lads who accompany them are the putters. The latter wear short drawers not reaching further down than the centre of the thigh, and a sort of legging extending from the ankle to below the knee. A great portion of the limb is thus, but for its covering of coal dust, left perfectly exposed, and one wonders at the impunity with which they ascend thus slightly clad, from the hot regions of the mine into the nipping air of wintry weather. But putters never think of colds or rheumatism.

All things being now ready, we will ourselves descend. If the visitor be wise he will change his hat for a cap, and envelop himself in his coarsest and oldest pea-coat. We then take our station in the cage. We shall be told to stand bolt upright, and keep our hands within the iron railings.

The hammer gives a tap to notify that all is ready below, the banksman tugs his lever, and the same instant—with a feeling strictly analogous to that which one experiences aboard a steamer as she shoots from the calm water of a harbour, and performs her first plunge into the trough of a seaway—the cage sinks beneath us, the faces of the people above, the buildings, and the sunlight, disappear as if by magic. For a second or two a faint grey glimmer of light shows the perpendicular walls down which we are shooting, with a rapid noiseless, and perfectly easy motion, and then all is pitchy darkness. The sensation now becomes curious. We are utterly unable to tell whether we are going up or down, but the suspense is speedily over; a minute or two, and our speed is palpably checked. A glimmer of red candlelight shines from below, and almost at the same moment we observe that the cage is descending so slowly as to be—to use the expression—feeling for the bottom; and as we touch the earth again, we see by the flicker of three or four rushlights stuck in lumps of clay, a dark uncertain sort of hole, with a dripping, as of falling water drops—a row or two of coal laden tubs, over which we have to clamber—half a dozen black hands put up to help us, half a dozen black faces grinning at our perplexity—a sleek horse or two standing motionless beside the tubs—caverned walls, dark and tunnel-like about us, and a curious warm earthy odour, not at all unpleasant, and mixed somehow up with the smell of stables.

One of the pitmen immediately hands us one of the lumps of clay which serve as candlesticks. The contrivance at first seems rude, but long ere you have travelled the pit you will find its excellence. The candles used are very small being sometimes forty to the pound, but they give a wonderfully good light. They are struck through the clay so as to show about an inch above it, and of course you push them up as they burn away. The clay candlestick can be moulded in a minute, so as to stick to any ledge or roughness in the walls. If it be required, two can be at once joined together, and there is a knack of carrying the lump in the hollow of the hand, so as to shield the flame from the draughts. I have seen a pitman carry an inch of candle thus for miles against the main ventilating current, when I have not been able to keep my light alive for a yard.

The workings where the people are actually digging may be a mile or two from the shaft; and while we are plodding our rough way towards it, through dark tunnels paved with little tramways, I shall endeavour plainly and intelligibly to describe the mode of laying out, ventilating, and working a coal-mine.

The spot for digging having been fixed upon, the operations are commenced by a gang of "sinkers", who are to regular pitmen what navvies are to regular railway servants. A sinker will sometimes take employment as a hewer, but only when no sinking work is to be got. As soon as he hears of a new mine he is off with his pick-axe and shovel at once. The work of sinking never ceases after it has begun, until the necessary depth is reached. The sinkers work in three gangs and relieve each other every four hours day and night. The turns are so arranged so as to give every man alternate spells of four hours' work and eight hours' rest. Their wages may average about 3s 8d per day—the daily work-hours numbering, of course, eight. During the early stages of the process the earth excavated is raised to the surface by a machine called a sack-roll—in other words a large winch. When the rocky strata are reached, a gin or capstan is employed worked by horses; and when the excavators are down some 50 fathoms in the earth, a steam engine which wlll be used afterwards for the general purposes of the pit, is applied. The bed of coal being attained, operations are continued by excavating roomy passages called rolley-ways, and which may be described as the principal thoroughfares of the mine, both for the passage of coal and air. By this time another shaft has most probably been sunk some dozen yards, more or less, from the first; and the main passages or galleries must always be so arranged as to communicate with both. Without such a disposition of matters there would be no means of forcing a current of air through the mine. Some pits, however, have only one shaft, divided into two air-tight compartments by wooden partitions called brattices. The ventilating principle in both cases is the same but I shall continue to speak of the double-shafted pits, which are the best, and happily the most common.

These shafts, of course, have different functions to perform, but in all of them a space is partitioned off for the exclusive purpose of conducting down fresh air into the workings, and letting it escape when it is done with. The shaft through which the ventilating current descends is called the downcast shaft—that through which the air ascends, the upcast shaft. Almost immediately under the latter, piled upon a great square block of masonry and surrounded by caverned walls, is heaped a vast roaring furnace burning night and day. The effect of this furnace is, of course, to rarify to a high degree the air beneath the up-cast shaft, and consequently to produce through all the mine a current setting towards it. Of course the cold air descends the other shaft to supply the vacancy; and it is then by a system of doors and traps, forced to traverse every foot of every passage of the mine before it is allowed, in popular terms, to be sucked in by the draught of the furnace. As I have hinted, this is rather the principle of the system than the actual plan adopted in all cases; for in many mines the air—moving at the rate of say 400 feet per minute, in the main passages, and creeping perhaps at only the fourth of that speed through the narrower corridors and workings—would take more than twelve hours to permeate the mine, and would return so impure as to be unfit for supporting healthy existence. The current is therefore by a combination of passages and traps, split into different branches, and sent to different districts of the mine, in proportions depending upon the number of people hewing and putting in each group of workings. In all the main passages of the pit the current comes by like the blowing of a steady breeze. In the galleries branching off at right angles from the chief rolley-ways, the atmosphere is hardly felt to move, but the slight flare of the candle reveals that the air is not actually stagnant.

The reader will, then, now keep in mind that, from the two shafts passages or corridors (all connected with each other) branch away in parallel or different directions, as the case may be; the passages connected with the downcast shaft being traversed by a fresh breeze running into the mine—those connected with the upcast, traversed by a breeze nearly as strong, but by no means so fresh. The rolley-ways are of course cut in the bed of coal, which may rise on either side nearly to the roof, or which may extend only three or four feet up the wall, like the strip of wainscoating in old-fashioned rooms. The next thing to be done is to work out the coals from the bed. Narrow passages are therefore cut, generally about four feet high, right into the coal, at right angles from the rolley way. These passages are called "headways". At a certain distance they expand into spaces of a greater width, of oblong square shape, formed of course by the excavation of the coals. These spaces or chambers are called "boards" or workings, and there the coals are hewn.

We will suppose that two "boards" are being wrought at once. The miners are therefore excavating two oblong chambers at right angles from the rolley-way, and leaving between each a great mass of solid coal. But the boards must be connected, or they could not be well ventilated. A passage is therefore dug from one to the other, parallel with the rolley-way, but at the depth of the board from it. Thus it will be seen that a great square pillar is left untouched, but that there is a free communication round it, its boundaries being the rolley-way on one side, the two oblong rooms with their narrow necks on two others, and the passage parallel to the rolley-way on the fourth. I am anxious that the system of "pillar" working should be fully understood, and therefore, at the risk of being tedious, I will add a simple illustration. Suppose two bottles to be inserted parallel to each other, and at a distance of a foot, in a bank of earth—their position horizontal, with their apertures just showing on the face of the bank. Now suppose the bottom of the bottles broken out and a pipe in the earth forming a communication between them, so that if you blew into the mouth of one bottle the air would come out at that of the other. This illustration exactly describes the method in which the mines are worked. Each pillar of coal left entire supports the roof, and the process is carried on, square after square being formed, until the boundary of the mine is reached, or until the difficulty of ventilating the labyrinth of boards puts a stop to progress in that direction. The boards are generally about five yards wide, and the pillars are generally about sixteen by twenty yards.

It will be seen therefore that the miner at first leaves nearly two-thirds of the coal untouched. The reason of the narrow passage opening into the boards is to facilitate blocking up after they are exhausted and after a "goaf" has been formed; and also to give conveniences for regulating the supply of air. The hewer is at his labour in the board, cutting down the coal; thus of course enlarging every hour the chamber in which he works, and filling from time to time the tubs which stand beside him, and which the putter directly seizes, and pushes upon narrow tramways back out through the boards and narrow necks into the rolley-way. The little trapper opens the door for him to pass—a door which were it not kept shut, would allow the air current to escape into the main corridor, instead of forcing it to make its way, as it will do into the next board; and the driver outside in the rolley-way, with his low platform-like train, receives and places upon it the coal-filled tubs, which the putter delivers into his hands, and, when his freight is complete, makes the best of his way with it out to the pit shaft.

Having carried his workings as far as is deemed practicable, the miner returns upon his steps, and attacks the oblong pillars of coal hitherto left untouched. As he digs them away, he inserts strong props to stay up the roof. This state of things, when a vast hollow in the earth is kept from collapsing by props, is called a "jud". But as not even a prop is lost, if it can be helped, in a coal-pit, the workmen cautiously withdraw them, beginning at first from the furthest end. As the supports are removed, the roof falls in with more or less rapidity. Sometimes tons of earth come tumbling down at once. Sometimes the descent is more gradual. Thus, by degrees, successive rows of props are taken away and the space in which they stood is occupied by a chaos of broken strata, heaped together with more or less solidity, but generally intersected with cracks, crevices, and hollow chambers, formed by the irregular shapes of the fallen rocks and stones.

This dreary space is called a "goaf" and every mine which has been for some time worked possesses one, the dimensions of which of course are being daily added to. Old mines of great extent have several goafs, and sometimes they each include dozens of acres of space. A mine thoroughly worked out will be all goaf, and probably the majority of pits, have a nucleus of falling and crumbling strata. These goafs are too often the plague spots of coal mines. Towards the centre they are supposed to be more solid and compact than nearer the edges; but as a vast quantity of coal has been extracted, and as the surface of the country above seldom sinks it is evident that there must be a vacant space left underneath. But goafs are seldom or never, indeed they cannot be, ventilated. Very often, in the expressive language of the pitmen, they are "lying dead", without a cubic foot of fresh air circulating through their winding crevices and splintered chambers. They then become the fertile generators of foul gases. The fire-damp rises slowly from these unwholesome recesses, and being one half lighter than common air, ascends to the caverned roof of the vault. There of course it is harmless. No one works near a goaf without a safety lamp, but occasionally—often on account of fresh falls from the roof—the space occupied by the vapour is lessened, and it struggles to set itself free, and gradually leaks through crack and crevice into the working parts of the pit. The terrible results the public are well acquainted with.

The Underground Features of a Pit

Our progress will be first along the rolley-way, our destination being of course the workings. The path is occupied by a single tramway, the space between the rails being taken up by short sleepers, laid as close as the rounds of a ladder. On one or both sides there trickle down to the well or "sunk", near the shaft, driblets in some cases, and rivulets in others, of salt and muddy water. Presently you may meet a party of pitmen returning from work. You hear their voices and you see the glimmer of their light at a distance; and presently they pass you—in Indian file – a ghastly-looking procession, seen by the flickering light of the single candle half enclosed in the hollows of the leader's hand. You will not go far without hearing the noise of an approaching train of waggons. The sound rumbles and reverberates, so that it requires a practised ear to distinguish in which direction the convoy is proceeding. Presently, however, you see the gleam of a light approaching, and very likely hear the shrill voice of a boy singing some popular ditty at the top of his voice. You stand aside, squeezing yourself against the damp wall, to allow the train to go by. It is drawn by a single horse at a walking pace, and may convey a dozen or fourteen loaded tubs. The platforms on which these are placed are not more than two feet from the ground. The driver is usually a lad under eighteen. He always sits just behind the horse, with his legs extended upon the low shafts between which the animal is yoked. He has a single light swinging in a lamp from the top of the foremost tub, but so placed as to be invisible, until you are close upon it. These drivers are paid, like the trappers, by the day and their wages may average about 1s 2d. They enter and leave the mines with the putters. Occasionally considerable portions of the way are inclined planes, where the services of horses are not required. The full wagons running down pull the empty ones up. At either end of the inclined plane, a couple of individuals, generally a man and a boy, are stationed to arrange the waggons. There is a bell wire in many instances running along the roof of the passage, and a vigorous tug at this by the man below announces to his coadjutor above that he may start the loaded wagons, which come careering down, like thunder, in the darkness.

The glimmer of light at what may be called the station is commonly afforded by a candle, stuck by means of clay to a post or the wall. We may now be supposed to have advanced some distance into the mine, and a difference is perceived in the atmosphere. The men generally tell you that they are quite comfortable; but however much they may be accustomed to the comparative closeness, a stranger is apt to feel an unpleasant sense of depression on the chest, accompanied with a slight degree of nausea. As soon, however, as the heated air produces copious perspiration, these unpleasant feelings go off—at least, they did so in my case; and I afterwards felt no inconvenience, when more than a mile further in, and away altogether from the main channel.

In traversing the Gosforth Pit I was struck with the aspect of a little workshop, excavated in the wall near the top of an inclined plane, and tenanted by a single old man, who has charge of all the safety lamps used in the mine. He sat at a bench with a great jar of oil by his side, busily employed in filling and trimming the lamps, which, when he had finished, he hung upon the wall on ranges of hooks, the initials of the miners being chalked below them. In the passages Davy lamps are not required, but in the distant workings apart from the main stream of air they are commonly used, whether the existence of gas be suspected or not. I inquired whether the men ever lighted their pipes at the lamps. The old man didn't know but what they might sometimes. It required good suction to get the flame through the gauze, but "some on 'em had a rare twist with the pipes in their cheeks". The old lamp-trimmer sat in his gnome-like workshop nine hours a day. There was a second small chamber off it, in which were placed a vice, hammers, files, and other instruments required for the repair of the metal parts of the lamps.

In following the track of a rolley-way you often observe examples of the "pitches" and "troubles" with which miners have to contend. Sometimes the seam makes a sudden bend upwards or downwards, involving, unless it speedily returns to its former pitch, the necessity of a change of level in the workings; at other times a band of clayey stone or shale intersects it. It is curious to observe the thin layers of unworkable coal, perhaps two or three inches thick, glancing like a black riband along the lighter-coloured strata through which the passage has been cut. In some points props are fastened to strengthen and support the sides, and in others the corridors are regularly built in with masonry so as to appear precisely like a railway tunnel. In moving with the current of air you feel its influence in a very small degree, and the reflux and agitation produced by the going by of a train is most refreshing. After having passed, it may be, several stations at the bottoms and tops of inclined planes—at each of which the attendants will probably be sitting upon lumps of coal or rude benches, or on the waggons, waiting for the moment when their services are called into operation—we reach a point whence we can diverge into the workings. A row of waggon frames stand here, opposite an aperture in the wall which may measure, say, from three to four feet square, and raised about two feet above the tramway, so as to allow the tubs pushed out of it to glide at once, without change of level, upon the framework.

We now come, for the first time, upon the putters. You hear a shouting and a clattering in the black hole before you, and in a minute a coal-tub emerges with a crash upon the locomotive platform; and you perceive a figure more than half naked, and of course, as black as a negro, who has looked out for a moment, exchanged a word with the driver, and then disappeared in the recesses of the "headway", shoving an empty tub before him. This is the putter and we shall follow him. Clambering over the waggons we find ourselves in a narrow passage, ruggedly cut among the rocks, and the painful stooping position generally necessary to traverse which speedily makes one think of taking to all fours as a luxury. At all events you almost envy the putter the tub on which he leans as he pushes it out and in. Here as in the rolley way, there is a tram-road, the rails being necessarily of a very narrow gauge. About half way to where the board opens up, we pass an air door, attended by a trapper. The poor little fellow sits squatted upon the ground in a recess, holding a cord in his hand, with which he chucks–to the door after the putter and his tub have passed. If he can beg or pick up any candle ends, the trapper has the luxury of light; if not he must sit quietly in the darkness. The trapper's wages are always 10d a day. The air is first forced into the boards by means of either a door or a barrier in the main passage, and then as it cannot escape back again towards the furnace by the nearest way, it necessarily courses through every part of the workings. Leaving the trapper behind, we can probably catch at length the faint click of the picks which the hewers are wielding, and presently the passage through which we are crawling opens into a sort of shallow chamber—the "board"—heaped with loose coal, the roof strengthened with short props and crossbars, and at the farther end of it the glow-worm-like sparks of the Davy lamps.

We are now fairly in the recesses of the pit, and the eye being by this time pretty well now accustomed to the darkness, we can watch the hewers at their work. The labour would be toilsome even in the fresh air; but in the deep recesses of a mine it must be very fagging. The short straight pick is the principal implement employed, with iron wedges, and mallets for driving them into the seam when the coal shows a tendency to come away in large lumps. Gunpowder is only employed in the more open parts of the mine. Of course, to fire a train where Davy lamps are habitually requisite would be madness. The toil of the hewer depends greatly upon the thickness of the seam, which prescribes the attitudes in which he is obliged chiefly to labour. Sometimes he stands, sometimes he works on his knees; sometimes he flings himself down on his side, to get at the lower part of the bed. The skill and the endurance of the hewer are mostly shown by the facility with which he can accommodate his postures to the nature of the seam, and the vigour and effect with which he can labour in them all. The coal is always pretty compactly lodged, and requires a smart blow to bring down even an ordinary shovelful; and this is the more felt from the cramping position, often among props and posts, in which the limbs have to be exerted. The men work in flannel shirts and short drawers, with the perspiration washing every now and then a new white streak in their besmirched faces. Close behind the hewer stand one or more empty tubs, which he has to fill. He then attaches to the staple fixed in the corner of each one of the little cords and wooden labels already described, and the putter wheels it out by main force through the narrow passages. The hewers of course take down with them as many labels as they expect to fill tubs. Their hours of work are at present eight or nine per day. Here and there a very hard-working man will work somewhat longer.

In some pits there are relays of hewers so as to carry the work on until late at night, but the following plan is more generally adopted. The hewers enter the pit at two or three in the morning, and set to work; the putters come to their aid two hours from the time they have commenced, so as to find coals hewn and ready to be carried out. In some pits another set of hewers enter at eight or nine o'clock; but this I repeat is not a general practice. As the putters arrive two hours later than the hewers, so they remain behind them to accomplish their task. There is one putter to every three or four hewers, and the like proportion of drivers and other labourers employed about the waggons and inclines to every three or four putters. These last are, as has been mentioned, lads generally under twenty. Their work requires constant stooping, and constant and severe muscular exertion. They have generally begun as trappers—then they have been team drivers—after which they have been promoted to putting, and of course look forward to becoming hewers. It is not easy for people who never saw the employment to realise to themselves what putting is. Let them, however, just try to fancy a pitch dark oblong hole, just big enough to contain an ordinary sofa. Then let them fancy the shoving and dragging of wagons holding about 7cwt stooping almost double and the thermometer seldom below 75 degrees. This is what is called "putting coals". Although mere lads are engaged in it, I fancied the muscular exertion to be even more than that requisite in the hewer's labour. Both hewers and putters are paid by the quantity of coals extracted, and the latter make nearly as much as the former, their wages 3s to 3s 6d per day. Of course the amount must depend on the quantity of coal picked by the hewers. The latter will earn if they do not restrict themselves, something like 3s 10d or 4s per day; and besides this they have certain advantages in the way of house accommodation, which I shall afterwards allude to.

The pitmen take what provisions they need during their working hours down with them. They have canteens and bags for the solids, called "bait pokes". No beer or spirits is allowed in any mine whatever, and the men all agree on the reasonableness of the regulation. In the canteens they have coffee, which they drink cold, milk and water. The putters consume an immensity of water, notwithstanding the heat and perspiration in which they are continually bathed. In many pits casks of the pure fluid are provided for these poor thirsty fellows. I have peeped into several "bait pokes", and generally found their contents to be great hunches of bread, with smaller portions either of meat or cheese. These small haversacks are hung to nails upon props, until their proprietors feel sufficiently appetised to attack them.

The hewers generally labour by threes or fours in the same board. They are, I was told by some good authorities, although the statement was denied by others, by no means fond of working alone, from superstitious considerations. Many of the old-fashioned ideas in this respect are dying away, but the mining population, particularly the hewers, are still very attentive to signs and omens before they commence their day's work. They count it specially unlucky to cross a woman on their way to the pit. Considering the hour at which they leave home, the conjunction does not probably often take place; but many a miner, if he catches a glimpse, or fancies he does so, of the flutter of a female dress, will turn on his heel and go back to bed again. A gentleman informed me that he had once unwittingly stopped the day's working of a pit by passing the "row", when the men were going to their labour, wrapped up in a light coloured plaid. He afterwards learned that there was a great consultation held on the bank, and that it was unanimously resolved that nothing could be more rash than going into the pit after several of the party had distinctly seen a ghost. The superstitions of the pitmen, however, form a subject on which I shall afterwards have occasion to touch.

The labour of the putter is at present being considerably infringed upon by the introduction of Shetland ponies, small enough to traverse the headways, and strong enough speedily to hurry out the tubs. The horses used in mines, after they are once brought down, seldom see the light again. They are generally in capital condition, the warm air making their coats sleek, and their docility is very striking. Indeed, unruly horses would never do for pit labour. The stables are usually situated close to the downcast shaft, and except being a trifle darker, are very like stables above ground. The horses are attended to by stable men, who do not interfere in any other work of the pit.

In returning from the recesses of the mine, which we may do by the up-cast passages, we have an opportunity of seeing the furnace, attended by its solitary watchman. The rush of air close to an efficient furnace forms a current which a sailor would call a top-gallant sail breeze. There are generally two fire-trimmers, who relieve each other night and day. The smoke of the furnace and the impure air escape by the up-cast shaft together. If you stand by its brink, you will observe the vapour rising like a dense steam from the pit. The pumping apparatus may be fixed in either shaft. Every thirty-three feet from top to bottom, there is a cistern, inserted in a recess cut in the side of the shaft for the purpose, and the water is raised by different sets of rods, from one cistern to the other, until it is elevated to the surface.

The Daily Life and Toil of a Miner

Until 1844, pitmen, and indeed everybody connected with pits, were always hired by the year. The "binding" as it was called took place at the end of March. The men then assembled at the colliery, and met the proprietor or his agents, who read the bond, detailing the terms to be paid, and the discipline and regulations of the mine. To this the labourers fixed their names or marks. Earnest money, called "arles", was then given. Up to 1804 the arles frequently amounted to two or three guineas. At that date the sum was reduced to half a crown, and since the strike in 1844, the custom has been totally abolished. The bond, as it is at present drawn out, invariably stipulates that the engagement on either side is terminable at a month's notice. The pitmen, I must say, are a class of people not always to be easily pleased. When the bond held them for a year, they urged that it placed them under an unduly lengthened thraldom. At present complaints are not wanting that the monthly system enables masters to dismiss their hands without giving sufficient warning.

The bond usually commences by binding all the persons hired to hew, work, fill, drive and put coals, or to do such other work as may be directed, and as shall appear necessary to the owners for carrying on with advantage the operations of the mine. Thus, at a pinch, any man is bound to perform any sort of work. The bond next sets forth, that the wages are to be paid fortnightly, and it recounts the rates to be adopted for the working of different seams—the coals to be in all cases sent to bank in a clean and mercantile state, and free from all refuse. The method of working to be pursued is then stipulated, and the allowance, if any, of gunpowder to the hewers set forth. Since the abolition of the yearly binding, powder is very rarely furnished by the owners. The rate of wages payable to the putters is next stated—that rate differing according to the distances which they will have to push the tubs. Next, the wages of the day labourers are set forth, and parents of trap boys are cautioned against deceiving the managers of the pits as to their children's ages. Stipulations are also commonly made for the weighing of the coals sent to bank. The allowance for deficient weight (if any), and the quantity of refuse permitted in each tub are then stated, with the penalties to be incurred if either condition be violated. Articles are then inserted, binding the workpeople to continue the servants of the proprietors, in the case of the working of the mine being temporarily discontinued, and binding the proprietors to pay a certain amount of wages for all such times of abeyance; the men, meantime obliging themselves, in consideration of these wages, to set themselves to any work which the proprietors direct. The day's work for a hewer is defined to be a day "not exceeding eight hours"; and the hewers are bound not to leave the pit until they have hewn and filled a corresponding quantity of coals. The day's work of the operatives paid a fixed weekly wage is commonly understood to consist of twelve hours—the period commencing with the hour when the engine begins to draw coals to the surface. When the hewers are required to act as putters, they receive a certain amount of extra wages called "furtherance". The bond then commonly goes on to provide that all persons to whom the proprietors assign houses, hold those houses not as tenements, but as part of their wages and to bind the recipients to give up possession within a certain number of days after the termination of the hiring. The bond sometimes, although by no means invariably, terminated with a clause binding the workmen to keep no horses, donkeys, dogs, poultry, or in some cases pigs. This provision, however, is now very generally exploded, or at all events if made, is not enforced. Pigs, dogs, and poultry, in especial abound in most colliery villages.

Such then is a general statement of the stipulated terms on which the pitmen descend to their work. I proceed to detail the habits of their daily toil and life. The hewer only requires tools. There are drills for boring into the seam when gunpowder is to be used, picks for separating the masses of coal, iron wedges and mells for loosening the mineral, when blasting is not permitted, and shovels for filling the tubs. The picks and drills are usually the property of the hewer; the mells, wedges, and sometimes the shovels, are found him. A hewer possesses at least a half a dozen picks. They may cost about 1s 8d each. He generally fits the hafts to them himself, and a blacksmith, partially paid by the colliery, keeps the iron part in order. The picks have to be sharpened every day, so each hewer when he ascends goes straight with his implement to the blacksmith's shop, and next morning finds it laid out in readiness for him. The hewer pays 2d per fortnight to the blacksmith. Gunpowder for blasting is, as I have said, in the great majority of cases, found by the men themselves. Sometimes they are compelled to buy their candles from the overmen, who occasionally supply the articles. The powder, which is very coarse stuff, costs 6d per pound, and hewers will often use from three to four pounds in a fortnight. They make the cartridges in which it is fired at their leisure. In some collieries the men have a powder and candle magazine established in a detached building, and attended to by one of themselves, whom they pay for the purpose. They are thus supplied with the articles at cost price. As an instance of the too prevalent recklessness of miners, I may mention that I found men smoking in a magazine with scores of pounds of powder lying in paper bags upon the shelves. The candles used are sometimes thirty, and sometimes forty, and rarely sixty to the pound. A hewer will require about two pounds of candles in a fortnight. Like the powder they cost about 5d a pound. Out of the fortnight's wages of a hewer are, therefore, to be deducted the price he pays for his gunpowder and candles, amounting probably to about 2s 6d a fortnight.

Davy lamps are always found and partly kept in order by the colliery. I have described the lamp-trimmer whom I saw in Gosforth Pit. The hewers on returning from work pass the shop—there are such in every pit—and the lamp man unscrews the bottom part of the lamps to be refilled and trimmed. The men carry the gauze cylinders home with them and clean them carefully, as, should the wire net work become partially clogged with coal dust, the danger of explosion is greatly increased. I have described the excellent pit candlesticks, made of lumps of clay. The clay is generally obtained by the wives and children of the hewers, who will sometimes threaten to "lie idle" unless they are kept well supplied. Men working with Davys have in a money point of view, a slight advantage over those labouring with candles, but they carry on their toil by a worse light, and of course in a more dangerous position. Drivers are supplied with lanterns—called I believe "mistresses", by the pit.

The poor little trap boys have no such advantage, and light is too expensive a luxury for them to buy. If the parents are indulgent, they will give them a couple of candles per day to light them in and out of the pit. These poor little fellows often complain grievously of sitting for twelve hours at a stretch in the dark. After the first few hours, the pitmen have told me that the constant cry of the trappers to all who pass their solitary stations is "What o'clock is it?" or "Will it soon be time to call kenner?"—the latter phrase signifying an expression shouted down the shaft by the banksman, and repeated throughout the workings, when the hour has arrived for knocking off and ascending to the surface. As might be expected, the trap boys are not by any means devoid of superstitious terrors. After an accident they are specially sensitive, and have a great aversion to going near places where the dead bodies have been laid previously to being brought to bank. For all this, however, it rarely happens that the parents have to use any compulsion to force a boy to work. The hewers are in the practice of taking the children very early down into the pit, and habituating them to its repulsive features; while if a boy has been at school he is generally delighted to change the discipline of the class even for work underground. The number of trap-door boys required at present is, however, far less than it used to be; the doors being now commonly constructed with springs so as to swing-to every time they are opened. As a general rule, a trap-boy is placed as near his father or brothers as is practicable. The putters who pass by the doors are notoriously careless as to whether the trapper does his duty or not. Indeed, this recklessness appears common to almost every workman in coal-pits. It is the business of the putters to push their tubs through the doors, and they appear to take no heed whether or no the portals are closed behind them. Indeed, I understand it is to be by no means unusual for the putter to run the tub with such precipitancy as to break or disable the door, which will probably remain for several hours in an imperfect state before it is repaired by the deputies.

The last-mentioned class of functionaries I have not yet alluded to. I may therefore now sketch their duties, along with those of another body of employees—generally classed with them—the overmen. Both overmen and deputies are ordinarily selected from the hewers. Their wages range from 18s to 25s per week, and to them are usually assigned the best houses in the pit village. The overmen in a mine hold analogous positions to boatswains on shipboard, or corporals in a regiment. They are the lowest persons in authority. The deputies are employed in fixing props and brattices, and generally in taking charge of the woodwork in a mine, a department on the efficient discharge of the duties of which the ventilation of a pit entirely depends. When gunpowder is used in safety lamp works, the deputy always fires the charge. Both classes of official are nominally, and no doubt often really, selected from the most experienced and most intelligent of the hewers; but an unpopular appointment of the kind is sure to result in a charge against the masters of partiality and favouritism. A number of the deputies, I have been informed by the pit-hands, are "blacklegs",—that is; men who have kept aloof from the Union, and generally declined to join strikes. It is the duty of the overmen and deputies to descend into the pit by midnight, or before it, and to traverse the whole of the workings, in order to see that there is no appearance of dangerous gases or of symptoms of fall from the roof. When anything wrong is apprehended, the inspecting party leave a rude caution in the shape of a prop or a shovel flung across the path as a token for the hewers, when they arrive, to go no further. Sometimes they chalk a word of warning upon the blade of a shovel, and stick it upright in the castle; but so profound is the ignorance of many of the pitmen, that an intelligent hewer informs me that shovels have been frequently kept until he made his appearance, when they were presented to him, with a request that he would decipher the mystic hieroglyphics.

There is generally speaking, a watch kept all night upon the pit heap; and at the proper hours, the sentinel, who is termed from one part of his duties the "callsman", proceeds round the colliery village to rouse the hewers—rapping at every door and proclaiming that it is time to turn out. A great number of the pits are worked by two shifts or sets of hewers— called respectively the fore-shift and the back-shift. In these cases the callsman proceeds on his first round about one o'clock in the morning. The hewers composing the fore-shift thereupon turn out and array themselves in their working dresses, which are generally left roasting before the fire. They let themselves out, falling-to latches being attached to the door, for the purpose of securing them thereafter, and proceed to the shaft, which they descend in parties of half-a-dozen or more. About two hours after the hewers have been at work, the callsman makes a second round, and summons the drivers, putters and trap-boys. By this time the hewers have filled a sufficient number of tubs to set their coadjutors at work, and as soon as the engine begins to heave up its first load of coals to the bank, the day's work, so far as regards those who work by the day, is held to have commenced. The back-shift of hewers "go in" about eight or nine o'clock in the morning. The fore-shift comes out about ten or eleven a.m., and the back-shift about four or five p.m. The men of each shift change hours every week, the fore-shift of one week being the back-shift of the next.

About eleven o'clock in the forenoon, then, the first party knock off work. They place their picks in the waggons, take them out again at the bottom of the shaft, and having ascended, proceed with them to the blacksmith's shop. By the time they get home, their well-earned breakfast is waiting them. But instead of sketching in general terms a fore-shift man's method of passing his day, I will transcribe, almost verbatim, the statement of one pitman—a statement which, upon very extensive inquiry, I find may be taken as giving a fair specimen of the habits of the body.

"Well, sir, when I get to the bank I'm very ready for my breakfast. We're all that. Pitmen have the best appetites. No one can beat the hewers in that way, except, perhaps, the putters. They've a wonderful swallow certainly. My mistress knows better nor to keep me waiting when I come to bank. If I expect to ride (ascend the shaft) at ten o'clock, she has the coffee hot by nine o'clock, in case I shall be sooner nor I thought. I don't wash until I have my breakfast. I'm too sharpset for that. Aye, aye, I must have my coffee and bread before I do aught else." Refreshment in the pit? "No, sir, I only take in a bit of bread in my bailpoke, or, maybe, wrapped in a bit of clout, and a drop o'water in the canteen. The drivers and trappers take down more, because they stay longer than us. Well when I've had my coffee—it used to be porridge, but we've got more genteel now—I warrant you I have a good wash—a wash all over. There's always warm water ready and soap. Cold won't bring the muck off, and besides warm's comfortabler-like—I get to bed." Too tired to wash, and go to bed without it? "Bless you sir, ask the mistress if she would let me do that. No, no. She has over-much respect for the sheets. Pretty sheets they would be if colliers got into them without washing. Well, sir, I have a sleep of two or three hours, till the afternoon; then I get up and feel quite ready for dinner. We don't get as much flesh meat as we could eat, I assure you. What a man has in that way depends on circumstances. If he has a large young family, its little enough, you may take your oath of it. Still, a man who works like a hewer must have nourishing meat. That's a necessity. He couldn't handle the pick without. A single man gets two or three pounds of meat in a week, but we make it go as far as we can. We have often suet puddings and dumplings. We never have any beer or ale at dinner—only water; but we generally manage to have some ale on Saturday nights, particularly on pay-weeks. Well, after dinner I generally have a lot of little things to do, perhaps about my tools, perhaps about my garden. Maybe I may sit down and make cartridges for the shots, or put new hafts to the picks, or I may dander in and speak to a neighbour, or have a game at quoits, or a walk to breathe the fresh air. Some of us that have a turn that way read books, or make small things in the furniture way, especially bird cages and little chests of drawers for ornament, or we smoke our pipes before the door. Then we have some tea and go to bed perhaps about seven o'clock or eight o'clock. Those who go in late in the morning have dinner when they come to bank, and then go to bed. They have tea when they rise again, and can do what they like till night, when they turn in in time enough to get up very well by seven o'clock, or six o'clock; and that sir, is a very fair account of a pitman's day."

The clothes used for the mine are, as I have said, made entirely of coarse flannel. Sometimes the wives are competent to shape and sew them. Sometimes they are purchased at slop-shops at Newcastle. A hewer's dress consists of a long jacket with large pockets, a waistcoat, a flannel shirt, a pair of short drawers reaching to the middle of the thigh, a pair of stout flannel trousers worn over them, with worsted stockings or "hoggers"— that is stockings with the feet cut away. Many of the hewers who wear hoggers envelop their feet in rags to prevent the coal dust getting between the toes. They all wear stout shoes. While at their work, the heat is commonly found so oppressive that the hewers often fling off every stitch save the short drawers. They generally, however, come to the pit mouth fully dressed. The putters on the contrary make their appearance, as I have already described, in the short drawers with or without "hoggers". A pit suit of good material and fair workmanship will cost about a pound. In spite of their grimy avocation, there are probably no members of the labouring classes more clean than the pitmen of Northumberland and Durham when above ground. They have a thorough scrubbing with soap and hot water every day of their lives, and they generally dress in a far better style than the ordinary run of labouring men. Indeed, it is difficult to believe that the clean, respectably attired person is the same begrimed, three parts naked being, whose white gleaming eyes and teeth you remember, as he turned round from the wall of coal, and held up his Davy lamp for your convenience. I was remarking one day how exceedingly black a putter looked, when half an hour after, I beheld him emerge from his home, his complexion almost as light as that of an albino, and a profusion of "lint white locks" streaming in dandified curls down his cheeks.

A Colliery Village

A pit row is like nothing whatever in the shape of a collocation of dwelling places that I know of in England. It is neither like a country village nor a section of the meaner part of a manufacturing town; but it appears to me to possess more than the inconveniences of the one, and more than the ugliness of the other. The shops, if anything worthy of the name exists at all, are of the meanest and most miserable description. From end to end there is not a single large house, a tree, or a church spire to break the shabby uniformity of the pitmen's cottages. The general run of chapels, principally belonging to Methodist bodies, which abound, may be distinguished from barns only by being far smaller and more paltry-looking. But I shall endeavour to sketch the *tout ensemble*. Fancy, then, in the vicinity of the pit-heap, a succession of rows of one-storied red-tiled cottages. Sometimes they are arranged in double lines of all sides of a square, leaving a black dismal vacancy in the centre. But more commonly they fill up an oblong space, the longitudinally-running rows being, however, unbroken by cross streets. Uniform as all the houses at first appear to be, a second glance will show that there are differences. In some rows the ridge of the roof is equi-distant from the eaves—the two surfaces of tiles sloping at similar angles. In others, a series of smaller houses in the manner of lean-tos appears to have been added to the original tenements; although in fact, the whole row was so constructed from the beginning. By this method of building, the houses have a one-sided appearance, fully twice as much of their bulk extending on one side as on the other. These peculiarities of construction produce three distinct classes of houses. The third, or lowest class, is formed by the back-house, or lean-to. The second class is formed of the front houses to which the smaller ones are attached; and a house of the first or best class is produced by flinging a front and a back tenement into one dwelling. Opposite the doors on either side of every row will be observed small detached buildings with the roof sloping in one way only, and here and there will be scattered little houses like miniature dwellings, but adorned with chimneys from which smoke occasionally issues. the first erections are pantries and larders, one of which is attached to every house; the second are ovens, at which the bread of a dozen families can be baked at once.

Let us now proceed along the streets of the colliery village. Almost without exception they will be found in a miserably filthy condition. Sometimes ash pits have been formed with singular judgement close to the larders, but most commonly the ashes and all sorts of domestic refuse are flung into the centre of the street. All the way along the dismal thoroughfare runs a sierra of "middens", with here and there a filthy pigsty. In a few colliery villages there is a feeble attempt at surface drainage, the liquid refuse in these channels being very frequently stagnant; but in not one pit-row out of the scores that I have seen, and in not one pit-row, I am told, in Northumberland and Durham, is there a single foot of underground drainage, calculated by means of sinks, to carry away domestic slops. And these rows, be it observed, were not built piecemeal by poor men, ignorant of the importance of drainage to health and life; they were one and all constructed wholesale by the owners of the neighbouring pits, for the accommodation of their workpeople, and they are the only houses in which these workpeople can possibly live.

But I have a more serious charge to bring against the owners of colliery villages even than that involved in lack of drainage. There may be exceptions to the general rule (if there be, I have not seen them); but the general, almost the universal rule in Durham and Northumberland is the construction of little towns—for many pit villages may be so called—without the erection of one single privy or cesspool, either public or private. The few privies which, in rare instances, do exist are rude constructions of boards, built by the occupants of the houses themselves, and generally located in the gardens. I repeat, to their flagrant disgrace, the owners of the pit-villages of the north have made not the slightest provision for public decency or public health in the respect in question. In the worst parts of Manchester and Oldham, I have found some sort of accommodation of the kind, exceedingly defective, and often exceedingly filthy. It was reserved for the pit-owners of Northumberland and Durham to set every claim of nature and common self respect alike at defiance. Of course the consequences of such a state of things may be imagined. I have dwelt upon the point because I have been over and over again most earnestly entreated by the pitmen to bring the circumstances before the public, as one in which not only the convenience and the health, but the feelings and the morals of the mining population are deeply concerned.

Housing in a Pit-Village

The houses of the pit village may, as I have stated, be divided into three classes. Those of the lowest class usually contain only one room; those of the second contain a large room and an attic. The best houses consist of two rooms on the ground floor, with generally an attic over one of them. In all cases, the sitting room door is the street door. It will be obvious that tenements so arranged furnish miserably deficient accommodation. The largest families have only two inhabitable rooms, the others being wretched lofts, with the tiles left bare, and so low that even beneath the ridge of the roof a man cannot stand upright. But two-roomed houses fall to the lot of perhaps only one-third of the mining population. The dwellings as I have stated are accounted part of the wages, and they are apportioned by the proprietor or his agents, not so much according to the family of each pitman as according to the family he has working, or likely to work in the mine. A young married couple go, after their union, into one of the back or lean-to houses. Here they remain until they have a young family around them. Then they are probably transferred to one of the second class dwellings, of one room with an attic, and by the time the boys begin to work in the pit the father can claim a first-class or double house. If the family consist wholly or principally of girls, they must make shift in the second-rate house. Parents with growing boys have always the preference in obtaining work in a coal-pit, and houses in a pit-village: indeed, married men without families are sometimes turned out of their own into inferior houses to make room for the more useful circle of juvenile labourers.

Practically, and for all purposes of living, the attic seems, from all I can gather, to be of small use; and the deplorable consequence is that more than one half of the pit population virtually live – each family – in a single room. Here is bedroom and kitchen – here the men and boys, on their return from the pit, wash their almost naked bodies, too often in the presence of growing-up daughters and sisters – and here too the women dress and undress, unless the presence of an absolute stranger, compels them to run across the street, in order, as I have over and over witnessed, to change their attire in the pantry. The men say that they cannot wash upstairs, as the water would plash through the frequently warped flooring down upon the furniture, and perhaps the bed below; and in the unfrequent cases of two-storied pit-houses, complaints are frequently made of the spillage caused by the occupants of the higher room. The best sort of houses in a pit-village are always occupied by the deputies, the overmen, and the principal waggon-drivers, and the range is commonly nicknamed "Quality Row". As a general rule a garden goes with every house, the ground being sometimes attached to it; but by far the most frequent plan is to subdivide a field into patches, wherein each pitman may grow a few pecks of potatoes or cabbages. The miners sometimes take pains with their gardens, but they are more commonly neglected. Besides his house each miner receives fuel, not quite for nothing but for 3d. per week, the trifling amount in question being nominally paid, not for the coal, but for the "leading" or carting it to the door.

Let us imagine then, if we would form an idea of a colliery village, some half a dozen rows of perfectly uniform one-storied cottages, the intersecting lanes dotted with ash-heaps and middens, with, in rainy weather, perfectly formed sloughs of mud round the hills of refuse. On the outskirts rise one or two, modest looking, dissenting chapels, as unadorned as though the line of beauty typified the path to destruction, and about as big as ordinary sized parlours. At one end probably rises the pit heap, at the other extends the garden field, and all around stretches a labyrinth of deep-rutted, miry cross roads, through which in this wintry weather, the wayfarer, as I have had woeful experience, wades rather than walks.

We will now enter one of the ordinary class of houses. In one respect, particularly in the cold season, the pitman's dwelling is especially comfortable; it is sure to have a blazing fire, the bright red reflection of which dances cheerfully on everything around. As a general rule the furniture is decidedly good; some articles are even costly. The visitor's attention will be especially drawn to the bed and the chest of drawers. In a great proportion of cases neither of these would be out of place in a house of some pretensions. The bedsteads are very frequently of carved and turned mahogany, and the bed, clean, soft, and comfortable, with white furniture and a quilted cover-lid. The chest of drawers is frequently an article which costs from £8 to £10. It commonly rises almost to the ceiling, only leaving room for a few old-fashioned china or stoneware ornaments to be placed upon the top. The chairs are sometimes deal and sometimes mahogany. The mantelpiece is generally crowded with little ornaments of china and glass; the plates, cups and saucers are usually kept in cupboards; but highly-polished brass candlesticks, placed on shelves or hung upon nails, glitter from the wall. Birds and birdcages abound. The songsters are generally fine canaries, or carefully bred mules, and the cages have often been manufactured by the occupant of the cottage. The stock of books is generally very small, but there is almost always a large folio bible to be found, often accompanied by a few Methodist tracts, and—strange literary jumble—assortments of dream books, "Oracles of Fate, as consulted by the Emperor Napoleon", and "Little Warblers".

The women are the great agents in getting the houses so well furnished as they are. They strive to outdo each other in the matters of beds and chests of drawers, the two great features of their rooms. When a young couple get married they generally go to a furniture broker in Newcastle or Sunderland, with perhaps £10 of ready money, obtaining a considerable part of their "plenishing" upon credit, and paying for it by instalments. Like the Manchester mill-hands, the colliery folks have a great notion of clocks; but unlike the cotton workers, a great proportion of the pitmen's timepieces are regular eight-day clocks with metallic dials. The floors of the houses are seldom or never boarded. Sometimes they are formed of a hard composite, but they are more often paved with red brick—here and there, perhaps, covered with strips of carpeting. Complaints of dampness are very rife, and the chimneys frequently smoke abominably. The attic is invariably gained by a perpendicular flight of steps and a trap-door. The pit-men represent that it is so bare and cold as to render sleeping in it in the cold season a matter of real suffering to people accustomed to the hot air of the mine while at work, or to blazing fires in their living rooms at home. I may add that I have seen houses of a decidedly superior class to those just sketched, but I have good reason to believe that most industrious pitmen can attain to the state of comparative domestic comfort above described.

Accidents in Coal Mines

It has been stated as a matter of regret before several Parliamentary committees, that no means exist of getting at, with anything like accuracy, the statistics of the loss of life underground. Except in the case of a catastrophe on a great scale, little or nothing is heard of coal pit accidents beyond the immediate locality of the mine. Many violent deaths occur underground which the coroner never hears of. An explosion perhaps kills a couple of men. There are numerous persons in authority interested in hushing up the matter. So the proprietors pay for the funeral of the victims—make some small money present to the widows, if there be any— allow them to continue in the possession of their houses, and little or nothing more is ever heard on the subject. One evil resulting from this state of things is, the facility which it affords to different parties of underestimating and over-estimating the probable number of yearly victims. For instance, on the late occasion of the opening of the Coal-Exchange a placard was extensively circulated in London, one of the statements of which was that since 1800 more than 20,000 human beings had been killed by explosion in coal-pits.

This estimate seemed so fearful that I have taken some pains in order to ascertain whether there were any exaggerations involved. There was a small pamphlet published some years ago by a working collier in which are given the number of fatal accidents, the several causes and results, with the name of the collieries in which they happened, in the counties of Durham and Northumberland, the register embracing the lengthened period between 1756 and 1843. I have gone carefully over this calendar, and the results are that according to the pamphlet in question, there perished in Durham and Northerland during the 87 years from explosion, about 1,491 persons, and from all other accidents common to miners, about 270 persons, making a total of 1,760 violent deaths. Now, taking the fatal accidents of Northumberland and Durham as amounting to only one fourth of those which occur in Great Britain, the general result would be an estimate far below that given in the placard in question. Let us try it by another test. The number of known deaths by accident and misadventure in 55 mining districts in 1838 was, from all causes, 349. This number taken as an average, and multiplied by 49, would give a total of about 17,000 fatal accidents. But out of the 349 deaths not above one-fourth were caused by explosion; therefore, still taking 1838 as an average year, it would appear that the fair estimate for deaths by explosion for forty-nine years would be about 4,250 instead of 20,000. I have already mentioned the increase in the total number of accidents from explosion which took place in the northern coalfield after the introduction of the safety lamp. By parliamentary returns connected with that inquiry, it appeared that in thirty-six years the loss of life in the northern coal district by explosion was 985. The South Shields committee reported that in twenty years 680 miners were destroyed by explosion in the valleys of the Tyne and Wear. These several estimates give approximate results to what is probably the truth of the matter; and although they contradict the exaggerated estimate of 20,000 lives lost by explosion in less than half a century, they still tell a terrible tale—it may be in some cases of carelessness and recklessness—but assuredly in all cases of the defective ventilation, which made that recklessness and that carelessness so widely fatal.

But accidents from fire-damp form only one category of those incidental to coal-pits. Mine catastrophes may be divided into three general classes – those in the shaft, those produced by the falling of the roof, and those the result of the presence of diluted carburetted gas. Shaft accidents are, perhaps, more frequently than any others, the result of carelessness. Since the introduction of the cage, for ascending and descending pits, the chance of casualties has been much diminished. I have already described the hazardous mode in which men were formerly pulled up from, and let down into the pits, dangling with their thighs in the loops. It was a common thing for a couple of men to descend thus. Each with a boy upon his knee, while half a dozen boys over them clung one above the other to the chain. These last grasped the rope in succession as it moved downwards into the pit; and of course a false movement in a moment's nervousness or hesitation might, and often did, cause them to miss their grasp and perish miserably. At present, however, where in the case of almost every pit the men traverse the shaft in cages, the principal danger to be apprehended is the breaking of the rope.

To guard against the consequences of this accident an ingenious invention has lately been patented, consisting of a system of springs, attached to the edges of the cage, which, when released by the pressure caused by the weight of the tubs, as they would be by the breaking of the rope, immediately start out in a lateral direction, and seizing the spears or guides down which the cage glides, arrest its progress and hold it suspended until a new rope can be attached to it. Experiments, considered by practical men to be satisfactory, have been made with this apparatus, which is the invention of Mr. Foudrinier. At the Usworth colliery in Durham, the apparatus was fixed to a cage, loaded to the extent of two tons and a half. The rope suspending this great weight was several times disengaged, and on every occasion the spring clasps leaped forth and held the cage stationary. A certificate setting forth the confidence of the subscribers in the invention, and stating it to be "highly important for the saving of life", was signed upon the spot by twelve viewers, four engineers and several other gentlemen connected with the scientific management of collieries. On another occasion four gentlemen actually confided their lives to the working of the apparatus, standing upon upwards of 40 cwt. of coal. An objection started to the invention, upon the ground of the risk from perhaps more than 200 fathoms of heavy rope or chain falling upon the arrested cage, has been met by the fact, that in the Usworth Colliery this casualty actually happened. Upwards of 200 fathoms of rope, weighing 37cwt, did actually, after an accident, fall upon the suspended cage, without overcoming the clutch of the springs, or injuring either cage or shaft—of course, the former is strongly roofed in. In talking over this invention with a very able colliery viewer, he stated an objection which seems unfortunately too characteristic of colliery management. He feared that such an apparatus would have a strong tendency to cause the use of ropes after they had become worn out and unsafe. In other words, the safeguard, in case of accident actually happening, would tend to supersede the means taken for preventing accident. It was so to a certain extent with the Davy. The lamp was intended as a protection when accidentally carried into foul air—a policy very like that of wilfully running a ship among breakers because a lifeboat is known to be at hand.

The falling in of the roof is most commonly caused by parsimony in using supporting timber, or by want of skill and care in withdrawing that timber when a goaf is to be formed. The men state that they have cause to complain in this respect, both from the insufficient quantity of props often employed, and from the lack of skill of the deputies by whom the props and other timber defences are arranged.

But the fearful scourge of the coalmine is the distillation from the mineral of carburetted hydrogen or fire-damp. The pure gas is inexplosive; but when mixed with eight times its volume of air, the fluid acquires powers more terrible than even those of gunpowder. A mine explosion is a thing unhappily often heard of; but its terrible features are not in general correctly realised. A light is brought in contact with the aerial agent. Immediately it bursts, with a smothered roar, into a vast sea of scathing flame, flying from passage to passage, and corridor to corridor, wherever the explosive compound exists, and dashing planking, brattices, and doors before it, as though they had been shattered by cannon-balls. In a pit near Newcastle three men were employed close to the bottom of a shaft, coaling up the entrance to an old deserted working. Behind them at a few paces distance, was a brattice or partition, extending down and across the shaft, and formed of seasoned three inch planking. A candle was fetched, the better to survey the masonry. Gas was present—it fired—and the three men were blown right through the three-inch planking, and smashed into pulp on the opposite side of the shaft. In other cases, men have been shot up out of the shaft like bullets out of a gun-barrel, and their blackened limbs picked up in the adjacent fields. But generally, the loss of life from actual flame, from being dashed against the sides of the mine is comparatively small. The worst comes after the explosion. No sooner has the sheet of flame spent itself than volumes of carbonic acid—the fatal choke-damp or stythe, one breath of which in its pure state is death—come rolling in suffocating fumes along the neighbouring passages. The explosion has frequently blown down the brattices and trap-doors; the ventilation of the mine is therefore, in a moment, suspended, and the stythe works its deadly will. It frequently happens that ten men are killed by stythe for one burnt by the fire damp. The poor fellows are found unscathed in face and limb, but choked by the suffocating vapour. Several men have given me descriptions of what they witnessed of the effect of explosions taking place in quite a different part of the mine from that in which they were working.

"I remember, sir," said one, "an explosion happening in our pit. It was far from us, and we heard no noise; but all at once the air was chopped off from our mouths. Then we knew what had happened. Not one of us spoke a word to the other but we cast down our picks and ran to the shaft for life! I did not think of death to myself, but I thought of Jane (his wife) and the five little ones. Thank God, we got safe to the bottom of the shaft; but if the stythe had chanced to come across we should have fallen down and died where we lay."

The miners know when they are in foul air by the appearance of the flame in the Davy lamp. It becomes elongated and presently, if the gas continues to pour forth, the ordinary flame is, as it were, lipped and haloed by a second bluish-hued fire, formed by the burning of the carburetted hydrogen within the gauze screen. It used to be not an uncommon practice for miners to continue working in the full consciousness of the atmosphere with which they were thus surrounded, and perfectly aware that their lamps were, as it is called "afire". Recklessness of this kind is now, however, by no means so common as it was. In such cases as I have mentioned, an accident to the lamp from a fall, or the chance blow of a pick, would have produced an instantaneous explosion. Still, however, men do not scruple to carry the Davy into an atmosphere which they know to be highly inflammable. A scientific gentleman deputed from Government was lately examining the scene of a fatal explosion. He was accompanied by the under-viewer of the colliery, and as they were inspecting the edges of the goaf, it was observed that the Davys which they were carrying were afire.

"I suppose," said the Inspector, "that there is a good deal of fire-damp hereabouts?"

"Thousands and thousands of cubic feet, all through the goaf," replied his companion, coolly.

"Why," exclaimed the official, "do you mean to say that we have nothing but a shred of wire between us and eternity?"

"Nothing at all," said the under-viewer, very tranquilly, "there's nothing where we stand but the gauze to keep the whole mine from being blown into the air."

The inspector made a wise and precipitate retreat. Occasionally when the men come to their work, they find, if the ventilation has been defective, a stratum, as it were, of explosive air floating near the roof of the working. A common remedy in such cases is for them to strip off their jackets and brush and sweep the foul air out towards the main passages, where the strong ventilating current carries it harmlessly away. In about eight to ten mines in the north, the Davy has been superseded by the Clanny lamp, a light which I have the testimony of many practical men for asserting to be superior in many respects to the Davy. The general principle, that dependent upon the wire gauze, is the same in both lamps; but in the Clanny apparatus there is an additional glass cylinder to protect the flame against draughts, and matters are so ordered that as soon as the air reaches the explosive point, the flame goes out. The Clanny lamp, besides being in this way safer than the Davy, gives out more than twice as much light. Its drawbacks are, being heavier, and as I believe more expensive. While upon the subject, I may mention that Dr Reid Clanny of Sunderland, the inventor of this lamp, had conceived and carried out the idea of availing himself of the non-passage of flame through wire gauze at least two years before the invention of Sir Humphrey Davy. Of course, all gases given out in coal mines are not explosive. Carbonic acid, although generally the product of explosion, is sometimes generated spontaneously. In this shape it is seldom fatal, because its increase is gradual, and it extinguishes the lamps, thus forcing the men to leave the place long before the air becomes absolutely poisonous to breathe. Sometimes carbonic acid causes lamps to burn so dimly that the men are forced to agitate them to improve the flame, and I have heard of cases in which boys have been employed at 1s 6d and 1s 8d per day to swing the lamps in order to keep them alight. The effect of hard and protracted labour in such an atmosphere must be palpable.

The facts stated above necessitate the conclusion, that it is not to the most admirably adapted lamps which science can invent, but to steady and well-regulated ventilation, that we must look for the prevention of explosive accidents in mines. To make things reasonably secure the current ought to play ceaselessly through every nook and winding of the pit. The smallest quantum of air which ought to be sent through the main passages of a fiery colliery is in the opinion of competent witnesses from 350 to 400 cubic feet per second; and in the better ventilated pits, upwards of 30,000 cubic feet do actually pass per minute. In this respect the Durham and Northumberland collieries are far in advance of the pits in other districts; but even in many of these there is great room for improvement. Among the working men there exists a very deep and natural feeling upon the subject, which is one of life or death to them. The topic is now under consideration of Government, and Professor Phillips is now engaged in inspecting, on the part of the Government, certain of the northern coal mines. The method adopted by the professor has been freely canvassed by the working miners, who conceived that a list of collieries furnished to him by the viewers, and which he is at present engaged in inspecting, included only the very best ventilated pits in the district, and was not calculated to convey a correct idea of the general condition of the coal-mines of the north.

Acting upon this persuasion, a deputation of the working miners, appointed at a public meeting of the body, waited upon Professor Phillips to request that he would also descend and examine an additional number of collieries, a list of which they furnished him. This deputation, composed of delegates from the different pits in question, had an interview with the professor on the 22nd of October last, when he explained to them that the list furnished by the viewers was drawn up in accordance with his own views, as he intended first, to examine a number of what might be termed model pits, and thus form a standard by which he could afterwards the better judge the condition of the inferior ones. The deputation then handed to the professor statements of the condition of things in the mines which they represented, every delegate detailing the condition as regards ventilation of his own pit. I have been furnished with copies of these statements, which I subjoin. They are to a certain extent ex parte documents, and must be viewed in that light, but they are of very considerable interest and importance, as expressing the opinion, rightly or wrongly entertained, by a large body of working men upon matters with respect to which they must be practically, if not scientifically, familiar and which (at all events) involve their chances of life from hour to hour. I am in possession of the delegates names, but have been requested to suppress them. The documents put into my hands I transcribe unaltered as regards arrangement and composition:

STATE AND CONDITION OF THE COLLIERIES IN TYNE, WEAR, AND TEES, WITH RESPECT TO VENTILATION, AND REPRESENTED BY A DEPUTATION OF MINERS TO PROFESSOR PHILLIPS, OCTOBER 22, 1849

North Hetton Colliery. The ventilation down the staple is very bad; the air is so slack that when men fire their shots [blasting the coal] the smoke from the same stands there all day, there not being a current of air to carry it away. The staple is about one mile from the main shaft, and is 12 fathoms deep. The Hazard Pit is about one mile from the main shaft, and is 12 fathoms deep. The Hazard Pit is very bad in the broken or pillar working; the safety lamp will not live, and is necessarily unfit for a man to work in six hours. The brattices are put in for 14 yards to the pillar, which is 24 yards, together with 12 yards of wall, being 22 yards before the air. The waggon and tramways are insufficiently propped—that is, the timber is too scant; and thus we are exposed to dangers from the falling roof. There are no parties to look after the same. Since the ponies [small horses] came into general use the air is much more soft, and we consider that the said ponies consume more air than was consumed by the putters, and they increase the danger by their superior strength in drawing, when the tub, or corf, is fast to the timber or props. Remarks: The tendency of the powder smoke to still further contaminate the air is obvious and clear; and it is also clear that the constitutions of the workmen must suffer in a corresponding ratio—nothing being more calculated to injure the health than contaminated air. Better to have pure air. Very many fatal accidents have occurred through insufficient timber, and when no one is appointed to inspect the state of the props the danger is increased. £10 per month would remedy all this evil—being but 2d per score for 60 scores per day, 5 days per week. What a great good for so small a sum as 2d per score.

Westerton Colliery. State of the ventilation on October 16, 1849: The men of the above colliery complain "That the air is not properly conducted in the working places." That there is a great deficiency of trap-doors and stoppings all essential to a proper conducting of the air, and bearing up to where men have to labour. That cases are of frequent occurrence where men have had to leave their work through an excess of the presence of carbonic acid gas, or stythe. We, the workmen of the above colliery, would respectfully respect to have a visit from the commissioner, and feel hurt at the Black Boy being chosen as a colliery to be inspected with a view to afford a criterion, which colliery is well known to be a better ventilated one than ours.

Washington Colliery. State of the ventilation, October 2, 1849. Pit fired at a place where a box is placed to convey the foul air out of the working, when it is mixed with the fresh air, and sent through the workings of two other districts or flats. The masters blame the leaving open of a door which stood in the headways course, at a place called the far crosscut [angular excavation] and assert that the lad, or boy, expressed his desire to have the door to mind, that the price paid for so doing might add to his scanty wages. Another explosion took place in July, 1849, when George Dang was so severely burnt that he only survived nine days. December last, 16th, 1848, four men were drawn over the pulley. Henry Hutchison and John Forster were killed; the other survived the accident. The coroner's depositions went to find fault with the engineman, he being too young, according to Lord Ashley's Act. The owners have never allowed the friends or relatives of the sufferers recompense; but the case is before a solicitor to compel proper damages. Examined the pit on the 19th and 20th October; went through the workings and the waste also. Took the west side of the rolleyway first, then the east to the staple, where all the returns meet. The staple is 7 feet diameter. The downcast shaft is 7 feet, and the upcast 7 feet also. We are working the Hutton seam and the Low-main. The furnace is in the Maudlin seam, 11 fathoms above the Hutton seam. The height of the Hutton seam is 3 feet 8 inches, the Low-main the same. We found the furnace slack in the up-cast shaft. Water was falling. There were places wanting brattices. Great improvements since we refused to work on account of the previous accidents. The ponies and asses that are used in the workings consume the air, and otherwise prevent its free circulation. The tubs are 7 cwt.

Castle Eden Colliery, near Hartlepool. State of the ventilation, October 1849. The owner, Gladstone Esq, Viewer, M. B. Robson. Resides on the colliery; is manager at Whitwell Colliery also. The subordinates are chiefly (to the best of my knowledge) selected for their capabilities in the science of ventilation, they not being capable of writing. The mine is worked with candles generally, but sometimes Davy lamps are used. The seams are the Low-main, and Main coal, liable to fire damp; evolves from the coal and roof also. The weather does not to my knowledge influence the discharge of gas. The shaft is 12 feet diameter, and is in three compartments, two of which are down-casts, and the up-cast being about one-third of the whole. The ventilation is by furnace. The pit works double shift, from Monday, at one o'clock a.m. till

Saturday, at twelve p.m. The hewers work double in walls, where two are turned away at one time, making four men in one board; when the heat from the perspiration of the men and the blasting of the coal renders it almost insupportable for life, and consequent injury to health. The brattices are much neglected, though there are printed rules stating that the brattice is not to exceed six feet from the face, yet they are sometimes twelve yards from the face. There are thirty six horses or ponies. The air passes through the stables and carries with it most unwholesome effluvia into the workings. There have been repeated solicitations to give a scale of air to the stables, and carry off to the furnace; yet it has always been refused. Where doors are thought necessary they are swing doors, and often will not fall close. The tubs are left in the face of each working place etc; in narrow places the men cannot get out, though in the same mine blowers are very frequent. The quality of air is mostly complained of as doing serious injury to our health; it is called damp air. The workmen's tools are frequently left in the workings, and are covered with mould or damp; a fungus is always hanging on the prop of timber. We are exposed to dangers in want of deputies etc. to prop the place, and when we complain we are told to do it ourselves, and if that does not suit, they [the workmen] may leave. The tubs are 25 pecks or 7½ cwt. The danger from want of timber is of common occurrence; and though representing our case to our employers they will pay no heed to our solicitations. 170 to the Hutton seam and 150 to the Low-main.

Crow Trees Colliery. State of the ventilation, October 1849. Three down-cast shafts and one up-cast, the last 7 feet diameter. There is a split at the bottom, and goes 150 yards along the rolley-way to the main door, takes to the east where 24 men work. No system of conducting the air to these men, there being no brattices; the air returns back through the goaf for about 300 yards, comes again into the waggon ways, and travels near a mile to another main door, and goes south where a few men work; no means are taken to convey the air to these men. Then takes over the goaf to another flat; between that flat and another there is a swing door, no other means being employed to convey the air to the men. Very often the men have to return without working for want of air; many are heard to wish there was a little gas. The air is so damp that when we lose our light no lucifer match will strike. The return, in a certain place and for some distance, has to traverse a passage not more than two feet high; indeed, men have to creep on all fours. The seam is 3 feet 3 inches high. Mr. John Robson, viewer and manager.

Orclose Colliery. State of the ventilation, October 1849. The diameter of the downshaft is 7 feet 3 inches; the diameter of the upcast shaft is 8 feet. There is a pumping set of three lifts, 10 inches in the bore, in the up-cast shaft. The men requested to examine the pit; but Mr. Willis, the overman, stated that he could not allow that to be done without leave of the head-viewer, Mr. Elliott. He promised to see him on the Friday, but did not; consequently we have not had the opportunity of examining the pit. The seam makes a very great quantity of gas of an explosive character, and frequently men have been burnt, one of whom died very lately (September 23, 1849). The boards are partially bratticed, but not wholly so; there is a want of system in that particular. Few doors in the workings and those are swing doors. There is deficiency of the known means to render the men's lives safe.

Wingate Grange Colliery. State of the ventilation, October 22, 1849. The workmen of the above colliery sent a man to be examined before Professor Phillips, the commissioner of mines. We send the following cases to which we can bear witness. We are compelled to drive the narrow places 5 feet wide, and to drive the boards from 20 to 30 yards to the pillar. The walls from 7 to 14 yards. We are compelled to drive them these distances without brattices or doors, and instead of main or sheth doors, nothing but swing doors, when they are any at all. The air is split six times from the main passage. A headways course is driven on each side of the mother gate board, at each flat. In some instances they convey the air into the workings with a wooden box eight or ten inches square. We frequently have to begin work in the morning with the Davy lamp, until the deputy thinks the place clear of gas, and then we get the naked light or candle. The gas has frequently to be dusted out in the morning even in the boards near the flat. The height of the seam is five feet, under the present mode of working by raking up the bottom stone and leaving the top coal, the height is four feet. The tubs are 3 feet 6 inches high, the breadth 3 feet 4 inches. The space for air to travel is but small. This is our condition at present: the men of Wingate Grange.

Cassop Colliery. State of the ventilation, October 22, 1849. The shaft is 12 feet in diameter and is divided into three partitions, two of which are downcasts, the other up-cast. The air splits at the bottom of the shaft, the one goes east and the other west. The air courses are driven six feet wide. The height of the seam is 3 feet 4 inches, and it invariably falls from want of wastemen and timber. There are not more than 2 square feet for the return air to the up-cast shaft. In consequence of the want of air before the boards are up to the pillar, the candles will not burn, and even in some cases two or three candles are lighted at the same time in order to get a sufficient light, all of which could be prevented if doors or brattices were provided to conduct the air up into the boards. When the men blast the coal, the powder smoke stands upon them all the future part of the day, which is found very injurious to the men's health. The old colliery has two shafts, one a downcast and the other one, up-cast. The air is split at the bottom of the shaft; after that it is split very often, but we cannot tell the number of splits; but in the workings there is a deficiency of air for the men to work in, which would be entirely obviated if a sufficient quantity of doors and brattices were provided. There is not much hydrogen gas, but chiefly carbonic acid gas, whcih we feel very injurious to our health. In the broken, or pillars, the Davylamp will not burn for want of air.

South Wingate Colliery. State of the ventilation, October 22, 1849. Owner, A. Seymour; viewer, Martin Seymour. There is one shaft divided into three compartments. Fire damp prevails. There were no brattices in the pit until a recent explosion, wherein two men and two boys were burnt severely. Brattices are now in the pit. The following particulars are from the mouth of one of the sufferers, and other workmen employed in the colliery. There is one engine on the colliery which draws the coals by day; when the ropes are taken off for the purpose of drawing water by night. The men were sent down on the day in question, and then the ropes were taken off; they then went into the working places, where many were; there being no brattices, no precautions were taken by the officers to inform of the presence of gas; one of them went up a board to get a shovel (a very common occurrence), when the gas ignited, burning him and three others. Had the explosion not driven itself out, there can be no doubt, owing to accumulation of gas in the other places, that all in the pit would have perished. Those who were burnt were brought to the shaft bottom, and the signal given to get them to bank, but without avail, all means were used in their power, by shouting and beating on the iron tubs to make a noise; it is evident that they were known to be there as the rapper was muzzled and coals were thrown down the shaft. The unfortunate sufferers thus lay in agonies 5 hours and 35 minutes before they were got up. The manager knew that gas was generated in the mines previous to the explosions. There is a stone band in the seam; this is thrown behind the workman; thus the boards are almost choked up, there being only a narrow passage to convey the coals out. Since the explosion, the officers state that the sufferers had orders not to go without a lamp; yet in the presence of the witness one of the sufferers denies the assertion and states he had no such orders. He is not likely to survive.

Trimden Grange Colliery. State of the ventilation, October 22, 1849. We, the workmen of the above colliery, will give you a correct statement of Trimden Grange Colliery. The down-cast shaft to the five-quarter seam is 6 feet by 8 feet 9 inches; the down-cast to the main coal seam is the same. There are two engines down the five-quarter seam supplied with steam from bank, with pipes 2¼ inches in diameter; there is a gas pipe in the same shaft, 2 inches in diameter, goes down to the five-quarter seam, which is a great injury to the men's health when they are at work. The air courses are six feet wide with waggonway. The return in the waste one is four yards wide, and is just high enough that a man can creep upon his belly, and we state that it is not sufficient to keep the pit in a working state. The men many a time have to leave their work after they have been at it 2 or 3 hours many a time insensible. In many instances they have to light two or three candles, to prevent their being in the dark, and we think it injurious to work in such places. The air is split in three different places, and there is nothing but fly doors, with the exception of one or two, and all of them stand open nearly the whole day. They are working the whole pillars from 24 to 40 yards, and no brattice in any of them therefore the air is quite flat, for there is no board-end stoppings.

Ouston Colliery. State of the ventilation, October 22, 1849. The owners are Mr. Henry Hunt and partners. The old pit is divided into two compartments; the air is split at the bottom, going north and west 1½ miles, going south and east 1 miles. The pillars are driven from 24 to 30 yards, without brattices or doors which causes the gas to accumulate. Sometimes the men have to work with their lamps red hot, which endangers their lives very much.

Seaton Burn. State of the ventilation, October 22, 1849. A great deficiency of air in the working places, in consequence of only one length of brattice [wooden partition] being put in at the board end, and there being no board-end doors. The boards are driven 30 yards to the pillar, the walls are ten yards, making forty yards before the air. The walls being 4 yards wide, the current of air is nearly stagnant in the headways course. The air is damp and cold, yet of that sluggish character, that the smoke of gunpowder, with which the men blast the coal, stands upon them all the future part of the day.

Ludworth Colliery. State of the ventilation, October 22, 1849. Sir, the men of Ludworth Colliery are labouring under very bad circumstances, which is ruining their health for want of better ventilation. On Friday, the 19th October 1849, the onsetter had to come to bank for the smoke going down the down-cast shaft which penetrated the brattice when ascending the up-cast. There is also a want of timber to support the roof in the workings, and our lives are in danger therefrom. The boards are driven 26, and some 30 yards to the pillar. There is but two lengths of brattice in each board, and both sides of the board nearly close. The large tubs (30 pecks) so fill up the narrow places that the workmen cannot get out should anything happen—that is, should the place explode, or should the roof fall. Chief agent; Mr. Thomas Wood, but does not reside on the colliery.

What the miners are almost to a man in favour of is, regular Government inspection of the collieries—the inspector having the power of enforcing his recommendations. Petitions to this effect have been in former sessions presented to parliament, and the question will again be agitated next year. Tracts are at present being published upon the subject, under the auspices of the delegate council of the Pitmen's Union. The men urge that of all classes of labour none has a greater claim upon the paternal vigilance of a Government than a dangerous and little understood toil, surrounded with special causes of peril, and carried on apart from the general eye, in the dark recess of the earth. They argue that while the factory labourer and the emigrant are officially cared for and protected, and while a train is not allowed to run upon a new railway until a scientific agent of the Government has minutely inspected and testified to its safety, that vast numbers of people are daily obliged to hazard their lives in an occupation which, for its safe conduct, imperatively demands constant vigilance, and scientific superintendence—a species of superintendence, moreover, carried on in a different spirit to that now exercised on the part of the owners themselves; and who, the men allege, in the management of coal mines, are very often apt to make the safety of the pit a secondary consideration as compared with its profitable working. For these reasons amongst others, the miners are anxious for the appointment of Government inspectors, men of scientific, and practical skill, able not only to recommend, but empowered to put their recommendations into practice.

Relations between Employers and Colliers

I have stated previously that the great strike of 1844 paralysed, if it did not temporarily break up, the miners' combination in Durham and Northumberland. More than one of the unionists have informed me that that strike was resolved in opposition to the earnest counsel of the most able men in the body; and a most intelligent individual, of much authority among the associated workmen, has deplored to me the fact that people always connect unions with strikes. The former he regards as a legitimate and necessary means of enabling labour to hold its own against the power of capital; but a "turn-out" he believes to be an expedient which, although sometimes it may be absolutely indispensable, is yet always and must be always attended with profound human suffering—with a dislocation of the great industrial machine, in the smooth and steady working of which all are interested—and a measure which ought, therefore, never to be adopted unless at the call of a stern and imperative necessity. Whatever may be its future operations, however, the Miners' Union is now again making head.

The association in the north is local, being confined to the counties of Durham and Northumberland. It numbers at present upwards of 7,000 members, of whom a few, and only a few, are boys. It employs six paid labourers to disseminate and enforce its views—comprehends upwards of sixty collieries, many of them amongst the largest and most important in the district—and holds regular fortnightly meetings, at which a delegate from each pit attends to consult and report progress. As one of these meetings, thus composed of working men, deputed by their brethren to represent their interest in the struggle between capital and labour, was held the other day at Newcastle, I deemed it my duty to attend, and state the nature of my mission in the north, so as to receive from the mouths of the men themselves their own version of their grievances. I am aware that any such statements will be generally regarded as proceeding from sources peculiarly interested in impressing the public with a one-sided idea of alleged wrongs. But I shall take care that both sides of the question are submitted to the world. I shall give the statements of the pitmen, and I shall add the counter representations of gentlemen also practically connected with collieries, but who, in their capacity as viewers or proprietors are naturally led to regard the same subject from a different point of view. If I shall succeed in fairly and honestly stating the pros and cons of a disputed matter which has occasioned numberless strikes and a vast degree of bad blood between employers and employed, I shall account my object as so far answered.

Leaving out of view for the present questions as to the rate of wages—always of course a fertile subject of dispute, but one continually changing its phases with fluctuations of the coal market—I proceed at once to state what appears to me to be the chronic source of bad feeling between the collier operatives and their employers. In working coal mines there are two sets of fines or forfeitures falling upon the men, which have been enforced more or less rigidly from time immemorial. Hewers are, as the reader knows, paid by the quantity of coals which they send up to the pit-bank. These coals are placed in tubs, and must amount to a certain weight, which, I believe, differs in a slight degree at different collieries. If, upon their arrival at the weighing machines at the pit-mouth, they prove to be, by a certain number of pounds (generally fourteen) under weight, then the hewer loses the whole amount due for hewing the tub-full. This custom is called "set-out", and earnings thus forfeited are said to be lost by "set-out". But even if the weight be found correct, there is another ordeal to be gone through. When the coals are tilted into the screen, a person appointed for the purpose, and called a "kecker", closely examines them, and picks out any stones, splint, and foul and inferior coal, which he can detect. If this refuse amount to more than one quart in some collieries, and two quarts in others, then the hewing of the whole tub is forfeited. This penalty is called "laid-out". Besides the screens there are generally placed shallow wooden trays, divided into different compartments, in which the refuse from each tub is "laid-out", to be shown to the hewer, who sends it up, when he comes to bank. These two customs of "laid-out" and "set-out" are at the bottom of a vast proportion of the disputes between master and man in the coal districts.

In estimating the amount of wages lost by the fines in question, the coal-owners and the coal-workers usually differ very widely. Much in the case of "laid-out" depends upon the quality of the seam in process of working. Sometimes the coal is pure and is easily wrought; at others it is to a greater or lesser extent intermingled with different mineral substances, the uniform rejection of which, in filling his tub, requires the constant care and minute attention of the hewer. In the report of Mr. Tremenheere for 1846, there is a calculation of the amount lost in fines in 120 collieries from 5 April 1843, to 5 April 1845. From this estimate the loss would appear to be, on the average, not more than ½d per day per man. In some of these collieries it is stated that the amount averages 2½d per man—in others, it is lower than ¼d.

I referred this statement to the meeting of delegates, and there was at once a unanimous denial of its correctness. They were not prepared with particulars at the moment; but the amount of fines lost on an average, they solemnly assured me, was much more serious. A number of cases in support of the general assertion were then adduced. First came the statement put forth by the "Committee of the Seaton Delaval Colliery", giving the account of the "laid-out and set-out" at that pit for five fortnights, beginning in last February. From this statement it appears, that during the ten weeks in question, there were drawn 35,881 tons 15 cwt of coals. The united "laid-out" and "set-out" were 1302 tons 7 cwt. The average price of working was stated at 1s 1½d per ton; therefore 1302 tons 7 cwt. at 1s 1½d per ton makes a "dead loss to the hewers of the sum of £71 17s 5d". In another colliery I was informed by the delegate representing it that 145 score, at 10s per score, had been lost to the hewers in nine months. In a third colliery—I refrain from giving names, but they are on my notebook before me—I was assured that as much as 6s, 7s, and 9s, had been lost by one man in a fortnight's pay. Of the fourth colliery—a southern one—the following statement was made. In one of the seams there are six or eight inches of "grey" or coarse coal. These the men have to "carve out", and if 6lbs of this coal be found in one tub the miner forfeits the whole of it. My informant said that working "to the greatest extreme"—meaning with the most extreme care—he had frequently lost his tub, which cost him each time 5½d. He added that it was all but impossible to distinguish the coarse from the good coal in the darkness of the bord. This statement was corroborated on all hands; and it has been confirmed to me by working men, both before and since, in several parts of the two counties. They state that although it is easy in the daylight at the bank to distinguish bad coal or coal stones, yet that in the pit—and more particularly if the hewer is using the Davy—the most practised eye is frequently deceived.

As to "set-out", I found the complaint general that, particularly in the cases where coals have to be conveyed a long way to the pit-mouth, there is frequently a waste occasioned by accidental spillage—principally in descending inclined planes, where the waggons are subjected to shocks and jerks. In fact the hewer has no one to look after his interests from the time when the putter moves away the full tub until the banksman jerks it out of the cage. At the weighing house the hewers have, in many collieries, an agent who checks the weight. In their anxiety to avoid the "set-out", it of course often happens that the hewers pile up their waggons with more than the standard weight. For this they are paid 1d for every 14lbs of overweight sent up. In a large colliery which I visited to the north of Newcastle, the checksman informed me that, previously to his appointment, the extra earnings had been on an average 1d per score in every six weeks. Now the men gained 3d per score per fortnight. My informant was of course paid by the hewers, at the rate of about 18s per week.

I return, however, to the statements of the delegates upon the subject. Having heard their representations as to "laid-out" and "set-out", I inquired whether they thought that the masters ought not to have some check upon the quantity and quality of the coals sent up. To this a unanimous and hearty affirmative was at once given. It was only just and reasonable, they said, that the masters should have a check. The men did not want to be paid for a greater weight than they had worked, or for stones or splent sent up instead of coal. But what they did complain of was, the loss of the whole tub for a trifling under-weight or a trifling mixture of "foul" coal. It was very hard that for some accidental spillage—perhaps taking place when they had no control over the tub—they should pay so heavy a penalty as its entire forfeiture. This was what they proposed: let the weight of the foul coal be by all means deducted, and let the hewer be paid for the net quantity of pure coal which he sends up. This arrangement they argued would be fair for master and man. They admitted at once that it would be absurd to expect an owner to pay putters and drivers, and keep machinery going, in order to bring to the surface a useless material but they submitted that the men, as their wages would be reduced by every pound of stone or splent with which they loaded their tubs, would have the same interest as their proprietor in keeping stone and splent out of them.

These statements I have laid before several gentlemen connected, as proprietors and viewers, with coal-pits, and their answers to them may be briefly stated as follows. In regard to "set-out", they admitted that grievances from spillage might have existed when the old-fashioned corves or baskets were in use, but they were unanimous in declaring that, with the square tub running upon wheels, and drawn to the bank in a cage, no appreciable waste whatever could take place. If, these gentlemen urged, the hewers were paid by the exact amount of coal which they sent up there would be no check upon their putting the whole lifting mechanism of the mine into operation to raise much smaller quantities than that mechanism was calculated to convey to the surface. If a hewer, they argued, can fill ten tubs in a given time, he can fill half these tubs in half the time. So far as regards his individual labour, he might be fairly paid by actual weight of the coals raised. But there is a great body of putters who are paid by the tub, whatever may be its weight—and a still greater body of drivers, banksmen etc., who are paid by the day—and an expensive system of machinery calculated to raise certain weights every time it is put into operation. It is clear, therefore, they argued, that if hewers are paid by the weight at the end of a day's work and not by the weight of each individual tub, the owners have no check upon their giving to the whole of the remaining working agents of the mine half only of that amount of labour for the performance of which they are arranged and paid.

With respect to "laid-out", I was requested to observe that the men are always paid at a higher rate for working seams much intermingled with stones and foul coal than for excavating seams containing little or nothing save the pure mineral. If they are, therefore, occasionally called upon to work slowly and circumspectly, they are paid accordingly. Besides, I was informed, it is always reckoned the duty of a hewer to clean the coals, and part of his wages are given to him in consideration of that special portion of his work. This statement the hewers themselves admitted to be correct. It is of course necessary, I was told by viewers and proprietors, that the coals should be cleaned by someone. The commonsense way is to clean them at the bottom of the pit, and so to avoid lifting unmarketable rubbish to the bank. This is therefore the plan adopted; and when the hewers send up foul coal, they break their agreement and are therefore equitably fined. To separate the valuable from the valueless mineral is a work involving a certain degree of time and trouble. If the hewer were permitted to shirk the task, he would be paid for a smaller quantity of coal in each individual tub, but his wages would not be reduced, because he would have more time to fill the tubs—while as in the case of "set-out", the whole machinery of the pit would be working to convey to the bank stuff which was of no use when it got there. The gentleman whose views I am stating observed that as to the vast majority of men, the penalties were merely nominal. One of them showed me several pit accounts—taken as I know perfectly at random—in none of which the amount deducted for "laid-out" and "set-out" rose in a fortnight's pay, higher than two or three shillings; while in two fortnights were respectively 3d and 9d out of more than £120. The same gentleman informed me that in a pit belonging to a near relative of his own, there was a seam longitudinally intersected by a strip of inferior coal, which was not worth while bringing to bank. The rule of the colliery was, that if a certain number of pounds of this substance was found in any tub the hewer forfeited no less than 5s. "The amount seems great," said my informant, "but the fine is never incurred. The worthless coal can only be shovelled into the tub from sheer carelessness, and that carelessness the fine prevents."

Thus then I have stated both sides of the question fully and I think fairly. It is not my business to decide between the conflicting views, I leave them as I found them, and return in the meantime to the meeting of union delegates, from which I have wandered in order to connect a subject discussed there before me with the replies subsequently entrusted to me to be made public along with the delegates' arguments.

The Educational, Moral and Intellectual State of the District

There being representatives present of so many and such important collieries, it occurred to me that I might with advantage seize the opportunity of acquiring some of the educational, moral, and intellectual statistics of the district. At my request, therefore, the acting chairman read, name by name, the list of collieries represented, and called upon the delegate of each to enumerate the number and nature of schools established in connection with his pit, stating by whom they were supported, and whether there existed any news-room or libraries for the adults. The required information was given by each delegate succinctly and briefly. The following are the results. I may add that I have appended the population of each colliery the name of which appears in the official documents furnished to the Newcastle Coal-Trade Office in 1844.

Seaton Delaval. Male working population, 626. Three schools and one library. Two of the schoolmasters supported entirely by the workmen, and teaching in Methodist chapels; the owners of the colliery finding the schoolroom of the third.

Cowpen. Population, 318. Several schools including an infant school, supported by the men. No library or reading room.

West Holywell. Population, 143. One National school. The owners were formerly in the habit of giving 8s a week towards the support of the schoolmaster. Recently this allowance was withdrawn, but they furnish a house and a schoolroom free. There was a library which had commenced operations only the previous Monday. The delegate added that for any deficiency in the means of intellectual improvement, the people were much more to blame than the owners.

Seaton Burn. Population, 296. One school mutually supported—that is the house accommodation found by the master, and the fees paid by the fathers of the scholars. No library.

Wall's End. Population, 255. Five or six schools mutually supported, and one library.

Buckworth. One school and a library, mutually supported. The owners give £2 a year to the library.

Branspeth. Population 111. Only a Dame school for the younger children and a night school, supported by the men, and taught by one of them. No library.

Woodfield. Population 76. Three schools, two of them supported by the men, the third in connection with the Established Church. One library.

Beachburn. One infant school. One night school, supported by the men and taught by one of themselves.

Trimdon. Population 619. One school mutually supported, and a reading room established by the owners.

Coxhoe. Population 368. Two schools supported by the men, and a library mutually supported.

North Hetton. Population 325. One regular school mutually supported; two night schools, supported by the men, and taught by members of their own body. No library. House accommodation provided by the owners.

West Cramlington. Population 315. One school mutually supported, the fees of the children being only one penny a week. No news-room but the owner wishes to erect one. "If the men will take one step he will take ten."

Pittington. Population 580. Three schools—one supported by the owners and two by the men.

Washington. Population 194. One national school. House accommodation free. Fees 1d per week. No library.

Ellmore and Appleton. Two schools mutually supported. No library.

Sherburn Hill. Two National Schools. No library.

Rainton. Population 500. One school for boys and girls, supported by the owner. No library.

Great Hetton. One National school mutually supported. Another school supported by the men. The owner gives a free house to a schoolmaster and mistress.

Marley Hill. Population 128. One school mutually supported. No library.

Castle Eden. Population 450. One school supported by the owners who will not allow any other school in the colliery. One library in which no "Liberal Newspapers" are allowed. The delegate himself had opened a night school and was compelled to give it up.

Wingate Grange. Population 625. One National school, mutually supported, and a reading room.

New Durham. One good school supported by fees. The children pay 3d a week for the elementary classes. No library; but the owner will fit up a room, and "give them a chance" of establishing one.

Shincliffe. Population 213. Two schools. One National. The other kept by a working man at night. No library.

Haswell. Population 305. One National school, mutually supported. Two other schools similarly maintained. A library, unhappily allowed to "lie dormant".

Cassop. Population 469. One National school and two others self supported. No library.

Heugh Hall. Two mutually supported schools. No library.

Grange. A school entirely supported by the men, and a library belonging to the Wesleyan body.

Broomside. One National school, mutually supported, and one self-supporting school. No library.

Belmont. Population 185. One mutually supporting school. No reading room.

Little Chilton. One school, mutually supported. The owner offered to set a library on foot; but prohibits political publications.

Hartley. Population 270. One school supported by the men. No library.

Hatherton. Population 246. One school mutually supported, and a library on a small scale.

Blackboy. Population 430. Two schools, mutually supported. House accommodation is provided for both master and mistress.

Roddy Mark. One school, mutually supported. No library.

Westerton. Population 184. One school connected with the Church. The fines go to purchase prizes.

Croppy Crooks. One school. House accommodation provided by owners; fees paid by parents.

Derwent (coal and iron works). Eight schools; five for boys and three for girls. Self supported. The use of the library is restricted to the clerks at the office and the foremen.

Ludwith. One National school, mutually supported. Children pay 1d per week.

Shotton. Population 676. One mutual National school, and a library, which is well supported. It belongs to the company.

Danton. One school in connection with the Methodist body. House accommodation provided for master and mistress.

Edmondsley. Population 275. One school; held in the Methodist chapel. The owners give £50 between master and mistress. Threepence per week is deducted from the wages of those who have children at the school.

Chalan. Population 150. One National school. No library; but the owners are about to establish one. Fifteen pounds has already been collected for books.

Kibblesworth. Population 129. One school supported by the men, and one library supported by the master.

Elswick. Population 146. One Dame school, a library, and a Sunday school, supported by the men.

Woodhouse Close. Neither school nor library.

Hunwick. Population 152. One mutually supported National school. No library.

Tanfield Lee. Population 283. One National school. The pupils pay 3d per week.

Walker. Population 357. Four or five schools. Two of them National. A library connected with the ironworks doing well, with 300 members, at 1d per week each.

Hebburn. Population 361. Two schools for males and females. Both are held in chapels and are self-supporting.

South Hetton. Population 518. One National school, mutually supported. A library supported by the owners.

Eldon. Population 218. No school at the colliery.
Mickley. Population 194. No school; no library.
Black Prince. One National school and a library, both mutually supported.

The names of several other collieries were called but the delegates did not happen to be in the room. Some little confusion was occasioned by the term "mutually supporting" being generally used only when the owner paid a sum of money to the schoolmaster; but I am given to understand that the rule of the proprietors giving a house and generally a garden and coals, to the teacher or teachers, is all but universal. The Marquess of Londonderry contributes about £300 a year to the schools upon his estates. They educate upwards of 630 children, each of whom pays 1d per week.

The list of colliery schools given above, although it leaves doubtless much to be done, still shows that progress in the right direction has, to some extent, been made. A dozen of years ago not one-third of them were in existence. In those portions of Mr. Tremenheere's Reports, devoted to the educational facilities afforded in the colliery districts, the phrase continually occurs when describing a pit seminary – "Until within a late period the only means of instruction for the people were dame schools". Many of the old class of schools taught by masters were also wretchedly inefficient – the teachers being frequently disabled workmen, and the number of their scholars forming but a miserable percentage of the work people of the colliery. The consequence has been that the mining population are exceedingly low in point of education and intelligence; and yet they contradict the theories generally entertained upon the connection of ignorance with crime by presenting the least criminal section of the population of England. Indeed, the disproportion between the mining districts of Northumberland, Durham and the average of England, particularly as regards the more trifling class of offences against property, is very remarkable; and great as this disproportion is, that of female crime in the mining districts, as contrasted with the general average, is still greater. In 1847, the number of persons offending against property in England and Wales was 28 out of every 10,000 of the population. In the mining districts including Northumberland, Durham, Cumberland and Cornwall, the proportion was only 7 in 10,000. Again for the three years ending in 1847, there were, in the mining districts only 9.33 female thieves out of every 10,000 women. The proportion in Middlesex was 34.69; while throughout England and Wales generally, the proportion was 17.67.

The author of "Tactics of the Times", in adducing these results, attempts to account for them on the supposition that the uncertainty of human life, caused by the frequency and the terrible nature of accidents in mines, produces a deep and salutary effect on the minds of the people. But the explanation seems very fanciful. A sailor undergoes at least as much risk as a miner; and sailors are not reckoned a particularly thoughtful race. Besides, taking one of the most exclusively coal-mining districts I can find

— that of Auckland, Teesdale and Weardale — the Registrar General's last report makes the general value of life within it as 1 in 49 — a higher proportion than that of London, and more than 20 per cent higher than that of Manchester. The fact, to some extent, appears to be that the naturally sombre and earnest mental temperament which distinguishes the people of the north of England in general, has, in the case of the miners, been fostered and wrought out into strong religious convictions through the agency of the Methodist bodies, who have obtained almost the entire spiritual control of the people; the efforts of the thousands of local and itinerant preachers being greatly aided by the comparatively isolated condition in which the mining population lives — seldom or never coming in contact with the members of any industrial class except their own, and little exposed to the influences and excitements of great towns.

Let the cause be, however, what it may, the miners are a reverse of a criminal population, and they are also the reverse of an intelligent one. An educational census of the people employed in the collieries of the Earl of Durham was lately instituted; and the results may, I believe, be taken as giving a tolerably fair view of the general state of education and intelligence throughout the coal districts. The number of people directly or indirectly connected with the Earl of Durham's collieries was about 4,500. This estimate includes persons engaged in a variety of occupations, having more or less reference to pit labour, embracing waggon-way wrights, waggon fillers, blacksmiths, engineers, banksmen etc. From the total number, more than 700 was deducted for children below five years of age; of the remainder, numbering 3,716 there were 1,461 who could read and write; 1,339 who could read only; and 916 above the age of five who could neither read nor write. This is the general result, applying to all the workpeople above and under the ground; but the details of the inquiry proved that while upwards of one half of the families — the males of which were not, strictly speaking, pitmen — could read and write, only one-third of the pit families were so far educated.

But a pitman's notions of reading and writing, I was informed by an intelligent member of their own body, are very modest. "Many a hewer and putter," said this individual, "will tell you that they can write; but they would be sorely puzzled to read the specimens they would give you." In a colliery in another part of the district, where an educational investigation was set on foot, the results were, that of 331 persons capable of being educated, only 165 could read the Bible. A schoolmaster with whom I conversed and who has had a lengthened experience amongst a pit population, estimated that only about 25 per cent of the children stay at school so long as to be really benefited. He said that their parents commonly professed to be very anxious about the education of their children, but that they sadly grudged the fees, and the boys were sent down to the pit as soon as they could earn a shilling. At many collieries, the pitmen have been found to prefer sending their children to schools taught by inefficient masters of their own class, rather than to seminaries managed by properly trained instructors. As in the cloth and cotton districts, Sunday schools have played a principal part in affording to the present generation of pit-labourers what degree of education they do possess. In every pit-village there are one or more Wesleyan or Primitive Methodist Chapels, and attached to every one of these is a Sunday school.

With the exception of what is done in these institutions, the education of a pitman may be said to terminate with the day that he first descends the mine to labour. He begins, perhaps, as a trapper, and sits twelve hours a day in the dark. Indeed during a considerable portion of the year, the trappers, drivers and putters never see daylight except on Sundays. They descend the mine before dawn, and ascend it after nightfall. The work of boys, both in driving and trapping, is, therefore, so drearily monotonous and sombre that they are very unwilling to undergo anything like additional restraint above ground — while the labours of putters and hewers is physically so severe and exhausting, that by the time they ascend to day, there seems to be but little left of that energy and vigour which, in so many instances, prompt the manufacturing operative to visit the lecture or the concert room. The pitmen as a body know little, and care little about politics. Their ideas are limited to the mine in a far greater degree than the spinner's or the weaver's are confined to the factory. If they have no particular technical grievances to complain of, they seldom disturb themselves about abstract political claims, or abstract political wrongs. I have been in scores of pitmen's houses and I do not think that I saw a newspaper in one of them. Where there were books they generally consisted of Methodist religious publications.

The Bible is, however, to be found in almost every house, and the religious feelings of the community, if unenlightened, are strong and practically binding. The Church of England is I believe from what I have seen regarded by a large proportion of the mining community with feelings of positive and active enmity. They almost invariably class it with the aristocratic institutions and influences which they believe to be hostile to them. The church clergymen, they say, take part with the masters, but the Ranters take part with the men; in fact most of the local preachers are themselves working men, addressing their comrades in their own patois, and treating every scriptural subject in the peculiarly technical tone of mind which is common to whole community.

The Family in the Mining Districts

In the mining districts, the family tie remains almost invariably unbroken until the marriage of the children. Trappers invariably give their wages to their parents. When a boy comes to be a driver he is allowed a small weekly amount of pocket money; and when he attains to the dignity of "putting", he either pays his father for his board and lodging, and clothes himself, or hands over the entire amount of his wages, requiring to be found in board, lodging and clothes, and demanding a certain sum, usually about 2s 6d, per fortnight for his *menus plaisirs*. The pitmen do not generally marry until they become hewers, and their wives are almost invariably chosen out of their own community. Whole villages are thus often related by marriage. Occasionally, but not often, a pitman's child will go out to service; but in the vast proportion of cases a hewer's daughter becomes a hewer's wife. Should she be left a widow she still remains in the pit-row, sometimes opening a small huckstering shop, and taking in clothes to wash and mangle. A disabled man also occasionally takes to dealing in small wares; and in some cases superannuated hewers will, in addition to what light jobs they can pick up about the pit, occupy themselves in collecting the clay used for the workmen's candles. A hewer is past his prime at forty. Pains and stiffness in the back and loins begin to come on, and he finds, particularly in difficult seams, that he can no longer send to bank the same quantity of coals as he managed ten years before. Old pitmen are very generally supported in whole or in part by their grown-up families — a filial duty, the performance of which is far more common in the mining than in the manufacturing districts.

The Amusements of the Miner

The amusements of the pit population are, as might be expected, somewhat limited. Dog and cock-fighting used to be prevalent, but both of these cruel sports are now dying out. The cocks when pitted against each other, are always armed *secundum artum* with steel spurs, and a few men still rear bulldogs for fighting purposes. The fights generally took place in slack times, or upon the Saturday following the fortnightly pay Friday. At present the sports most in use are quoit playing, foot racing and bowling. The latter game, as it is understood in Northumberland and Durham, means simply trundling a ball of stone, iron, or heavy earthenware, along a certain distance, either upon a road or across a moor – the victor being the player whose bowl traverses the space propelled by the fewest number of throws. Foot races are often got up at public houses, for such stakes as pints of ale. Putters are the usual performers; hewers soon get too stiff in the joints to do much in the running way.

A piece of Christmas mummery, now dying out, was formerly much in fashion, and it appears from the descriptions I got of it, to have very much resembled the chimney-sweeps' antics on May-day. The exhibition is called the sword dance, from five of the performers going through evolutions armed with weapons of the kind.The whole party consisted generally of about ten persons; of those, five were dancers. One was called the "gunner", another the "clothes carrier". The two principal personages were termed "Tommy" and "Bessy", and a performer on the fiddle usually made up the troupe. All were more or less fantastically dressed. "Tommy" and "Bessy" especially wore masses of fluttering ribbons of the gayest colours. The part of the lady, be it remarked, was always enacted by a man. The functions of the "clothes carrier" are explained by his title – the party proceeding across the country from colliery to colliery, at each of which they donned their masquerading attire, and were made very welcome. After due obeisances had been made to Tommy and Bessy, the dancers drew their weapons, and proceeded in peaceful fashion to use them. They capered about, clashing the cold steel, and as it was necessary in some of the evolutions that every man should grasp the end of his partner's blade with one hand while he held his own with the other, the sharp edges were carefully concealed beneath a lashing of rosined cord. Meantime Tommy and Bessy carried round the hat, and at every fresh largess the report of the gunner's musket saluted the liberality of the donor.

The pitmen are, generally speaking a decidedly temperate race. Dram-drinking for instance is unknown amongst them. Ale is their usual festive beverage; but except on Saturday nights, they very seldom exceed in it, and often do not touch it. Once a fortnight, however, there is a general *gaudeamus* at the public-houses in or near the colliery village. The men assemble in great sociality at the sign of the "Pit Lad" or the "Davy". Pipes are lit; songs, in the curious patois of the district – which sounds like broad Scotch ill-spoken – are roared in chorus; the strong ale does its duty; and the wives who have come to coax their good men home find themselves on a bootless errand. Unhappily, however, a very frequent termination of the festivities is, or rather was — for the pitman is improving in that respect as in many other — a quarrel, a scuffle, and a battle royal, fought by the whole of the dramatis personae. Sometimes the apple of discord appears in the shape of money transactions. At others, squabbles and little jealousies between the women are broached and discussed — the husbands, brothers and sweethearts taking different sides; and occasionally, says my informant (himself a pitman), they begin to boast of each other's personal prowess. "I'se a better mon than thee'st," one self-satisfied gentleman will remark to his compotator. A deprecating rejoinder of course follows. "Debate arising," as the journals of the House of Commons say, a general row is the issue. "Pitmen," remarked my informant, "will fight fair and mainly with their fists, if they are one to one; but in a general scuffle each will catch up and lay about him with anything handy. I have seen candlesticks, pots, and even chairs flung about; and in one public-house in particular the landlord was obliged to keep the poker chained to the hearth."

It is however to be distinctly understood that these descriptions refer to a state of society in rapid process of change for the better.

The Superstitions of the Mining Population

I have had some difficulty in getting at even the traditions of fancy which were once generally and devoutly believed by the coal-workers of the North. The old men I have been frequently told, have still a lingering faith in the legends of the mine; but the young men only laugh at them. The class of superstitions which still maintains some hold is that involved in the belief in omens, tokens, dreams, and lucky or unlucky occurrences. I have already mentioned that a pitman dislikes meeting a woman when he is going to his work. The walk from home to the pit-mouth, often performed in the dead of the night, is the period most rife in the warnings of some fatal result which the day's labour is to bring forth. A supernatural appearance, of a warning character, was often supposed to cross the miner's path in the shape of a little white animal like a rabbit. In fact, anything moving and white, was held to be an omen of impending disaster. Mental as well as visual warnings abounded. The miners had frequent presentiments that something was about to go wrong, and the teachings of the inward monitor were very carefully attended to. The pitmen of the Midland Counties have (or had) a belief, unknown in the North, in aerial whistlings ringing through the night air and warning them not to descend the shaft. Who or what the invisible musicians were nobody pretended to know. One therefore feels somewhat surprised at their having been enumerated and found to consist of seven, thenceforth designated the "Seven Whistlers".

I have only heard of two actual goblins known to haunt the mine. The one is a mischievous elf, whose presence is only indicated by the damage which he perpetrates. He is called "Cutty Soams", and appears to employ himself only in the stupid device of severing the rope-traces or soams by which an assistant putter, honoured by the title of the "foal", is yoked to the tub. The strands of hemp are left all sound in the board at night; in the morning they are found severed in twain. "Cutty Soams has been at work," says the putter dolefully, knotting the injured rope. The second goblin was altogether more sensible, and indeed, an honest and hardworking bogle — much akin to the Scottish brownie, or the hairy fiend whom Milton rather scurvily apostrophises as a "lubber". The supernatural personage in question was, in fact, a sort of ghostly putter, and his name was "Blue Cap." Sometimes the scared miners would behold a light blue flame, or "low" flicker through the air, and settle down on a full coal tub, which immediately moved towards the rolley-way as though impelled by a stalwart putter. Therefore once a fortnight Blue Cap's wages were left for him in a solitary corner of the mine. If they were a farthing below his due, indignant Blue Cap would not pocket a stiver. If they were a farthing over his due, conscientious Blue Cap left the surplus revenue where he found it. I asked my informant whether, if Blue Cap's wages were left out for him nowadays, he thought they would be appropriated.

He sensibly replied that he had no doubt that they would be pocketed by Blue Cap — or somebody else.

Regulation of Output

I have already alluded to a combination among the coalowners for restricting the amount of coals brought to market, and thereby keeping up the prices. This combination, or, as it was called, "Limitation of the Vend", after having existed at intervals for many years is now extinct. A practical "Limitation of the Vend" still, however, exists as regards a considerable proportion—more than one-third—of the Durham and Northumberland pits. This restriction, or, as its participators prefer calling it, "Regulation", is the work of the men themselves; and although they will not admit that it is an offshoot of the union, and although it may not exist in all pits connected with the union, it never exists save in such pits. This "Regulation" is a rule among the men themselves not to send up to bank more than a given quantity of coals per day per man. The amount is fixed by each colliery for itself, and the arrangement is always spoken of as perfectly voluntary, and one which any hewer may take part in or not as he pleases. The practical consequence, however, is that the regulation, wherever it is introduced into a pit, speedily becomes all but universal. The proprietors do not sanction the arrangement, but I cannot find that they are violently opposed to it. The fact is that it stands them in some respect instead of the old "Limitation of the Vend". I have not neglected to make inquiries into the working results of the "Regulation", as well as into the policy of its champions.

The first practical effect of the "Regulation" is of course to curtail, and in some degree to equalize, the rate of pitmen's wages. These wages I have generally reckoned as from 3s 6d to 4s a day, with a free house and garden, and coals almost at a nominal rate. The drawbacks, as I have stated them, may amount to about 1s 6d per week. As in the case of all work paid by the piece, the inquirer into the remuneration of coal-workers is presented with the most contradictory estimates, but the above calculation I believe to be pretty near the mark. In one of Mr. Tremenheere's reports there is an estimate of the average of wages, as connected with this subject of restriction, which a number of pitmen to whom I have shown it pronounced partial and over-rated; but which these very individuals have given me data for believing to be under, rather than over, the mark.

In this calculation the average earnings of the hewers in the Tyne and Blythe Collieries are estimated at 3s 9¾d per man per day, those of the Wear at 3s 7¾d, and those of the Tees at 3s 9½d. The highest average in the several pits are – in the first district, 4s 4d per day paid at Wallsend, 4s 4½d paid at Cramlington, and 4s 8¼d at East Holywell and Seghill. On the Wear the highest averages paid are 4s 3d at South Hetton, 4s 3¾d at Garmondsway-moor, and 4s 10½d at Kelloe. On the Tees the highest averages are 4s 3d paid at Auckland St. Helens, 4s 3¼d paid at Westerton, and 4s 11¼d paid at Craggwood. The lowest averages in the same districts are as follows. On the Tyne, at Lowmoor, 3s 1d per man per day; at Pelaw Main 3s 1½d; and at Cotlodge 3s 1¾d. On the Wear, at Elnet, Washington, and Kerpier Musgrove, 3s; at Beamish and Crow Tees, 3s 1d; and at Shotton 3s 1½d. On the Tees at Hunwick, 3s 1¼d; at Greenwood, 3s 4½d; and at Brancepeth and Etherley, 3s 6d.

This statement was furnished by the viewers and owners of the different collieries, and as I have remarked was pronounced as exaggerated by several practical hewers. In the course of conversation with one of these individuals, he told me of a "hewing match", formerly an ordinary occurrence among pitmen, in which his brother had been one of the competitors, and which he himself had witnessed. The seam of coal performed upon was, as I understand, one of fair average height and hardness. The parties performed a regular day's work of eight hours and at the conclusion of the trial, the winner had hewn 12s 10d worth and the loser 12s 2d worth of coal. The average between the two was thus 12s 6d. Now, subtracting the 6d for fines and drawbacks, and accounting an ordinary eight hours work as one-third of the labour performed during an eight hours' match – surely no extravagant estimate of the toil which a man can, as a general rule get through – the product is 4s, a higher amount by 2½d than Mr. Tremenheer's highest averages. Taking then 3s 9d as the average of wages before the restriction came into play, I find from calculations drawn from the source already indicated, that the average fall on the Tyne has been, including fractions, 7d per day, each hewer voluntarily mulcting himself of that amount. On the Wear the fall has been 6d, and on the Tees 9d per day; making the general restricted earnings 3s 2d in the first district, 3s 1d in the second, and 3s in the third.

At the Wallsend Colliery, one of the men who had them in his possession, produced a number of packets of pay-bills, showing the amount, all fines deducted, actually received throughout an extended period by the men. From the mass I selected the bills of one fortnight, and after making a careful average, I found that the wages actually paid during that time amounted to only 2s 9d per man per day, counting six days to the week. The average during the existence of the restriction, given for Wallsend in the official documents, is 3s 4d, showing a wide difference, which, however, may be easily accounted for on the supposition that the colliery was not working fulltime during the fortnight selected—a state of matters of very frequent occurrence—and also that there may have been one, or perhaps, two Saturdays of broken or of suspended labour during the period in question.

In the Thornley colliery calculations have been made upon a surer basis than those which I was enabled to frame, from the data above stated—the gross number of days worked being taken instead of the number of hewers.

The figures are, without cavil, those which stand in the books of the colliery and in the pay-bills in the possession of the men: and the result of the most extended calculation is, that 22,645 restricted days' work were paid for by £3,816 12s 7d, or at the rate of 3s 4½d per man per day. From this deduct 1¾d for fines, and the net product is 3s 2¾d. I may add that the estimate was framed with a view quite different from that of ascertaining the actual amount of wages. I fully believe then, on all these authorities, and on many other statements derived from *viva voce* intercourse with individuals, that good hewers, when working unrestricted can earn 4s and more per day, and that inferior hewers can earn 3s and more per day. It follows from the averages I have given, that the brunt and hardships of the restriction falls upon the best men in each pit. Coal-owners have informed me that it operates advantageously for slow or lazy men, because the fact of their superiors restricting themselves to a certain sum acts as a powerful stimulus upon them to approach that amount as nearly as possible. "Many and many a man," said a hewer to me, and I believe with perfect truth, "is not touched by the restriction at all. He can't come up to it." It would follow that the best men lose by this restriction at the very least 9d, and many of the less skilful more than 4½d a day.

The reasons why they subject themselves to this very serious deduction from wages which they are admittedly capable of earning, were detailed to me by an individual, who, I have good grounds for knowing, possesses the full confidence of the restricting hewers. These reasons were much to the following import. "The restriction is fixed at what we consider a fair day's work for a man with ordinary powers and endurance, engaged in the toilsome and exhausting labour of hewing. We believe that working men in this country work too long and too hard, and we would like to see the time and the fatigue both abridged. Beside we think it fair to stand by each other as a body, and not to go on competing the one with the other. We feel assured that if we worked to the utmost that we are capable of, we should suffer severely in health, and perhaps ultimately in wages. We know that there are more men in the trade than are requisite to raise the coal required for average vend; but by restricting each individual's work, we compel the masters to employ all, or nearly all of us, and thus to bring into operation what, under the competing system, would be the surplus labour. We conceive that this arrangement, while it benefits the body of hewers, does not injure the masters, because they are only asked to divide the same amount of wages amongst a greater number of men; the only hardship upon them, and we think it a very slight one, is, that there may be the loss of part of the interest of the money laid out upon the machinery, because that machinery does not work every day so long as it was calculated for. But we have also this reason—we think and so did the masters when they had the limitation of the vend, that this restriction limits the quantity of coals brought to market; and in our opinion if the quantity be limited, prices will rise and our wages will—or at all events, ought to—

rise with them. It may be very well to say that if the price of coals rises, so much will not be bought. But we know what we are about; we know that coals must be had. This country could no more go without coals than without meat. That is our vantage ground. Every steam engine—in every factory—on every railway—on board every boat and ship—depends upon us, and if we chose to be united we could stop them all. We therefore are of opinion that, were the restriction universal—and we are trying to make it so—we could not only shorten the hours of labour, but cause the hours which we do work to be paid for at a higher rate."

This I believe to be a fair and uncoloured view of the opinions of an overwhelming proportion of the pitmen—of those of them at least, who have opinions at all; and this section always leads the remainder, who follow the advice of those of their own class whose abilities they feel to be superior to their own, with the blindest confidence and the most unerring exactitude. I had much conversation with the individual to whom I am indebted for the above explanation of his comrades' views, and I found that he was deeply impressed with the logical truth of the position which they held, notwithstanding the untoward result of several strikes which had been more or less upon the principles above indicated. That there is a considerable quantity of surplus labour existing in the northern coalfield is admitted by masters and men; indeed one of the objects of the restriction is to provide employment for it. A portion of that surplus labour was of course caused by the population increasing faster than the trade; but a still greater proportion was the consequence of the various great strikes, every one of which introduced a fresh infusion of working men, from the Midland counties or from Wales. In the strike of 1831–32 more than 2,000 strangers were brought into the trade. In the strike of 1844, the Marquess of Londonderry alone imported Irish to labour at one of his pits. A great number of Welsh miners were also induced to immigrate, and there can be no doubt that the amount of extra labour introduced was such as seriously to interfere with the balance of industrial supply and demand.

But even at the time of the strike there were many more hewers and other labourers than were required for the work to be done. An address to the colliers, drawn up at the time by, as I am assured, a competent authority, estimates that in 1830 there were employed underground, deducting all persons in command, about 12,700 men and boys. In 1844 the number had increased to 22,700, being a rise of 79 per cent. The increase of vend during that period was 53 per cent. But in 1830 it was contended that even then there was 25 per cent surplus labour in the market, so that the surplus labour of 1844 amounted to upwards of 30 per cent; in other words, there were 22,749 persons employed, while 15,924 were competent to raise all the coals which the masters wished to raise—that is all for which they could find a profitable sale. This disproportion is now increased. The restriction no doubt prevents it from being felt with such severity as in other circumstances it would be; but I need only hint that the line of policy which degrades the best men to the pay of the worst, and the tendency of which is to crush down all superiority in energy or skill to a dead level of mediocrity, is hardly one of which the long continuance is, or ought to be, expected.

Evictions in a Colliery Village

I now pass to a part of the coal system from which springs much bad blood between employers and employed. It is not, as has been already explained, the tendency of the coal-raising trade to create inland towns. Every pit has its village, exclusively inhabited by the people employed in the mine; and almost as a matter of course the dwellings in which they live are erected by the owner of the works, nobody else having any interest to speculate in the building of cottage-villages. These cottages, as I have also stated, are held not as tenements but as wages. It follows that on occasions of strikes the payment of wages and the right to the occupancy of houses cease together. Hence frequently arises a system of evictions which I believe not only to be productive of the worst moral consequences to the people, but to be continually sowing seeds of bitter grudges between them and their employers. The mere act of ceasing to pay wages when men cease to work, has in it something so perfectly and obviously natural, that it involves no idea of hardship; but turning a man out of his house, particularly when, as must happen in the very nature of things in the coal district, he has much difficulty in finding another roof to get under—such a proceeding is regarded, by those who suffer from it, and by those who sympathise with them, as harsh, if not tyrannical. They do not readily recognize an abstract idea of right—and not only of right but even of necessity, on the coal owners' part—particularly when all their household goods are overturned by its exercise.

A strike followed by an eviction has very recently occurred at a colliery called Kepier Grange, a mile or two to the south of Durham. Hearing that the turnout workpeople were huddled together, principally in the public houses in the neighbourhood, I proceeded to the spot, and was conducted by several of the hewers to see what they termed the "tender mercies" of the coalowners. First, however, I requested the workmen to give me their version of the causes of the strike. It was partly for higher wages, partly on account of an alleged grievance in the weighing of coals. In a handbill published by the men, they state that the price paid them for hewing a tub of coals of the weight of 6 cwt. was 2¼d, and that no allowance was made to them for underweight. They had asked ¼d per tub more—were refused—and so turned out. In their verbal communications with me they stated that the atmosphere of the pit was exceedingly damp, and that in some places the workings were very wet. For coals hewn in the wet workings they were paid not 2¼d but 4d per tub; but the tubs were not weighed when brought to bank, because it was contended that the quantity of moisture which they contained made them apparently heavier than they really were. Thus, they said, although a workman might lose a tub which was a pound underweight, he reaped no advantage from a tub which was ten pounds overweight. They argued that they had lost more in this way than the extra sum which they were paid for working in wet places. They had no grievances in the way of "laid-out", to complain of; but they added that the people of the adjoining colliery were paid more than twice as much for a tub as they were. This difference of course resulted from the difference of the seams worked—the fact of there being little or no "laid-out", showing that the coal at Kepier Grange was clean and unmixed with refuse, while as regards the pit referred to, I had subsequently woeful accounts of the difficulty of working its seams owing to their extreme shallowness.

I proceeded to inspect the condition of the people who had been turned out. In the public house which I first entered there had been 28 persons accommodated. The back-yards and out-houses were crammed with the coarser furniture, while the better articles were stowed away within. In one room three temporary beds were spread, and I was told that others were nightly made up on the floor. The huddling together of families in this way—the sleeping arrangements being quite unscreened each from the others—cannot but produce the worst moral and social effects. In another public house close at hand a similar state of matters prevailed. Three uncurtained beds were placed at the head of a room, so close that each touched the other, and in the night time mattresses were laid all along the kitchen floor. Bad as all this was, I was given to understand that things had been even worse, but that the strike having now continued about a fortnight, the people were being gradually absorbed into Durham and the villages round it. In one small house, consisting of one small room, situated close behind one of the empty and evacuated dwellings, I found that eleven persons had taken refuge. The owner of the place was a single old man, who had received a family of ten from the neighbouring cottage. There was but one bedstead in the room, and upon that the mattresses and bed-clothes, which served the whole family and their host, were piled nearly as high as my shoulder. At night they covered nearly every available inch of the earthen floor up to the fireplace.

The father and mother complained bitterly of the manner in which they stated they had been evicted. It was already dark, they said, and a cold stormy night, when the police officers arrived to turn them out. Their furniture was seized and rudely flung in heaps into the muddy road. They pointed out a ditch into which tables and chairs had fallen pell-mell. On the bank of this ditch one of their boys lighted a fire in a pot. A policeman said that they had no business to kindle it, because the coals, as part of their wage did not belong to them any more than the house—and he kicked the lighted embers into the ditch. The family then attempted to find partial refuge in the recess of the door of their late habitation. The snow was falling fast, and they were in a dreary condition of cold and wet, when their charitable neighbour came forth and took them in.

This was the statement furnished to me. The evicted individual affirmed that he had had no warning that he was to be turned to the door on the day when the catastrophe took place; but all of the miners readily admitted that, in striking work they knew that they had rendered themselves liable to eviction. I had some conversation with one of the leading men amongst them. He said that they did not complain so much of losing their houses, which they admitted were part of their wages, as of the eviction being conducted harshly, and with unnecessary haste. "The house too was standing empty. The owners might as well have let us keep them until they got somebody else to put into possession. It would be no loss to them and a great favour to us." Without passing judgement upon the reasonableness of this idea, I must mention that the tone adopted in urging it was quite an appeal *ad misericordium*. With respect to the length of notice given of intention to evict, I was subsequently informed that it generally depended upon the length of the notice which the men gave of their intention to strike—in fact, that the men virtually gave their own notice of ejectment. If they signified their intention of striking in a fortnight's time, they knew that they were liable to be turned out at the end of a fortnight. If they struck without giving notice, the masters could turn them out of their houses without notice. The owners of the deserted colliery were, when I visited it, making great exertions to obtain a supply of labour. "They would employ you for a hewer in a minute if you wanted the job," was remarked to me by one of the turn-outs.

A great number of the body seemed to be lounging all day in and about the public houses, smoking and discussing the chances of the strike. The publicans gave them lodging for nothing, charging only for provisions; and those of their poor neighbours who could, appeared very ready to make room for as many as possible. Whilst I was standing at the door of one of the taverns in question, a man went by escorted by one of the rural police. The hewers told me that he was a tailor, who had taken employment in the pit, and they laughed at the notion of his pseudo-guardian. "If we wished to injure the man," they said, "it wouldn't be a single policeman who could prevent us."

I have thus stated the case of the men as given to me by themselves, omitting or modifying no particle of it. I applied, however, to the owners of the colliery for their version of the matter, and was courteously furnished by Mr. Sinclair, the viewer, with the following elaborate reply, dated a day or two after my visit to Kepier Grange.

TO THE SPECIAL CORRESPONDENT OF THE MORNING CHRONICLE

Sir, I am very glad to have the opportunity of assisting you in the object you have in view, as expressed in your note of the 12th, which I have just received, the more so that I feel that the more public a true statement of the relative position of the pitmen and their employers can be made, the sooner will a stop be put to those ruinous strikes among the pitmen, which have unfortunately been of too frequent occurrence.

The disagreement between the owners of the Kepier Grange Colliery and their pitmen is a most striking instance of the folly of a body of pitmen giving up employment where they were earning good wages with a moderate amount of labour, and which, after being unemployed, for nearly a month, they would now very gladly have if they could obtain it.

The pitmen sent a written notice to the owners, in which they stated that they were not adequately paid for their labour, and that unless certain additions were made to the different prices, they would cease working at the expiration of a fortnight, which is the length of time required for notice at this colliery when a pitman either leaves or is discharged. The owners, after taking the matter into consideration, replied, through me, that they could not give any advance of price, but that they thought that the men had acted properly in giving the requisite notice, and that they could leave the colliery at the expiration of their term of notice if they thought they could get better employment elsewhere—at the same time giving them notice that if they did so they must leave the cottages they then occupied, which were allowed them as part of their wages, as the cottages would be required by the new pitmen who would be employed. At the expiration of the term of notice the men ceased working but did not leave their cottages. Other workmen were employed, and on the second night after these men began to work, the window of the cottage in which one of them lived was broken by a volley of stones; another man had some of his furniture injured by stones having been thrown into his house, This intimidated the men who were working, and I was obliged to apply to the superintendent of the county constabulary to send some of his force to protect these men and the property belonging to the owners of the colliery. Until this occurred I was unwilling to turn out the pitmen who had ceased working, and I still wished them to remove their own furniture to wherever they might choose to put it; and on consulting with the owners of the colliery they agreed to give the pitmen a week to remove their furniture, and I had to get a sufficient force and remove it for them. This was done so as to give them as little annoyance as possible.

From that time until yesterday I had no application from the men to be allowed to return to the colliery, and I employed other workmen, who were working as many coals as we wanted. Yesterday they came in a body to my office, and asked if I would again employ them, I told them that I could give no answer as a body of men; but if they came singly into my office and applied for work, I would employ as many of them as I wanted; this they did, and I have again employed about half of them on the very same terms as they had when they ceased working—

whilst the other half will, I believe find very great difficulty in obtaining employment as pitmen at this season of the year, and would be very glad to have again the employment they have so foolishly lost.

I will now give you a statement of the earnings of these men before they ceased working, and also of the earnings of the men who have been employed since the others ceased—some of the latter never worked coal before, but were working as labourers eleven hours a day for 2s 2d. I must also beg you to remember that the pitmen have good cottages with gardens, and firecoal, in addition to what they earn in the pit.

On referring to the paybills I see that during the fortnight ending November 3, before notice was given by the pitmen that sixteen men who worked 151 days, earned £34 5s 6d, or 4s 6d a day; the remainder averaged 3s 10d a day, the average of the whole being nearly 4s a day. During the next fortnight, after they had given notice, twenty men, who had worked 184 days, earned £40 14s or 4s 2d a day, and the remainder 3s 9d a day; the average of the whole being 3s 10½d a day. None of these men worked more than six hours a day, and many of them not five hours. During the next fortnight, after the pitmen ceased working, the new men earned as follows:

> 3 men earned in 50 days £10 8s 4d or 6s 3 ¾d a day
> 2 men earned in 20 days £ 3 18s 5d or 3s 11d a day
> 5 men earned in 35 days £ 6 3s 2d or 3s 6¼d a day
> 4 men earned in 32 days £6 15s 10d or 4s 3d a day
> 6 men earned in 27 days £6 2s 0d or 4s 6d a day
>
> ———————————————————————
>
> 20 men earned in 164 days £33 7s 9d or 4s 7½d a day

These men worked six hours a day. During the present fortnight which will end tomorrow, we have had more pitmen at work; and although I cannot yet be certain what their earnings will amount to, I am sure it will be above 5s a day; three of them having in one day, when they worked eight hours, made £1 14s 6d, or 11s 6d a man a day.

I have now I think, given you all the information you require on this matter; but, should you wish for any further information, I shall be happy to give you any that I can.

I am, sir, your very obedient servant,
EDWARD SINCLAIR
Viewer of Kepier Grange Colliery
Kepier Grange Colliery, Durham, Dec. 14.

The cases are frequent in which evictions give rise to tumult, and even to bloodshed. On the very day that I visited Kepier Grange an eviction took place at Charlaw, a colliery not very far distant. In this case there was also a strike, and the men had had repeated warnings that they would be forced to give up possession of their houses. On the Friday they were told that all those who did not begin work on the Monday following must find other homes. A few complied; the rest remained firm; and a body of police were despatched to carry out the ejectment. Before, however, any steps were actually taken, and while the policemen were in the act of descending from the vehicle in which they arrived, a rush was made at them by the miners, prefaced by a shower of stones—and in the scuffle which followed, a policeman was severely hurt about the head, and one of the attacking party had his skull fractured. This seems to have put an end to active opposition. The people left their houses without resistance, but at night I understand that a good many of them broke through the windows and took possession again. They were to be proceeded against for trespass.

Such scenes as these—however justifiable or necessary the evictions (in other words, the stoppage of all wages) may be—such scenes it must be admitted, are very deeply to be lamented. They form one of the most painful features of coal-strikes, and one the remembrance of which rankles longest in the miner's breast. I believe that the cases are very few indeed in which wanton harshness is displayed on the part of the masters; but the very nature of the system, under which wages cannot be stopped without rejection of the recipients from hearth and home, seems painful and unsatisfactory. How it can be remedied is the difficulty. There is no choice of lodgings for the workman and besides he finds a free house and garden exceedingly convenient; while on the other hand, the master will not willingly give up an arrangement by which he possesses so strong a hold over those whom he employs. Some of the pitmen say that the fact of their employers being also their landlords involves the truck system; but they admit that almost in every case there are no houses other than their employers' for them to live in—so that if the arrangement does involve the truck system, it does so from the pure necessity of the case.

I have found few differences in respect to grades of house accommodation, worth noting, in my tour through the colliery villages in Durham and Northumberland. I saw pit-rows attached to old and to (as they are called) "young" mines. The later-built houses were generally more substantial and roomy than the old ones; but the plan continued exactly the same, and the room accommodation was just as deficient. Near the Walker pit there are a few detached houses of two stories, formerly used for the works connected with a deserted shaft, and now patched up into dwellings—each family occupying a single, unventilated and crazy room. At Framwellgate-moor I found that from the working of the mine being partially continued, the owners were letting out a fair row of cottages, after their sort, at the easy rate of 6d per week. The floors of all these houses were of some composite stuff, in many cases broken away. At a place called New Durham there is a large colliery village, containing a great number of houses, below the average in point of comfort. Outside, the whole place was a perfect waste of filth; and within the houses, the furniture I found to be in many cases meagre in quantity, and poor and shabby in quality. The people complained bitterly of the construction of the chimneys, which they said were continually smoking, in spite of all doctoring. In one range of two-roomed houses, fires could only be lighted in one apartment at a time. This range was known in the village as "Smoky Row". The floors of the several houses were miserably damp, and the whole of the ashes and the domestic filth were flung out before the doors. The people in this village were uncomfortable in several respects. The place is an exception to the general rule, in being situated nearly two miles from the shaft. This distance the fore shift and all the putters and drivers have to travel at least once a day in the dark, through the miry fields. The workings, again, are fully a mile from the bottom of the shaft so that the hewers and putters are forced to walk upwards of six miles above and beneath ground, going to and coming from their work. Besides, one at least of the seams now being wrought is an exceedingly severe one, the height of the coal being only nineteen inches, with nine inches additional cut for the behoof of the putters—making a total height of twenty-eight inches in which the hewers work. One of the latter sat down before me on the floor of his house in the attitude in which he laboured. It was an uncomfortable sitting posture, with the right leg extended sideways, the left foot planted on the ground, the knee drawn up and the head stooped, so as to bring the chin upon a level with the most elevated part of the limb. The hewer sat upon a very low stool, raised hardly two inches and called a "bracket". His wife said that the work was breaking his back.

At Collier-row, on the property of the Marquess of Londonderry, I found some fair cottages, constructed of wood and double-roomed. The usual ridge of ashes and filth extended along the rows, and across the road by which I reached the place two streams of water were flowing. Middle Rainton also belonging to the Marquess has a very favourable *prima facie* look. One range of houses lines the turnpike road. These are two-storied structures most substantially built. They accommodate two families, one on each storey, the arrangements being two good rooms and a pantry for each. The lower floor was paved with flags and altogether the aspect of things in the row was decidedly pleasant. Penetrating, however, to the back, I found quite a different condition of affairs—wretched houses of one small room each, the floors below the level of the refuse-piled streets, and the whole place wearing an aspect of dreary poverty and filth. There are some decidedly good houses in all the Marquess's pit villages, but the majority seem to be very much akin to the general run of pitmen's dwellings—no better and no worse. The people informed me that for certain improvements made, some time ago, they have to thank a visit of the Marchioness. The Marquess, however, is on the whole rather a popular person with the pitmen. In the strike of 1831 he offered himself as a mediator between the labourers and their masters, and was the means of obtaining for the pitmen a concession of their demands.

Miscellania

Hewers are apportioned to different seams, and different parts of seams, by lot; or as it is technically called, "cavil". The cavil takes place once a quarter. The men's names, written on scraps of paper, are placed in a hat, and the first name drawn settles the place of its owner, and through him the place of his comrades, according to a predetermined arrangement. It not unfrequently happens under the present system of monthly hiring, particularly if the demand for hewers is brisk, that a workman who has had a "bad cavil"—that is, a place in a hard or difficult seam—gives his month's warning and betakes himself to another colliery, in the hope of meeting with better luck. That the proceeding is obviously unfair does not prevent it from frequently taking place. In cases of removal, the old plan was for the new master to pay the expenses of the "flitting", but this has been discontinued, and the colliers must now transport their goods and chattels from place to place at their own cost.

In a great number of collieries within a reasonable distance of Newcastle, the proprietors send in one or more carts every Saturday, to carry out the marketings of the women, who proceed to town to lay in their stock of groceries etc. for the ensuing week. The carts put up at some central point in the town. Thither the tradesmen send the purchased goods, which are thence conveyed to the doors of their owners without any expense, other than the pence paid by each family to the driver of the vehicle.

In cases of fatal accidents in coal pits, the widows of the men killed are almost invariably allowed to retain houses rent free in the pit-row—although if they occupy double tenements, they must often remove to smaller ones. Women placed under these circumstances seldom or never quit the colliery. They set up little huckstering shops, and take in washing. The owners always pay the funeral expenses of men killed in their employment, and make a money present to the surviving relatives. One or more benefit societies are run in connection with each pit. They grant allowances on their largest scale in cases of accident; on a smaller scale in cases of sickness; and they commonly also afford small superannuation pensions. Generally speaking, some light sort of work about the pit is found for hewers who have grown grey in the service. The fines from "laid-out" and "set-out" are sometimes set apart by the owners for charitable purposes. But there are cases—the Haswell Coal Pit afforded a recent case—in which the men have absolutely refused the offer of the proprietors to apportion the fines in this way. "If you take them," said the workmen, "you take them unjustly, and you may keep them." The tone occasionally adopted by the pitmen may be judged of by this reply.

The small chapels which abound in colliery villages are "served" three Sundays out of every four by "local preachers", themselves working men. These persons proceed from mine to mine agreeably to a regular printed arrangement, a copy of which may be frequently found suspended from the walls of a hewer's cottage. They officiate gratis, generally dining at the table of any zealous member of the congregation. These local preachers exercise the deepest influence over a very large proportion of the coalmining population. Their sermons are usually couched in the homeliest patois, and are very often full of technical allusions and illustrations.

Transportation of the Coal to the Market

From every pit a tramway runs, either to join a neighbouring railroad or to connect the mine with one of the thousand "staiths" which form so prominent a feature along the banks of the Tyne and Wear. These "staiths" are high wooden jetties, generally running so far into the river as to allow vessels of considerable burden to lie afloat at their extremities, even at low water. The tramway runs from the pit to the end of the staith—the latter usually forming an incline, down to which each heaped-up waggon as it descends pulls up an empty one. The ship to be loaded lies, of course, below. The full waggon under charge of a brakesman lodges upon a species of an ingeniously balanced framework, calculated to swing down with the weight from the end of the staith, and to come to a rest exactly over the open hatchway of the vessel beneath. The brakesman or rider accompanies the waggon in its descent, and removing a bolt, the bottom of the vehicle gives way in a trap-door fashion, and its load sinks into the hold—the well-balanced platform immediately rising as the weight is removed from it, and restoring the waggon to its position at the extremity of the staith, up which it is pulled by the next descending load. There is a brakesman to every waggon, assisted by an off-putter, whose station is at the extremity of the staith, and who keeps an account of the number of waggonfuls shipped. The wages of the waggon-rider are about 15s, those of the off-putter about 18s or 20s weekly. The latter frequently goes on board vessels, so as to pilot them to their proper position at the end of the staith.

The largest class of collier loading at a staith will have her cargo aboard in a tide. In the hold there are a gang of "trimmers", whose duty it is to stow away the coals as they are poured under hatches. The trimmers are paid 3s 6d for each keel of eight Newcastle chaldrons. The crews of the colliers never meddle with the shipping of the cargo. They work the vessel and do nothing more.

Occasionally, instead of the vessel ascending the river to a staith, she lies at Shields, in the Tyne, or at Sunderland, in the Wear, and has her lading conveyed to her by keels, and shovelled on board by keelmen. These keels are the coal barges of the North. They are heavily built craft, partially decked, the hatchway being in general so large as to leave the impression that the boat has merely a ledge of deck running inwards from her gunwale. These keels are slop-rigged carrying a mainsail and jib, the blackened canvas of which forms one of the characteristics of the northern coal rivers. Each keel has an after cabin, or "huddick", in which the crew occasionally sleep. The huddick is furnished neither with berths nor hammocks—two or three mattresses and as many blankets, laid on the floor round the stove, affording the necessary accommodation. Keelmen form a sort of cross between hewers and sailors. They wear a peculiar costume, consisting of a large jacket, or rather doublet, with loose breeches, made very wide at the knee, and not descending further. The wearers of this costume are, or at all events were, a proverbially unintelligent, ignorant and intemperate set of men. One keelman, it used to be said, could drink out three pitmen; and there is a species of traditional story, well known in Newcastle, and which has long passed current as illustrative of the intelligence of those whose duty it is to make the "keel row". According to this legend, a keelman, seeing alongside his craft a hoop inside of which an unbroken mass of froth had collected, leapt overboard to secure the prize, taking it for a floating grindstone! Having been pulled out, he was narrating his mishap to a comrade, who vastly enjoyed the tale, but gently reprimanded the adventurer, telling him that he ought to have seen at a glance that the floating object was not a grindstone, because by his own account, it had not a hole in the middle!

The keel trade has been much injured by the railways, which convey coals to Sunderland and Shields more cheaply and speedily than they can be transported by water carriage. A keelman told me that in the old days he had often made £2 10s a week. His gains at present are from 15s to 18s. Sometimes a large colliery maintains a fleet of keels, but generally they are the property of comparatively poor men, each of whom acts as the skipper of his own craft. A keel is paid by the tide, that is, by the trip between the staith and the ship's side, whatever may be the distance between them. The freight is always one guinea, the keelmen for this shovelling the coals aboard. Formerly each keel was manned by three men and a boy, the latter called the "paydee". The guinea was divided between the three men in nearly equal shares, the skipper having only 8d per tide over and above the portion of each of his crew. The "paydee" had 1s 6d per week and his food. Since the keel trade has been slack, however, his services have been in general dispensed with. Before the period in question a keel not unfrequently made ten tides per week, but a third of that number is now reckoned fair average employment. Sometimes but not often, the keels venture into the open sea to load vessels which cannot conveniently come over the bar. The seamen who man the coal-brigs of Northumberland and Durham are almost all north countrymen. If engaged by the month their pay is 50s. A great proportion of these collier brigs, however, are London traders. They may make from ten to twelve trips back and fore per annum. And the pay of each seaman, his food being found, is always £4 per trip. As I have already stated, he takes no part in loading the cargo in the north. The keelman or the staithman performs that part of the work in the Tyne, or the Wear—the coal-whipper clears the hold in the Port of London.

II

STAFFORDSHIRE

The South Staffordshire Collieries

Introduction

In the southern part of Staffordshire—touching upon the town of Wolverhampton, then running in a north-easterly direction towards Bloxwich, from thence stretching to the south, and comprising within its limits Walsall, Wednesbury and Tipton, and extending as far as Dudley—lies the South Staffordshire Coalfield. It is a great basin of coal and ironstone seams, frequently running in alternate strata, and in some places especially towards the northern skirts of the field, approaching so near the surface as to be capable of excavation by means of rude and inexpensive, though in the end very uneconomical, machinery. This coal and iron bed has been diligently worked for many years. Above, for dozens of miles together, the country is literally a waste of cinders and refuse coal dust, studded with flaming iron-works, countless engine houses, and thickly clustered groups of dismal, squalid villages, any one of which it is as hard to distinguish from its neighbour, as it is to make out the individual pitmen, when their faces are all one black mask of coal-dust and grime. Underneath these iron works, engine-houses and swarming villages, the country is absolutely hollow—the rent and cracked walls, and tottering buildings marking where the superincumbent strata have been crushed down into the caverns gradually formed beneath them.

The vast majority of the inhabitants of the region are engaged in the employment which the nature of the soil has made the staple industry. The working men are exclusively iron-smelters and forgers and colliers. Indeed, the two trades hereabouts seem like branches of one occupation. When the iron trade languishes, the coal trade is depressed; and yet closely linked as the twin branches of labour are, there are wide social and physical differences between the two classes of labourers.

The Midland iron districts exhibit some of the very worst phases of manufacturing life. The working population are rude and unintelligent beyond those who people either the cotton or the woollen country. In the Wolverhampton district, out of 1,133 marriages which took place in 1846, not less than 649 men and 833 women signed the register with their marks; and in the Walsall district, out of 327 marriages, 153 men and 218 women similarly attested their want of education. From an estimate, the calculations for which extend over some years, it would appear that in the iron districts generally, 57 per cent of the women and 39 per cent of the men are enabled to write their names.

In point of criminality, Staffordshire is worse than the average of English counties. It is indeed, the twelfth in point of immorality, as measured by committals—standing in this respect between the agricultural counties of Bucks and Wilts. A considerable portion of the shire is, however, purely rural, and game-law offences form a large item in the list of convictions. In 1847 the criminality of the mining districts of the north was represented by 6.81; that of the silk district stood at 10.15; that of the agricultural districts at 14.80; that of the cotton districts at 18.52; and that of the iron districts at 20.24. The average of England and Wales was 15.90. The proportion of female offences in the Staffordshire iron and coal districts is great. The women work at rude and unsexing labour at the pit-mouth, partly assuming their habiliments and altogether adopting the coarseness of the men.

The houses are far inferior to the ordinary standard of the industrial districts, and they seldom or never have gardens. The people are often both dirty and intemperate. At Bilston it is calculated that 5,000 miners spend annually £50,000 in ale; and at Moxley there is one beer shop to every twelve dwellings. The value of life at Wolverhampton is about one in 40; at Westbromwich one in 45; and at Walsall one in 43. The population of the district of Wolverhampton in 1841 was 80,721; that of Westbromwich was 52,578; and that of Walsall 34,253. The number of illegitimate births in Wolverhampton in 1846 was 188; in Westbromwich, 100; and in Walsall, 107.

In the Parliamentary borough of Wolverhampton, including the towns of Bilston, Ledgley, Wednesbury and Willenhall there was in 1841, a labouring population of 79,259, including upwards of 30,000 children under fifteen years of age, dependent upon cheap public schools for education. Of these it was estimated that about one-fourth attended day schools of some kind, and that about one-half attended Sunday schools—leaving upwards of 15,000 children in a space of a few square miles growing up in dense and total ignorance.

The principal seam of coal which traverses the Stafford mineral district is no less than ten yards in thickness. The centre of the basin may be near Tipton. At Wolverhampton, to the north-west, the ten-yard seam begins to crop out in the surface and disappears; and the pits thereabouts principally work the lower lying strata, which run in masses from three to nine feet in depth. The "new mine" belt of coal lies beneath the ten-yard seam. Where the latter dips deeply, it is almost the only one worked—as at West-bromwich; but when it rises towards the edges of the basin, the pitmen sink their shafts to the inferior strata, which, of course, heave themselves up towards the surface at a still greater distance from the centre of the field. It is calculated that the gross contents of the ten-yard seam are about 40,000 tons per acre; but owing in a great measure to the rude style of working practised, the actual yield per acre is at present not much above 16,000 tons.

1. An explosion in a coal mine

2. Interior of a coal mine in Northumberland

3. Various positions assumed by hewers in digging at the coal

4. Holing coal

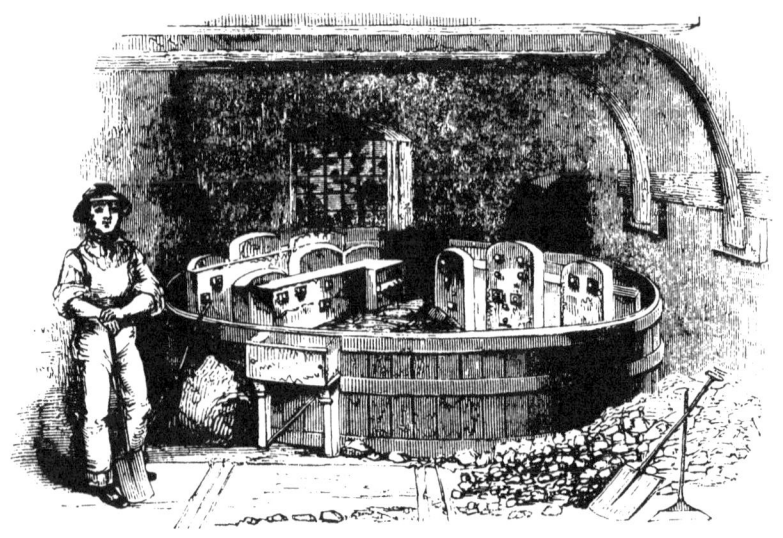

5. Flint-grinding

6. A potter's wheel: the thrower, ball-maker and wheel turner at work

The Working of the Collieries

The change from the collieries of Northumberland and Durham to those of Staffordshire seems like going back at least a century in the art of mine engineering. On the banks of the Tyne and the Wear, science the most profound, and practical skill the most trained and enlightened, are brought to bear upon the excavation of coal. The pits are worked under the constant superintendence of regularly educated viewers, each of whom has a staff of assistants, of more or less scientific and practical skill, to carry his directions into execution. In the Staffordshire coal district, on the contrary, everything seems to be done by the roughest rule of thumb. The pits as regards depth are mere scratches compared with those in the North; and except in the case of a few of the thick seam mines, they are ventilated solely by the agency of the vast number of shafts with which the whole coalfield is honey-combed—anything like artificial means for creating a current of air being seldom or never thought of. The workings in such excavations are, of course, very limited. The labourers could not breathe at any considerable distance from one of the shafts; and the consequence of the whole system is that the coal is worked in the slowest, most dangerous, and least economical fashion.

The appearance of the country around Wolverhampton, Willenhall and Bilston, where the thin seams principally lie, is strange in the extreme. For miles and miles the eye ranges over wide-spreading masses of black rubbish, hills on hills of shale, and mashed and mudded coal-dust, extracted from beneath, and masking as it were the whole face of nature. The earth hereabouts seems, as far as the eye can reach, to be literally turned inside out. Here and there a sterile-looking field may chequer the black prospect, but the general landscape may be correctly described as a perfect desert of coal dust, mud and refuse. This uninviting-looking region is honeycombed with pitshafts, and many of the surface undulations which catch the eye are the result of the earth having fallen in and collapsed on insufficiently propped workings. Dotted thickly over the coal expanse are scores of rudely-built engine-houses with short chimneys, and miserable hovels used as places of shelter for the above-ground workers, with here and there rows of dilapidated cottages; and there is hardly a building or wall which the continued sinking of the earth has not thrown off the perpendicular. Engine-houses lean this way and that—great cracks and rents opening in their walls; and the visitor is sometimes shown spots where rows of houses have been engulfed altogether in the earth. The tramways which wind through these dreary wastes are of the rudest construction; and here and there, labouring to load the waggons or pile the coals brought to the surface, are groups of swart-faced women—but with every womanly feature and attribute ground out of them by the coarse and filthy toil.

The spectator will observe that from every engine-house there extends, as from a common centre, a number of chains, sometimes passing over wheels working close to the ground, sometimes supported by means of rude stakes, at varying heights—the altitude becoming greater as the distance from the engine-house increases, until each chain passes over the apex of a triangle of posts, and then sinks perpendicularly down into the shaft beneath. The engine thus works three, four, five, and sometimes as many as seven shafts, all leading into the same pit, and all lying within a circle of a couple of hundred yards or so in diameter. The chains are so arranged that one-half of them wind up while the other half are being let out. The working of this mechanism is wretchedly slow, while the chance of shaft accidents is, of course, immensely increased by the fact that there is often necessarily employed three times the length of chain requisite for simply descending to the bottom. The pit may be but thirty fathoms deep, but probably there are nearly a hundred additional fathoms of chain requisite to stretch from the bank to the engine.

The chains used are generally composed of flat links of iron and there is always a heavy lump of metal attached to them just above the "skip", which serves to keep the horizontal extent of iron links from slackening when the load is at the surface. The beautiful contrivances in use in the North for warning the engineman that the tub is near the brink of the shaft, are here unknown. Sometimes a bundle of rags is attached to the chain some half a dozen yards above the skip, and the appearance of this rude token suffices as a signal for the slackening of the engine. In many of the South Staffordshire pits, the engineman does not know whether he is regulating the ascent of men or coals. "Look at that wire," said one of them to me at a mine near Bilston—pointing to a rusting thread of iron trampled into the coal dust; "it used to be fixed to a bell in the engine room, and when men were coming up the banksman rung it. But it got broken somehow—nobody will be at the trouble or the expense to repair it, and so I can never tell what sort of cargo there is in the skip." At another pit, a rude telegraphic sign, by the motion of the banksman's arms, announced to the engine man that miners were ascending. I asked how the sign was managed at night. "Oh," said the banksman, "then I wave my arm before the fire here; but we're not very particular." So indeed it appeared.

There are scores of coal-pits scattered through the Wolverhampton district, worked without any steam-engine at all, simply by the aid of a rude gin and a blind old horse. This gin is a species of capstan—the cylinder, on which the rope winds, being usually about six feet in diameter. It is strengthened by a rude but massive scaffolding, and the horse is harnessed to a strong circulating bar. A gin is seldom employed to work more than two shafts. The ropes used are common round hempen ones, and each winds in a different direction upon the cylinder. In these small pits there are usually about ten men underground, and a couple of men and as many women at bank. In no case which I have seen is the shaft furnished with those wooden partitions and guiding spears down which the cages slide so smoothly in the North. The hole has the appearance of a huge well, and the skip has ample room to oscillate as it swings up or down along the greenish slimy brickwork.

The system of working pursued in Staffordshire depends upon the thickness of the seam. The ten-yard seam is, as its name imports, a vast bed of mineral thirty feet in thickness. In removing this deposit, vast pillars are necessarily left to support the roof, and the men frequently work on ladders and stages fixed in the face of the coal. The boards or workings are generally about three yards wide, with a pillar six or eight yards square left between each. At almost every thirty yards a larger pillar, forming an immense block of coal, called a "fire rib", is allowed to stand—each group of workings opening out a cavern of about forty square yards, the roof supported by four pillars, with a fire rib on each side. Efforts are now being made to improve this manner of working, and to dig away great portions of the pillars, leaving the remainder to be crushed down by the weight above, and to form vast gas-breeding goaves. In the mines where the seams worked are not above five feet in height, the pitmen proceed "longwall" fashion. They drive a rolley-way, or, as it is here called, a "gate-road", right from the bottom of the shaft to the extent of the boundary and then commencing at the furthest extremity, they "howk out" almost the whole of the seam, temporarily supporting the roof with earth and rubbish, but so efficiently as to make it certain that it will ultimately collapse or "scrounce in" behind them. The iron-stone seams are worked in the same way, although as these last are generally thinner than the coal belts, the work is more severe; and a great number of boys are employed to load the refuse into small iron skips called "dans", and to trundle it out of the way of the excavators to those portions of the pit which, having been hollowed, require, partially at least, to be filled up with supporting masses of rubbish.

The general want of system, and the almost total absence of anything like scientific management, make great portions of the Staffordshire coalfield almost as dangerous to those who live on the surface as to those who work beneath it. I shall afterwards minutely describe the state of the hundreds of ruinous houses which I have found inhabited, although actually sinking into the moving and crumbling earth. As regards a great part of the district, nothing like authentic marks of the underground excavations are preserved. The workmen proceed partly by guess, partly guided by the position of the old shafts around them. Very often one mine runs beneath another; and it continually happens that the gas accumulating in old deserted workings leaks into pits in the course of excavation, and produces fatal results. Fortunately, however, the thin coal-seams give out very little carburetted hydrogen. On the surface, it not uncommonly happens that old shafts are left entirely undefended. Some of them, indeed, are walled around—others are built in with circular roofs, looking exactly like gigantic beehives—but I have seen many shafts down which an unwary step in a dark night might precipitate the wayfarer. When an open shaft exists near a cluster of houses, the inhabitants frequently dig a drain running into it—the mine in this case forming an undeniably handy cesspool. It sometimes happens that when a shaft is deserted, some poor vagrant family squat themselves down in the "hovel" upon its brink, which they are allowed to occupy either rent free, or for about sixpence a week. This is a practice which has given rise to many accidents, especially those of children falling down the shafts. Occasionally, too, the apparently solid earth gives way—the descent taking place suddenly, and producing a hole, of no great depth perhaps, but a fall into which, when the opening is recent, is exceedingly dangerous, from the volumes of gas which very frequently ascend through the newly loosened earth. Three people, residents in a hovel, lost their lives in this way a few weeks ago.

The Organisation of the Mines

The Staffordshire coal mines are almost universally worked upon the "buttie" system. The buttie is a sort of middleman or contractor. Generally speaking, he has been a working man himself, and still preserves the appearance, dress, and style of living of his original condition. The buttie is, in most cases, an entirely uneducated man. He may be, and usually is, a person of practical experience, and often of much natural sagacity; but it frequently happens that he cannot write, and can hardly read—and to this individual the whole working and management of the mine is entrusted. The engine and the machinery belong in the majority of cases to the proprietor of the royalty. He pays the buttie a certain sum for every ton of coal extracted, and leaves the mode of working entirely to his agent. The engineman and some few of the people employed above ground are sometimes paid by the proprietor, but all the underground workmen are hired and remunerated by the buttie, who, in fact, is at once a commercial agent and a managing engineer. The buttie has always a foreman called a "doggie", who passes the whole day in the pit, superintending and aiding in the proceedings of the workpeople. The doggie is paid regular wages, generally either 4s or 4s 6d per day. The great mass of the workpeople are either "holers" or "bandsmen". The holer answers in some respects to the northern hewer, but the manner of working the seam is different. The Staffordshire labourer commences operations along the seam by hollowing under, or undermining the ledge of coal. Squatting himself on the ground, or lying on his side, he hacks out the supporting strata to the depth of about eighteen inches, extending his operations along the seam, and pausing from time to time to support the coal thus deprived of its resting place, by means of short props called "sprags". Close to him stand the iron carriages already mentioned called "skips" and which look like great metal salvers upon wheels. Upon these skips the coal is piled, the mass being steadied by movable iron hoops, placed one above the other, so as to girdle and support the lumps of mineral. These carriages are loaded by the bandsman; but our business at present is with his comrade.

The holer is paid by the stint—this stint being the undermining of a certain breadth of coal, differing, of course, with the hardness and the difficulty of the seam. The present remuneration for a "stint" is 2s 3d. Many holers are able to work at least a stint and a half a day and are paid accordingly. The greater number, however, I am assured, do not earn at the present prices of coal, more than 2s 6d per day. The holer may ascend as soon as he has completed his stint, or he may remain until the termination of the twelve hours, or twelve hours and a half of daily toil. The holers who can and do earn their two stints a day are, I am informed, exceptions to the general rule. A few years ago when the coal and iron trades were in a more prosperous condition than they are now, there were great complaints of the self-restrictive system upon which the pitmen worked. In 1847, Mr. Parker, of the Chillington Iron Works, near Wolverhampton, stated that the colliers were then restricting themselves to eight and nine hours daily work for only five days in the week, their wages being on the average, 4s 4½d per day. He added that if the men would work twelve hours more per week, the difference would suffice to make up the quantity of coal and ironstone required, and that three pits out of every twenty might be then closed up. I have said enough however previously to show that this is one of the questions on which the men conceive that their interests, and those of their employers, lie in quite opposite directions. At present, however, the trade is too slack for anything like restriction to exist. The men are only overglad to get what labour their employers can afford them. I have made inquiries in many quarters among the working men, and they tell me that the coal union is extinct in Staffordshire. "They may get it up, again," said one of them, "in the North—but we're people from a great many counties here, and we don't trust each other."

Next in position to the holer comes the bandsman or bondsman. This functionary completes the work which his comrade began—breaks down with mallets and hammers, and sometimes blows down with gunpowder, the masses of coal already undermined by the holer—and then piles them upon the skip. In the majority of coal seams no putter is required. The horse which draws the skips comes close up to the workpeople, and from thence tugs his burden to the bottom of the shaft. In very many pits there is only a single horse below ground. It is in the ironstone mines, where the seams are often very thin, that putters are necessary. They are always mere boys and the tubs which they "put" or "pitch" are the small skips called "dans". The bandsman is paid by fixed wages varying in different pits from 4s to 4s 3d per day. For this he remains underground for twelve hours, descending at 6 a.m. The holer generally keeps beforehand with his work, so as always to leave the bandsman plenty to do. The boy who drives the horse and attends to him is paid from 2s to 2s 3d per day; and about the same amount of wages is earned by the hooker-on, a functionary who attaches the skips to the chain at the bottom of the shaft, and gives the signal for hoisting.

Upon the bank of the mouth of each shaft there are two or more women, superintended in their operations by a man. It is difficult to conceive of anything more utterly or coarsely unfeminine than the aspect of these persons. They are lean, haggard and grisly creatures—their skins engrained with dirt, which is very often never washed off from Saturday to Saturday—while, as for their ages, the great proportion actually seem to be of any age between 20 and 50. They generally wear men's coats buttoned over their dresses, and squat flattened bonnets, often crowned with a wisp of straw done up in a clout, on which to lay the basketful of coals which they often choose to carry upon their heads. These women seldom use spades or shovels in emptying the skips into the waggons. They work amongst the lumps of mineral with their bare hands, and they are altogether in their persons and their minds, melancholy examples of the effect of rude coarse toil in absolutely unsexing the women who are employed in it. The lowness of the wages paid to the individuals is the chief reason why the butties employ them, since frequent shaft accidents occur through their heedlessness. Their pay is sometimes a shilling, but more frequently they have only 10d or 11d a day, and many of them assured me that sometimes they do not make more than 3s. per week. As tolerably long intervals take place between the arrival of the different skips, the banksmen and women are unoccupied for a considerable portion of their time. They then retreat into the "hovel", a wretched hut built of loosely piled stones, furnished with a coarse bench, and in the winter time with a brazier of blazing coals. One of these "hovels" stands by the mouth of every shaft. The boys employed in the Staffordshire coal-pits are not numerous. There are few or no traps for them to attend to, and their principal work consists of waiting upon the men, carrying their picks to be sharpened and put in order, and holding and trimming their candles. The provisions of Lord Ashley's Act so far as regards the ages of boys working in coal-pits, are, I have reason to know, habitually set at defiance in South Staffordshire. In none of Mr. Tremenheere's reports which I have by me is the subject alluded to; but when I have inquired of the people themselves, I have almost uniformly been answered by a laugh at the absurdity of the question. "Not till they're ten years old! Ah, sir, they're in the pits long, long before that." The women have never been in the habit of working underground in this district.

The Daily Life of the Staffordshire Miner

There is nothing particularly characteristic in the dress of the Staffordshire miners. It generally consists of coarse loose flannel jackets and trousers with thick heavy shoes. At their work both holers and bandsmen labour naked to the waist. The latter set up the props, or "trees" as they are here called; but as one of them remarked to me, "There isn't much timber used hereabouts; we takes rubbish instead; it's not so good nor timber, but it's much cheaper, and that makes all the difference." The Staffordshire coal workers, behind their brethren in most respects, are especially so in point of cleanliness. The aspect of the beds in the cottages is alone sufficient to prove this. I should be loath to suppose that the statement is true generally—but it was asserted to me by a Northumberland pitman, who had passed many years in Staffordshire and Lancashire, that "he knew many a holer and bandsman whose legs were never washed since their mothers washed them". If such things can be, one ceases to wonder at the terrible ravages of cholera in Wednesbury and Bilston—especially when we remember the general intemperance of the working people hereabouts.

The Staffordshire colliers take all their meals, except supper, in the pit. The general dinner-time is one o'clock, and an hour is allowed for the meal. The whole "pit's company" then assemble at the bottom of the shaft, while their wives, sisters, and daughters make their way to the bank with the respective dinners. Each portion is placed in a bowl, tied over with a handkerchief or rag, very often none of the cleanest, and marked by some peculiar token which guides each man to his own mess. "Some people," said a woman to me, "will sew a button on the rag in a particular way; others will pin on a bit of the skirt which their husband knows the pattern on." The men fetch home the bowls at the end of the day's work. The dinner almost always consists of a portion of meat, with plenty of bread and potatoes. "My husband's dinner," said the wife of a bandsman near Bilston, "is usually half a pound of bread, half a quartern of potatoes, and a piece of meat—bacon very often—more or less of that according to how the money is, and sometimes none at all." "Well—yes—I do generally have meat to dinner," a miner answered to my inquiries, "but it's darned seldom that I have so much as I could eat on it. Only on Sundays we does manage a little bit extra." This man showed me his basin, which certainly did contain a rather overwhelming proportion of potatoes.

When times are better than they have recently been, the colliers of Staffordshire live well. Their pleasures are essentially animal, and it was said to me by a gentleman who knows the population intimately, that if every man had £5 a week he would spend it in eating and drinking. In Bilston, says Mr. Mosely, the Government Inspector of Schools, the improvidence of the people may be studied with advantage in the market place. "No other market is supplied with finer poultry, or, comparatively to the population, in greater abundance; and this is chiefly, if not entirely, for the consumption of the labouring classes—for the resident inhabitants not of those classes are few in number. There, sordid and ill-favoured men may be seen buying on Saturday chickens and ducks and geese, which they eat for supper, and in some instances of which I was informed they drink bottled porter and wine. Yet so little have they beforehand in the world, that if the works were to stop, they would begin within a fortnight to pawn the little furniture of their cottages for subsistence or for drink." This extract applies perhaps rather to the iron workers than to the miners; but to a great degree I believe it at certain times to be true of both. The supply of poultry in Bilston Market is a fact which I can corroborate both from inquiry and from personal observation.

When the dinners of the workpeople are all collected at the mouth of the shaft, they are placed upon a skip and let down en masse. The women then fill a basket of coal, to which each who has a male relation in the pit is entitled and they walk off, very often with more than twenty pounds weight a-piece upon their heads. Soon after noon, the Willenhall, the Bilston and the Dudley roads are lined with these women marching uprightly and steadily under their well-poised burdens.

In the northern coal-pits the most rigid teetotalism is enforced underground; but in Staffordshire the butties themselves find their workpeople in beer. I am bound, however, to say that from what I hear of the quality of the liquid, not much danger can be apprehended as likely to accrue from it to the sobriety of the consumers. The beer which the workpeople can "command" is, by the custom of the country, that sold at 2d per quart; but they tell me that the buttie very often sends them down stuff which would make them sick to drink. Adults claim an allowance of a quart, and boys of a pint. The liquor is sent down into the pit in huge wooden bottles, each containing several gallons. The forgemen, however, are the most enormous beer and ale drinkers. The severe muscular fatigue and scorching heat to which they are subjected, are supposed to render a constant consumption of liquid absolutely necessary for them. "There is a 'shingler' " (the appellation will be explained hereafter), said the landlord of a public house near Wolverhampton, in answer to my inquiry, "who sometimes comes in here, and drinks eleven quarts of ale at a time. They're capital good customers them iron-men. Bless you, they're always drinking, and they've got such good pay, a lot of them, that they can afford it. There's several men, at the works nigh here, who spend 3s in ale every day of their lives." And indeed the vast number of beer shops which abound throughout the district amply corroborate what I heard as to the immense trade driven by the publicans. In Bilston there are eleven churches and chapels—several of them very small—and 142 public houses. In this parish I may also add, that although there are hundreds of pit-shafts, and although the whole country is hollowed out, there is not a single resident engineer. The butties and the doggies dig and blast away, each after his own fashion.

A more miserable class even than the bankswomen are the poor creatures who come out to pick coal from the rubbish heaps at the pitmouth. Sometimes they are suffered to make the black gleaning in peace—but at other times, perhaps, if the buttie or the doggie happen to be not in the best of humours, they are given in charge, and hurried off to gaol for stealing coals. "I go to pick at the pit-heaps," said one poor woman to me. "It's the only way I can get fuel to keep me from starving these cold nights; but I must be very careful, and not go too near the shaft. There were two poor creatures committed to Stafford gaol last week for stealing coal, and they were only just picking out a few bits from what the pit people throw away for rubbish." Children are often sent out from Wolverhampton to pick.

There does not seem to be any regular grievance, such as the "laid-out and set-out" rankling in the minds of the Staffordshire coal workers. Occasionally they summon the butties before the magistrates for stopping part of their wages on account of alleged insufficient work; but the only special hardship which seems to be of a chronic nature is "builtass work." The derivation of the term is curious. Builtass is, or was, an abbey or religious house in Shropshire, which, as tradition states, was constructed by the forced labour or corvée of the peasantry. The name has been imported into Staffordshire, and "builtass work" there signifies forced labour. Applied to the coal-pits, the phrase implies a day or half a day's work, periodically imposed by the butties, and for which no wages are paid. The toil consists in clearing the mine of those accumulated masses of rubbish which, were they not periodically got rid of, would seriously impede the working of the pit. This gratis labour, whether or not it be objectionable in principle, hardly appears, however, to be very oppressive in practice.

The Staffordshire miner seems to have little superstitious feeling about him. His strongly-developed animal propensities appear to keep him often in a state of actual mental stagnation. If he dreads anything as ominous, it is the appearance, as he goes to his labour, of that unlucky creature—a black cat. But the only strong and general feeling which approaches to superstition is the uniform abandonment of a mine in which a fatal accident has taken place, until the victim shall have been buried. So long as the corpse is above ground, I am assured nothing will tempt the survivors to resume their labour. The notion that it is unlucky to meet a woman before descending the shaft has no place here. Indeed the employment of so many women upon the bank effectually neutralizes any idea of the kind.

Ventilation in the Mines

During my rambles over the coalfield around Wolverhampton, Wednesbury, Bilston, and Bromwich, I have had frequent conversations with the men upon the ventilation of the mines beneath. I find that they trust implicitly to the shallowness of the pits, and to the close collocation of the shafts. "The air is sure to get down some way or other," seemed the grand motto of their engineering; and, in fact, as the heat beneath is generally greater than that of the atmosphere, there is a languid ventilation which renders it possible to exist in the limited excavations in question. The shaft down which the air descends is called the "drawing" and that by which it escapes, the "driving" shaft. "Sometimes," I was told at the mine, "if it is very hot close weather, and the pit feels very choky, we light a fire at the bottom of the driving shaft, but in general we can breathe well enough without it." At another pit, worked by a gin and a horse, there was a sort of iron funnel-shaped machine, from which a tube stretched down the shaft, and which, being turned round to face the wind would, no doubt, in a smart breeze, conduct a refreshing current of air below. A second shaft, however, communicating with the pit, had recently been sunk at about 100 yards distance—and the buttie, being of opinion that the new aperture would afford sufficient ventilation, was, while I was on the spot, bargaining to sell his "blower", or ventilating apparatus, as old iron.

The Staffordshire Collieries at Night

I have been more than once overtaken by the night upon the dreary expanse of coal refuse which heaps so many square miles in this part of Staffordshire. A more singular sight than that which is thus presented to the wayfarer would be difficult to find. The earth, so far as it can be seen, seems like a great black sea of swelling mounds and hollows, dismal and pathless. Neither tree nor shrub, nor aught but crumbling coal ridges, stands up against the sky—but flaring and flickering close by you, and shining steadily at greater distances, burn hundreds and hundreds of the fires kept alive at the mouths of the shafts, showing you by their flashing glare the dismal scaffold-like apparatus of rope and beam which overhangs them, and surrounded by dusky figures, now relieved against the blaze, now retiring into the night. But these are not the only fires which give a character to the scene. Every mile or two roar the furnaces of great forge and smelting works. The red flames, as they curl up to and over their brickwork barriers, fling into the sky an uncertain lurid glare, which alternately fades and brightens like the quivering of the Northern lights. Girdling these perpetual well-springs of red fire are the dusky outlines of sheds and engine-houses, with a partially illumined streak—the side of the tall chimney next to the furnace light—towering high above them into the air. Over these vast fires, columns of smoke and steam careering by come for a moment visible, and then pass into the darkness—if it indeed can be called darkness, when the whole sky glows with the gleam of the thousand fires beneath. There is something almost terrible in the unwonted aspect of all around—the shale and cinder-covered earth crackling under the tread—the furnaces glowing all around—and the ceaseless murmur of escaping steam and clanking mechanism, borne by every gust of wind over the cinder desert. And almost all this transformation of the natural features of the soil has taken place within the memory of a few old men still living. "I can remember, sir," said an aged person whom I met in the outskirts of Bilston, "when all this country was as green and pleasant as any spot of England. There were coal-pits, to be sure; but there were fields and meadows and hedges between them. Now, you see, nothing green will grow, for the level of the country has been changed by these pit-heaps, and the sulphur smells, and the bad gases comes up out of the very earth."

Housing in the Collieries

Defective as are the dwellings occupied by the pitmen in the North, they are an hundred per cent superior to the tenements of their brethren in Staffordshire. The coal population in the latter county live sometimes in poor detached cottages—sometimes in detached rows or clusters of houses, sprinkled here and there amidst the rubbish waste, or along the roads—sometimes in overgrown villages, of each portion or quartier of which a smelting or a forging work forms the nucleus. These villages or small towns are, like the northern pit-rows, only to be paralleled by themselves. The Rev. Mr. Owen, the excellent vicar of Bilston, has felicitously sketched one of these jointed, yet still disjointed—crowded yet scattered—collocations of dwellings, describing it as "broken up into thick paranthetical tufts of population in three or four separate *faubourgs*, baffling the visitor, as he emerges from suburb after suburb, to discover which of them is the town, till he finds that there is no town in particular, and no suburb above another, but that the suburbs are like their inhabitants, all of a class—all of a piece; street after street and man after man—continual duplication of each other . . . black red streets and black red men, equally indebted to the everlasting coal and smoke for their home and complexions."

The majority of houses belong to small proprietors, and fetch, considering their accommodation and construction, high rents. The tendency in building cottages in this part of the country is not only to make the shell very diminutive, but to split the interior up into almost infinitesimal rooms. I have found four chambers in a cottage, the largest of which was not above seven feet by five. The ground floors are hardly ever boarded, being almost always paved with brick, and very commonly sunk beneath the level of the road. Were it not for the cheapness of coal, which allows the people to keep up almost perpetually blazing fires, these rooms would be so damp as to be hardly habitable. As it is, the interstices of the bricks have always a humid, slimy appearance, and the mode of cleansing in use increases the disadvantages of the flooring. Instead of scouring in the ordinary fashion, the people mop their apartments, emptying buckets upon the kitchen floor, which, particularly where the level is under that of the road, absorbs through its joints a greater portion of the moisture than the mop can possibly dry up. Excepting the tendency to small rooms, there is no particular phase of cottage construction which seems peculiar to the district. The detached cottages and the rows of cottages, if not generally, have, not unfrequently, back doors and yards, the latter usually in a filthy condition. Entrance to the second floor is, in the majority of cases, obtained by a staircase, rising from the principal apartment beneath. The windows are commonly constructed of small lozenge panes in metal frames, the glass often broken and patched with rags, and altogether the interior aspect of the tenements in question is paltry and squalid.

I have already learned by ample experience never to expect good furniture in ill-constructed and inconvenient houses. The dwellings of the South Staffordshire colliers confirm the rule. They exhibit neither the well-stocked cupboards, the well-arranged crockery racks and shelves and the gaily-painted clocks of the Manchester operatives—nor the handsome beds, ample and polished chests of drawers, and burnished teapots and candlesticks of the Northumberland and Durham pitmen. In the dwellings of the poor, the degree of comfort of their occupants may be very fairly gauged by the bed and bed-linen. In the South Staffordshire cottages, both are very commonly mean, uncomfortable, dirty, and neglected—of course there are exceptions, but I state my general impressions after having visited scores of pitmen's dwellings. The furniture is of a piece—paltry and huddled. There is seldom or ever a carpet, and the accommodations for cooking are very deficient. In many living rooms I found washing going on, the place reeking with the peculiar fumes of soap and hot water applied to dirty linen, and everything splashed and uncomfortable. I was struck by the almost total absence of newspapers and books—a few dirty tracts and paltry collections of songs, lying enwreathed with dust in the window-sills, being the only things literary to be seen. In many of the houses the evidence of slatternliness was just as visible as that of poverty. Dishes lay about unwashed, unswept grates were littered with the grey ashes, and beds were very frequently left unmade, their whitey-brown sheets presenting anything but a pleasant spectacle. The ornaments in the South Staffordshire colliers' houses are few and paltry, consisting almost entirely of little earthenware figures, rudely painted and the meanest description of plates. In the north there is hardly a pitman's room but is enlivened by the song of canaries and gold-finches. Cage birds are few in South Staffordshire, and when they do exist, their shabby rushed prisons are quite a contrast to the large and elaborately woven wire receptacles which the northern pitmen themselves delight to fashion for their songbirds.

Gardens are quite unknown in the coal and iron districts of Staffordshire. Indeed, for mile after mile, nothing green will grow. Here and there an individual has attempted to form a sort of artificial garden, by bringing soil from a distance, and laying it upon the coal refuse, but the constant smoke kills every bud and sprout.

I have already alluded in general terms to the cracked and dilapidated state of the immense numbers of the houses, owing to the continued sinking and shifting of the earth. This is one of the worst features of the district. It makes great numbers of the houses uncomfortable — almost uninhabitable — and not a few absolutely dangerous. A visitor to the western outskirts of Bilston, in the direction of the village of Ettingshall, might well imagine that he gazed upon a tract which had been recently convulsed by an earthquake. He will see dozens of dwellings in absolute ruins, the walls partially sunk, and the second floors lying in masses of wet and rotting timber. Other houses, not quite so bad, he would observe torn by great rents from top to bottom, one portion leaning one way — another portion another way; the ground floor partially collapsed, partially hove up, so far as to fix the half-open doors immovably. I measured the crack in one house near Ettingshall — it was seventeen inches in breadth, and surrounded by numerous minor rents. The houses on either side of this one, although far off the perpendicular, and with wavy crevices running all along their walls, were both inhabited. Nothing is more common than to see a couple of windows sloping in different directions, a door broader at bottom than at top, or vice versa — the two gavels leaning towards or from each other, and stacks of chimneys apparently nodding to their fall.

Still the people continue to live in these dilapidated dwellings with the coolest indifference. "Between Birmingham and Kidderminster," says Mr. Mosely, "there are hundreds of paralysed hovels with scarcely a lintel or door-post in its place. One of them gave a loud crack, and out ran the inmates. It was evidently on the eve of falling; but the husband on inspecting it thought 'it would last another week', and back they all went to stay out the week." In a small grocer's shop which I visited near Ettingshall, I found that I could see daylight shining through the walls from the ceiling to the floor. I called the attention of the proprietor of the place to the fact. He had just been disclaiming against the truck system prevalent in the district, and hoping that it would be thoroughly exposed; but on the dilapidated condition of his own house and those in the vicinity being brought on the *tapis*, he very coolly said that that was quite a different thing, that the cracks made the houses airier and healthier ("they were as good as windows"), and wondered very much what people meant by coming prying about his property, and saying that it was in a dangerous state when it had stood with all its rents and cracks about it for twenty years.

The tenants of the rickety houses do not, however, as might be expected, survey the condition of their dwellings with the same complacency. Custom has made many of them reckless to the danger, and in some degree habituated them to the discomfort; but others complained bitterly of the wretched hovels which they were compelled to occupy. One woman in particular, hearing of my errand, ran after me and begged me to come and examine her house. It was one of a row, cracked, distorted and crumbling from end to end. As I stood by the fireside, I could pass my fingers through a crack into the open air. This crevice was partially stuffed with brown paper, and partially nailed over with rough boards, one of which the woman of the house tore down to let me see the extent of dilapidation. Upstairs, matters were still worse. The inmates could lie in bed and see the sky through half a dozen chinks. Those immediately above the beds — for there were two close to each other, and occupied by two married couples – were partially stuffed with brown paper and rags, while boards in the fashion of gutters, were fastened so as to lead the rain away from the beds, and let it fall upon the floor. Notwithstanding, they often wakened with the bed-clothes drenched. The wall facing the Bilston-road was especially crazy, and the head of the bed in which the woman slept was set close to it. "The bricks have yilded here," she said, "several inches, just a short time ago, and I am sure we never go to sleep without being afraid that in the middle of the night the wall will go altogether, and we shall be pitched out, bed and all into the road." The rent paid for this place was 1s 6d per week. The husband of this woman was a bandsman, in only partial work. The week before my visit he had earned only 6s 10d. They would leave the house gladly, but they were a little in arrear of rent, and they knew that if they attempted to "flit", their things would be seized on the instant.

I proceeded into the next house, which I found in a precisely similar condition. The rain came freely into the living-room and bed-room, and the occupants said that they did not consider their lives safe. The ground beneath them was entirely hollow. The landlord did not expect that the houses would stand much longer and so he would do nothing for them. There had been two cases of cholera in this house, and the whole row had suffered more or less. It was impossible not to observe that in few or no cases had anything been done in a workmanlike way to keep these rickety houses together, and diminish their danger to their occupants. The brown paper stuffings and boards were merely intended to keep out the rain and cold. The only instance I saw of architecture suited to the requirements of the locality was in the case of a most unique-looking church at Ettingshall, which is absolutely bound together by girding timbers and strong iron buttresses. If this building ever sinks into the earth it will go en masse.

Near Wolverhampton, on the Wittenhall road, there is a row of miserable one-storied cottages — the history of which is characteristic of the locality. Where they stand, a row of two-storied dwellings formerly existed. These last sank into the earth, and out of the ruins of their upper walls and roofs the present cottages were constructed. This row of houses was severely scourged by cholera. In a short distance along the road, of which the row occupied about one-half, there were more than sixty deaths. The first house which I entered was a small detached hovel, not above twelve feet long on the outside, and yet divided into four miserable earthen-floored rooms. There was no ceiling whatever; the bare tiles could be touched by hand. On the side away from the road, a sort of lean-to was added to the house, forming one of the very worst sleeping places I ever saw. At its highest pitch the roof was not above five feet from the ground, while at the other side, the face of the furthest over-sleeper — and there were two in each of the beds — literally grazed the sloping tiles. In this hole there was neither window nor opening to the outside, but quite enough of cold air penetrated between the loosely laid tiles. Of course the place was pitch dark.

The mistress of the house, a haggard, care-worn looking woman, told me that sleeping places constructed in a similar way were attached to almost every house in the row. In 1832 she had lost her first husband by cholera. Last autumn she had lost her second by the same disease. It raged awfully all around, and many of the people fled and left their friends dying and dead. At that time the houses looked even worse than when I saw them — for they had since been whitewashed, and the windows improved. When the ravages of the cholera became known in Wolverhampton, the sick people were allowed to want for nothing. They had proper food and medicine; but the close choky air of the small unventilated rooms, and the foul dunghills around, were terrible. The police and the gentlemen from Wolverhampton smashed in the windows and broke holes in the wall to let in light and air. One man came crying into her house for the loan of a hammer to knock some of the bricks out of the wall of the back room where his wife was lying ill. He got the hammer, and while he was breaking a hole to give his wife fresh air, she died. My informant laid out the body. Often and often there was no proper person to prepare the corpses decently for interment. Her son, a young man of twenty, had laid out the bodies of several young women. They were buried in their best gowns. The people got panic-struck when the disease was at its height, and wouldn't go near the bodies. One woman died on the floor. She lay with her cap off and her hair all "staring" about her face, and her legs and arms cramped and drawn up under her. A female went to lay her out; but as soon as she caught sight of the body she rushed back, crying that she had never seen such a corpse, that she couldn't lay it out, or look at it, and that she was a dead woman herself. So indeed it proved — for she was taken ill, and died the same night.

In one of the cottages in the neighbouring row, out of a family of eight, a father and mother of six children, all except one child, were swept away. I proceeded to this house and found it tenanted by two Irish families, consisting of thirteen or fourteen persons. The damp floor was more than a foot beneath the level of the road. The few articles of furniture — broken old chairs, benches and crockery-ware lying on the earth — could not be worth half a crown. A big navvy-looking fellow had on his knees three or four children, with whom he was sharing a scanty dinner of bread and tea. Some of them slept upon rugs upon the floor, and others occupied two wretched beds in an airless hole, similar to that which I have already described at the back. The rent paid for this place was 2s per week.

The next house presented a still more miserable scene of poverty. The furniture of the living-room consisted simply of two broken chairs and a pot. The woman who lived here had four children, and expected in two months to be confined again. She looked more than half-starved, with pinched-in cheeks, and black livid rings round each of her eyes. Her husband was an engineman, but he had been out of work for twenty-two weeks, mainly in consequence of bad health, produced by the bursting of a blood vessel when exerting himself to clean a boiler. Before that event they had had a good house of furniture, but they had since lived by selling it piece-meal. Except the two chairs, the pot and an old worn mattress and rug, they possessed nothing but what they stood upright in. They dared not sleep in the bedroom, it was so damp, but they dragged the mattress into the living-room every night, and laid it down where the heat from the grate had dried the brick flooring. The ceiling was not six feet high, and the floor was a foot beneath the road. They paid 2s 6d a week in rent – at least, they had paid it so long as they were able, but now they were in arrears because they had nothing more to sell. The coals they had she picked at the heaps, but she was continually afraid of being taken up for it. They lived entirely on bread and coffee, but latterly they had sat, children and all, in the house for two whole days without food. It is to be hoped that the fortunes of this poor family are mending. On the day I visited them the husband had gone out to undertake the first work he had been able to get for near five months.

In a third house in the row I heard a story which illustrates the buttie system of working coal. The house was, like all the others, squalid and reeking with moisture. The husband worked in a neighbouring pit, and the wife, a thin care-worn litle woman, was preparing three small Swedish turnips for boiling.

"Ah," she said, "this has been a bad week for us. We are well nigh clemmed with hunger. My husband came home last Saturday night without a penny."

I said I feared that he had been at the public-house.

"No, no, nothing of the kind," replied the wife. "There's not a more sober man in the country than my husband — but he wasn't paid. Not a man in the pit was paid for the week's work."

I inquired the reason.

"Just," she answered, "just because the buttie had a cold and wouldn't go to the pit-mouth. He said that the men could wait till next week, or till he was better. At all events he was too ill to come out of his house; so after waiting till it was late, all the hands had to go away without getting a farthing."

I inquired whether they had had any money in hand to go on with.

"Not a penny," was the reply. "We get too little to save anything from one week to another, and how we['re to] get on this week I don't know. This is Tuesday, now I'll tell you what I did yesterday. I went out and borrowed a sixpence, and this is the way I spent it. I bought three-halfpence worth of bacon, and a twòpenny loaf, a half ounce of tobacco which cost threehalfpence, one half-pennyworth of beer, and two farthing candles, one of which we burned last night, and one which we have for tonight. I made the sixpence go as far as I could, and today I've got these three swedes" (pointing to the turnips), "which I'm going to boil; but it's poor watery stuff for a hard-working man, that has had no dinner, to make his supper on."

This miserable piece of petty tyranny, or wanton neglect, on the part of the buttie seemed to be taken without anything like indignation, just as a matter of course. The rent cleared by this wretched row, in which not a ceiling is higher than six feet, in which every floor is damp, and every wall crazy, and in which the cholera carried off a fearful proportion of its inhabitants, exceeds for the eight houses of which it is composed, a pound a week, and it has very frequent parallels throughout the district. The cracked and torn house which I have described in detail may be taken as a specimen of the condition of hundreds of dwellings round Wolverhampton, Willenhall, Wednesbury, and Bilston.

The Educational, Moral and Sanitary State of the Population

The mortality in Bilston from cholera considerably exceeded the proportion of deaths at Paris. Out of a population of about 24,000, more than 700 people died in seven weeks. In the neighbouring district of Cosely the mortality was also great. There had been repeated strikes for wages in the collieries around, and the dietary of the people had consequently been so poor as to render them especially liable to the disease. Bilston is almost exclusively inhabited by colliers and iron workers. Its population is, as I have stated 24,000. But of these I was informed that about 5,000 persons attend the different churches and chapels, while 11,000 never go near them. There are about 4,000 children connected with various Sunday and day schools, and upwards of 400 Sunday School teachers. Out of 5,000 miners in the neighbourhood, it is calculated that 4,000 never attend any place of worship whatever. The prevalent ignorance is, of course, deplorably gross. "Many butties," says the Rev. Mr. Owen, "come to me to prove wills, often to the extent of thousands of pounds, and in nine cases out of ten they affix their marks." Complaints are very rife in the district of the unwillingness of the colliers to make any sacrifice whatever for the education of their children, or even to send them to their school *gratis*. Mr. Parker, the proprietor of very large iron works in the neighbourhood, once offered to pay 2d a week for any of the children of his workpeople whom their parents would send to school. Out of 1,500 workmen whom he employed, only 30 embraced the offer.

The active and enlightened exertions of the Rev. Mr. Owen, of Bilston, to infuse something like intelligence into the population by which he is surrounded ought to be known. The rev. gentleman does not confine himself to religious instruction but wisely labours to promote the advance of that general intelligence and information without the existence of which the raw mental material can hardly be brought into any shape. Through Mr. Owen's exertions a series of familiar lectures, suitable to the capacities of the audience, have from time to time been given, principally by clergymen of the church. On the list of lectures at present in course of delivery, I find an account of a trip to Snowdon, with notices of Wales, and an explanation of the process of floating and hoisting the Menai tubular bridge — a narrative of the escape of Charles II from Worcester — a history of the American Revolution, and an exposition of "Popular Proverbial Errors". These lectures are when practicable illustrated by simple diagrams and dissolving views. When I was at Bilston, I found Mr. Owen actively preparing a lecture on the Bosjesmen, whose presence he had procured from an exhibition room in Wolverhampton. These lectures are attended on the average by about 600 persons; and here I found for the first time in the mining districts, the dissenters in a great minority as compared with the church. The clergy of all persuasions, however, work harmoniously together; and indeed, the field seems amply wide for the labourers. Mr. Owen informed me of the somewhat curious fact, that not one single regular member of the Methodist body at Bilston had died of cholera. This he attributed to the general sober habits of the persons in close communion with and strictly under the discipline of the persuasion in question. The great proportion of deaths at Bilston were amongst the dirtiest and most intemperate of the population.

The vast proportion of the town is, however, pitiably behind-hand as to sanitary matters. Only about one-third of it is drained, and the sewage of that third flows into an open and filthy brook, which runs through the lower part of Bilston, and on the banks of which more than 100 persons were swept away by the epidemic. Lining this open sewer, for such it is, are groups of small unventilated houses, without back doors and surrounded by masses of mud and filth. In the brook itself, domestic refuse and the garbage of slaughter-houses abound, and at one part of its course the water is used for the steam-engines of an iron works, and then partially discharged in a heated condition and sending up the foulest vapours. The cholera was particularly fatal in the vicinity of this dirty pond of steaming water. It is a curious fact that in both visitations, the first case at Bilston took place in the same house. I visited it. The building consists of two stories, each of a single room. In the lower chamber there is an oven common to all the neighbours—the place being, in fact, a mere shell, with shattered windows, open to all the winds of heaven. Above it is a small squalid room, for which its female tenant pays 1s 8d weekly rent. The brook bathes the walls of the house. All along the banks of this foetid stream are shallow wells. From any one spot they may be counted in twos and threes. These contain the only water used for drinking and cooking, by a large proportion of the inhabitants of the poorer part of Bilston. I tasted the fluid, which was mawkish and nasty beyond description, and charged, as was very evident, even to the eye, with solid matter held in suspension. This water is mere surface drainage. The mines have absorbed all the springs in the vicinity. "The wells", said one man, "always rise and fall with the brook." "Aye", added a woman, "and when the brook is dirtiest, they're dirtiest." In some of the wells which I looked down I could see the oily glancing of the scum as it floated upon the top of the water. Only an inconsiderable portion of the public-houses have pipe water, which is brought from Tipton. The local authorities have made efforts to cleanse the dirtiest portions of the Bilston-brook; but the nuisance itself, it seems, cannot be suppressed under the existing law. A deputation waited upon the Central Board of Health in London upon the subject, when it was ascertained that no clause in any of the Health of Towns Bills applied to the particular circumstances of the brook, it being a natural stream, and neither a ditch, drain, watercourse, or sewer.

The Ironworkers of South Staffordshire

The iron works are of two general kinds — the smelting or blast furnaces for separating the pure metal from the stone, and the forging mills where the metal is "puddled" and rolled into sheets, rods, bars etc. It is calculated that each blast furnace gives employment altogether to upwards of 200 men. Some ironmasters keep their furnaces continually blowing, except when they are obliged to quench them to repair the brickwork. The men are divided into day and night shifts, and on each alternate Sunday the whole twenty-four hours work is done by one of the shifts, so as to give a fortnightly rest to the others. Some ironmasters occupy their hands upon Sunday in repairing the accidental damage and wear and tear of the week, and only a few partially suspend operations on the first day of the week, so far as to content themselves with a single instead of a double cast, or extraction of the molten metal. The injury done to the physical powers, as well as to the moral character of the men, by Sunday labour, can be well conceived, and is only too notorious in the district. Many of the ironmasters contend that the system is one of necessity. Others who do not pursue it maintain that it is not required by the exigencies of the trade, but that, on the contrary, a better week's work is done by labouring in six than by toiling seven days. For Sunday labour, extra ale is allowed; and "very often", says a gentleman connected with one of the largest iron works in the district, "there is much more attention paid to the ale than to the work." The masters who allow their people rest on the Sunday, adds the same authority, have, as a general rule, the steadiest and best hands in the district. Their work, both of repairs and production, is very generally turned out in a better style than that of their Sunday-toiling competitors. The wages of the blast-furnace man, in the Staffordshire district, averages about 21s or 22s a week, ranging from 18s to 25s; but always fluctuating with the state of the iron market. At present and for some time back, the demand for labour has been slack, and the wages at their lowest point. The consequence has been very general distress amongst the working population.

The iron labourer, it is the concurrent testimony of all who are best acquainted with the Staffordshire district, is improvident to a degree far beyond the average of working men. As a general thing he and his family live well in the beginning of the week, while the money lasts, although by Saturday a portion of the furniture or the wardrobe may be on the pawn-broker's shelves. There are hundreds of families who habitually pawn their Sunday clothes every Monday morning, and take them out every Saturday evening, paying, of course, a month's interest on the loan. A strike of a couple of weeks, or the suspension of work for that period at a forge or mill, always suffices to crowd the pawnbrokers' shops in the vicinity. The men at the forge mills earn higher wages than those at the blast furnaces. In both cases the work is kept up night and day, the shifts changing places every week.The forgemen are exposed to more continuous heat than the blastmen, and their work is on the whole heavier, although by no means unremitting. I abstain here from any description of labour, as such will appear in its proper place, when iron-forging comes to be more particularly the subject of discussion. I shall merely add that the wages of the forgemen range from 25s to 30s per week; those of their boys or "Underhands", from 7s 6d to 10s per week; and those of the millmen from 16s to 25s per week. A few of the hands, however, will make even still higher wages than those specified. Women of a class similar to those who labour at the pit banks, are employed about the blasting furnaces and the coke ovens. The wages earned by these persons seldom exceeds 1s, and is more frequently only 8d a day.

The Truck System in South Staffordshire

I have now to direct attention to the great and flagrant social and industrial evil of the truck system. In many portions of the iron and coal district of South Staffordshire the law upon this subject is so habitually and grossly violated as to be all but a dead letter. Employers of all classes, and of all the staple trades are, in this respect, equal sinners. I found that the very worst "Tommy-shops" in this district are kept not by the ignorant butties, but by great ironmasters—vast capitalists who employ men by the hundred—and regularly mulct them out of five, six, ten, or even more per cent of their wages by paying these wages in goods—the latter sometimes, but not always, of inferior quality, and in the case of many articles charged at least five per cent above the market price of the country. I have not, indeed, been more startled by any phenomenon in the course of my researches than the constant and daring violation of the Truck Act in Staffordshire, and the utter helplessness of the people under the oppression of the Tommy masters. I am told that not a few magistrates are themselves notorious truck store-keepers. Of course their names are not openly displayed over the Tommy-shop door, but the fact is just as well known as if they served behind the counter.

The truck system in Staffordshire is part and parcel of what is called the "long reckoning" system. The ironmasters and coal contractors who practice it have nominal settlements with their hands, sometimes once in three weeks, sometimes once a month, and occcasionally not oftener than once in six weeks. This involves the dodge by which the law is evaded. They say, "We are obliged to pay in money, but we shall only pay when it suits us. In the meantime you (the men) may have what goods you want to go on with. These are not given in payment of wages, but merely as private arrangements to enable you to keep afloat until pay-day comes round; and when that epoch arrives we shall of course settle in money." This is the general principle on which the act is evaded. The details of the contrivances differ widely. Sometimes wages are paid on account by cheques upon distant banks, there being always a clear understanding on either side that the cheque is never to be presented where it is payable. If, indeed, it be cashed at all, the recipient has an immediate notice to quit his employment; and instances, I am told, are not wanting of the distant banks, when actually applied to, refusing or delaying, upon the ground of some alleged technical informality, to honour the draft. The cheque system is generally adopted by the truck ironmasters—the order being of course intended for presentation at the Tommy-shop, and sometimes there is an understanding that a certain portion of the amount, from ten to twenty per cent, will be paid in money. The butties, however, and some of the ironmasters, give direct orders on the Tommy-shop, the former being a line of intimation that the shopkeeper may trust the bearer to the amount of so-and-so, being the sum standing to the credit of the latter in the pay-books of the concern. This kind of order is always paid entirely in goods. At the large iron-works the Tommy-shop is usually on the premises, but the concern is entirely local. A number of butties, on the contrary, will have a Tommy-shop between them.

Sometimes the shopkeeper is merely the agent of the employer. In other cases the business is effected in the following manner. The employer agrees with a general shopkeeper to make all his men deal at the establishment of the latter. Then orders are issued for 10s and 5s worth of goods each—the cheque, of course, clearing the master of these amounts of wages, and the shopkeeper giving what quantity and quality of goods he pleases for it—in other words charging his own prices. When the cheques amount to a certain sum—say £100, the shopkeeper makes out his bill, deducting from it 5, 7 or 10 per cent, according to agreement—the deduction, whater it is, being of course so much clear gain to the master, and so much absolute loss to the men. It is right, however, to state, that in making bargains of this kind, some of the ironmasters stipulate that the goods supplied should be of fair quality, and shall be retailed at prices not higher than a fixed price. In the majority of instances, however, the price charged is just sufficiently low to keep the workpeople from breaking out into actual defiance of the system. I ought to mention that it commonly happens that different Tommy-shops sell particular articles cheaper than others. Thus one establishment will have a comparatively good character for butcher's meat—another for groceries; but as a rule, the prices range higher than those charged by fair tradesmen—in proportions which may be estimated by the particulars given below.

The ordinary prices of the ordinary articles of consumption in Wolverhampton are as follows: mutton 6½d; beef 6d; pork 5d; back of different qualities 7d, 6½d, 6d, and 5d, flour 1s 9d, 1s 8d and 1s 7d per peck; cheese 5d and 4d per lb; salt butter 10d, 9d, 8d; fresh butter 1s 3d; herrings 1d each; potatoes 10d or 11d per peck; oatmeal 2d per pound; tea 4s per lb; the best coffee 1s 10d; inferior kinds, 1s 6d and 1s 8d; sugar 4½d; candles 5½d per lb. These last are made as small as 20 to the pound. Best brown soap 6d, and inferior soap 5d per lb. Now, the general assurance I received from the working people who have "tommeyed" was that the truckmasters charged from 2d to 3d out of every shilling higher than the fair traders—on some articles a fraction more, on some a fraction less. A strike having reference to the truck system lately took place at Darlaston, a small town in the district, the staple trade of which is gun-lock filing. Two statements were published by the turn-out purporting to be a fair comparison of truck and ordinary prices. From the first of these I transcribe the following table:

	GROCER'S PRICE			TRUCKMASTER'S PRICE	
		s	d		s d
Cheese per lb		0	6	Cheese per lb	0 3
Fresh butter per 22 oz		1	0	Fresh butter per 22 oz	1 4
Bacon per lb		0	5	Bacon per lb	0 9
Ham per lb		0	7	Ham per lb	0 11
Sugar per lb		0	5	Sugar per lb	0 7
Salt butter per lb		0	9	Salt butter per lb	1 0
Flour per strike		7	0	Flour per strike	8 4
Total grocer's price		10	8	Total truck prices	13 7

Taking this statement as correct, the profit realised by the truckmaster over and above that of the fair dealer would be more than 27 per cent. A second statement corroborative of the first, soon made its appearance, and supplied a numerous list of articles upon which the alleged profit of the Tommy-shop keeper was still higher. As thus:

	GROCER'S PRICE		TRUCKMASTER'S PRICE	
	s	d		s d
Tea per oz	0	3	Tea per oz	0 5
Coffee per 2 oz	0	3	Coffee per 2 oz	0 5
Rice per lb	0	2	Rice per lb	0 4
Soap per lb	0	5	Soap per lb	0 7
Candles per lb	0	5	Candles per lb	0 7
Raisins per lb	0	5	Raisins per lb	0 7
Currants per lb	0	5	Currants per lb	0 7
Red herrings per doz	1	0	Red herrings per doz	1 10
Total grocer's price	3	4	Total truck price	5 4

The statement goes on to contrast the prices of the truck materials used by the gun-lock filers when purchased at the fair and at the Tommy-shops:

	WHOLESALE HARDWARE (IRONMONGER)				WHOLESALE HARDWARE (TRUCK)			
	£	s	d			£	s	d
Iron per bundle	0	3	3	Iron per bundle		0	4	6
Steel	0	17	0	Steel		1	1	0
Files 11 in. 3-square, per dozen	0	9	0	Files 11in. 3-square, per dozen		0	12	0
Files 8in. 3-square, ½ round, round edge, per dozen	0	3	6	Files 8in. 3-square, ½ round, round edge per dozen		0	4	6
Files 6 in. 3-square, ½ round, round edge per dozen	0	2	4	Files 6 in, 3 square ½ round, round edge per dozen		0	3	6
Total fair price	1	15	1	Total truck price		2	5	6

The next comparative statement refers to the drapery goods. It is as follows:

	DRAPER'S PRICE		TRUCK PRICE	
	s	d		s d
Good worsted shawls	4	6	Good worsted shawls	9 0
Gown pieces	3	6	Gown pieces	6 0
Half-handkerchief	0	5	Half-handkerchief	0 9
Stockings, per pair	0	7	Stockings, per pair	1 0
Total fair price	9	0	Total truck price	16 9

I submitted these figures to several respectable tradesmen—themselves sufferers by the truck system—and they assured me that both sets of figures were in several instances exaggerated— the fair selling prices much too low, and the truck prices much too high. Fifteen per cent was, however, the amount which two of the authorities in question agreed in rating the truck above the ordinary prices. But, perhaps, the literal truth, both as regards prices and other features of the system, will be best come at by giving verbatim the information which I collected from door to door. My informants were uniformly women, the men being, in all cases, at their work.

The first woman I questioned was the wife of a coal bandsman, living in a very dilapidated house on the confines of the parishes of Wolverhampton and Bilston. She spoke nearly as follows: "My husband is tommeyed. We're nearly all tommeyed hereabouts. I go to the Tommy-shop every week with an order. I get half money and half goods. They put down the whole of the money on the counter; but I only take up half of it: or if I do take up the whole, it is only to give it back again. Of course I know that if I do not spend 5s out of every ten shillings my husband will never have another day's work in the pit. But, after all, our tommy-shop is much better than many others. At -'s (naming an establishment kept by an ironmaster), the poor people never get one shilling in money—it must be all taken out in goods. I pay 11d a pound for butter, such as I could get in Wolverhampton for 8d and 1s 9d for a peck of such flour as I could get there for 1s 7d. At -'s they won't give you not even one penny to buy barm to bake your bread, if you were to pray for it. Very few of the tommy-shops keep barm. My husband is always paid, when reckoning comes, in a beer shop. I have heard say that that is unlawful. The buttie keeps the beer shop. My husband must spend at least 6d in ale for 'his shot'. The buttie wouldn't like him if he didn't. The reckoning comes once a month. Very often there is not 2s for us in money. The rest has all been taken out, half in goods and half in cash, from week to week."

Another woman, a neighbour of the first witness, dealt at a similarly conducted Tommy-shop. "We spend there 10s out of every pound my husband earns. I pay 1s 9d for flour, and 6d for the sugar which I could get for 4½d in Wolverhampton. Every week we have a draw, that is, the men's names are sent in on a list to the Tommy-shop, with a sum of money to each, and we have goods for half of it. The women always go for the draw. I think that the goods I get are of fair quality, and some things are not dearer than they are at the small shops around. Still I would like that we had our money paid to us direct. I could lay it out far better. I would go in once a week to Wolverhampton, and get the things I wanted. Formerly we dealt at -'s (naming the place already referred to). That was when my husband was in the employ of—. Then we had nothing at all but goods from one reckoning to another. My husband was making good wages, but I solemnly declare that for six weeks together I have never had a single penny of ready money. The money we got at the reckonings all went to pay the rent and to get clothing. I have had to borrow a penny to buy barm to bake with." (It will be observed that two women, examined separately, made use of the self same illustration of the tactics of the same tommy-shop.)

An engineman whom I talked to at the pit-heap said that at the Tommy-shop kept by the buttie who worked the mine, flour was 4d a peck and butter 2d a lb dearer than at Bilston. He had often heard of men being discharged because they would not deal at the shop. If a man wanted to go to the pit he must go to the shop, that was the rule; and he reckoned that it was pretty much the same thing with most of the colliers.

A butcher at Swan-hill, West Bromwich said, "I believe that round this place, within two miles, there are from 2,000 to 3,000 men tommeyed. It is ruination to honest tradespeople. If the masters want to keep shops, why don't they do it fairly, and try to sell better and cheaper than we do. But there's no chance for us; because whatever price the truckmen ask the workmen must pay. I am now sellings ribs of beef for 4½d, and roasting pieces for 3d. The Tommy-shops are charging 6½d and 7d for the same meat. I sell mutton at from 5d to 5½d, the Tommy-shops will sell it at 6½d a lb. The masters hereabouts say that the reckonings come once a fortnight, and so they do, nominally; but then they are continually being put off, for one reason or another."

At Wednesbury, a master miller informed me that flour was retailed by the truckmasters at 1d, 1¼d, and 1½d per peck dearer than the ordinary market price. On the western outskirts of the same place, a married woman stated that she dealt at a Tommy-shop which she thought was better than most of them. The reckoning was sometimes once a fortnight, and sometimes once in three weeks. She took orders to the shop, and for every pound she got 4s in ready cash, the rest in goods. Sugar, she thought, was about ½d in the 1lb dearer than at the shops. Cheese was a 1d and 1½d dearer. She need not go to the Tommy-shop; but then if she didn't her "husband would not be thought so well of". Another woman stated that their reckoning only came about once in five weeks; of course, they had to deal at the Tommy-shop. They paid 7s 4d a strike for flour, and 9d a lb for bacon. She did not think that meat was much dearer than at the shops about. But she could lay out the money much better if she had it all to spend when she liked. "If a man works for money he ought to get money."

The following is the testimony of a gentleman connected with a large ironworks, and who has taken much interest in the condition of the labourers throughout the districts: "The truck system produces the worst of feelings between the masters and workmen—and no wonder. The ironmasters usually pay in cheques upon distant banks, but if any of the banks dare to cash them their services would very soon be dispensed with. Instead of the banks, they carry their cheques to the Tommy-shops, the masters pretending that the workmen must find the shop handy. I feel quite sure that many of the colliers do not get above 2s a week in money, and that almost all goes to pay the rent. The reckoning is often delayed for five weeks. In fact, the time of payment is at the caprice of the masters. The people are thus often put to great shifts for money. I have known a woman go to the Tommy-shop—get a pound of sugar at 6d a lb—and sell it to a neighbour who was not tommeyed for 4d, just in order to raise the ready cash."

All the clergymen with whom I have conversed bear testimony to the moral and social, as well as physical evils caused by this system. The working people are cheated and the fair traders are cheated by the truckmaster just as much as they would be by smugglers. That the compulsory paying for labour in goods is fostered and made practicable by the "long-reckoning" plan which, in a great measure, enables the truckmasters to evade the law. "There is," says the Rev. Mr Owen, "a text in Deuteronomy, which I have more than once publicly referred to"; and certainly the verse in question—the fifteenth of the twenty-fourth chapter—does strikingly apply to South Staffordshire. The employer is thus commanded to treat his labourer: "At his day thou shalt give him his hire; neither shall the sun go down upon it; for he is poor and setteth his heart upon it; lest he cry against thee unto the Lord and it is a sin to thee." The rev. gentleman is of the opinion that no legislative enactment will put down the truck system, until the long reckonings be abridged by the interference of Parliament. The best class of masters, "the honourable masters"—as those who do not tommy their men are emphatically called—settle regularly once a fortnight. The butties, as I have said, often pay in beer-shops, in the face of the law, which enacts that all payments so made are null and void. Prosecutions are sometimes set on foot against the truckmasters, but the difficulty of adducing legal evidence is so great that the stray convictions now and then obtained have little or no real effect in putting down the system. In Darlaston, I believe that the people are really bestirring themselves, and making head against it; but in Wednesbury, I was told that two new Tommy-shops had been very recently opened. The local press is overawed by the ironmasters. The people fret and chafe under the exaction, but are compelled to submit to it; and thus, by notorious, flagrant, and habitual violation of the law, workpeople, tradespeople, and "honourable masters" are alike made subservient, and alike suffer through the cupidity of men who ignore every consideration save that of profit.

The Potteries

Introduction

The case of the Potteries is one of those curious instances so often to be met with in examining the field of British industry, of a certain branch of manufacture setting itself arbitrarily down in a certain locality, without any particular or obvious reason for the selection. It is no doubt impossible to produce crockery-ware without an abundant supply of coals. That supply is to be found spread over wide fields in the west, the centre, and the north of England. Yet the trade of the potter is practised, as a staple branch of industry, only in that insignificant stripe of North Staffordshire through which run the infant waters of the River Trent—there a mere brook, fresh from its sources in the moorlands. Pottery establishments may be scattered here and there over the kingdom; there are several upon the Tyne, and the Wear, about Newcastle and Sunderland, but in the trifling strip of Staffordshire called par excellence, "The Potteries", are manufactured nineteen-twentieths of the crockery, coarse and fine, porcelain and earthenware, used in England.

The Pottery district is about ten miles long, and two or three broad, running north and south in the valley of the Trent, and consisting mainly of a chain of large villages, or small towns, or perhaps to speak more correctly, neither villages nor towns in the ordinary acceptation of the terms, but straggling districts more or less built over—the streets here clustering thickly together—there spreading out in long arms, which just extend far enough to connect the main groups of buildings; the intervening patches of country sometimes consisting of pleasant fields and undulating pastures, sometimes chequered with isolated manufactories and detached rows of smoky houses, surrounded by plots of waste ground, heaped with cinders, scoriae, and fragments of broken pots, which have not stood the fire—the whole being diversified here and there by those black mounds and grimy buildings which denote that a coal shaft is sunk beneath them. The North Staffordshire Railway binds together the range of the Pottery towns like a thread stringing beads. The general sweep of the country is bold and undulating; and from the heights on which the village of Hanley stands, some really fine panoramic glimpses can be caught of green undulating hills, with far-spreading breasts, mapped out by tree and hedgerow into arable field and pasture meadow, dotted with the smoky appurtenances of coal pits, the tower-like forms of windmills, and here and there by dusky clusters of houses, grouped round a pottery with its tall engine chimney and its bee-hive-like furnaces.

As for the Pottery towns, there is hardly more distinctive individuality between them than between the plates and saucers of the well-known willow pattern, which they produce in such abundance. In Hanley alone there is a market-place, distinguished by some new and handsome ranges of buildings. But you may wander from township to township and parish to parish, and still imagine from the aspect of things around, that you have not moved an hundred yards from your starting point. Everywhere there stretch out labyrinths of small, undistinguished, unpaved streets, the houses generally of two stories in height, and built of smoke-grimed brick. Here you will find a new row of cottages, the uniformity of the walls slightly broken by stone facings; hard by may be a cluster of old-fashioned houses, with lead-latticed windows, and perhaps some attempt to cause ivy to train up the wall. Every few steps bring you in sight of a plain brown brick chapel—a Sion, or Ebenezer, or Bethesda—and numerous as are the Methodist places of worship, I regret to say that the public houses are more numerous still. I thought that Bilston and Willenhall, in the southern part of the county, were unsurpassable in this respect; but I have repeatedly seen localities in the Potteries where every fourth or fifth house was a tavern.

Diverge from the main thoroughfares—into regions of backyards and little gardens, and outhouses, and waste patches belonging to potter establishments—and you find yourself in a curious chaos of old tumbledown sheds, littered with crates, broken crockery-ware, and straw—of walls and lean-tos, built of old "saggars"—in other words, of great, coarse yellow dishes of the commonest ware, used for containing the pots while being burnt—diversified here and there by brick pits, clay-pits, smoking engine-houses, and great coal heaps, dismal wastes of muddy ground, more or less strewn with the eternal pavement of broken stone-ware, the whole landscape enlivened by glimpses of barges deeply laden with piled-up clay or flints, lying by wharfs, or slowly moving along the narrow canals; for the potteries are most abundantly supplied with the means of inland navigation.

Indeed, had it not been for the genius of Brindley, the white clay of Devon and Cornwall, and the chalk of Kent and Sussex, would never have been worked up into ware in Staffordshire. The great scheme of the Bridgewater canals may be said to have developed itself in the district of the Potteries. It was near Burslem, I think, that the first sod was turned, in breaking ground to join the waters of the Mersey and the Trent; and the first or one of the first, of the great canal tunnels was cut in the neighbourhood beneath the Air Castle-hill—a somewhat ominous name, which, while the project as yet existed but upon paper, was of great service to the small jokers of the district. Nevertheless the hill is now pierced by two tunnels—the old canal and the more recent railway one. These excavations run different courses, and at different levels through the earth, crossing each other in the centre of the hill.

In sketching the outward and obvious peculiarities of the Potteries district, I must not forget the significant number of Old Testament names to be seen on every sign-board. Moseses, Jacobs, Seths, Joshuas, Daniels, and Enochs, meet you at every turn. The same peculiarity of nomenclature will be recognised by anyone acquainted with the well-known names of many of the principal pottery firms. Wesley himself planted his church in the district; and at Shelton near Hanley, is one of the very largest Methodist chapels in the kingdom.

As a whole, the appearance of considerable portions of the Pottery towns is not very unlike that of the iron and coal districts which are in the south of the county. The population, however, from the nature of the occupation look clean and respectable. At meal times, or in the evening, they pour out from the manufactories—men, women and children—with aprons and sleeves plentifully besprinkled with dashes as of liquid white clay. Here and there, however, you see a symptom of the neighbouring coal mines, in the appearance of men and boys, in coarse besmirched flannel clothing and wooden clogs, with faces and hands like sweeps.

The Pottery towns are Longton, or Lane-end, Stoke-upon-Trent, Hanley, Shelton, Fenton, Burslem, and Tunstall. The conjoined Stoke and Wollstanton district, which comprehends the greater portion of the Potteries, with a district not strictly belonging to them, is treated as a whole in the Registrar-General's returns, so that there is no obvious way of ascertaining the separate rates of mortality, and the separate educational condition of each individual township. By the general return it would appear that the number of persons living in and about the Potteries to one death is about 38. The population of the double district in question in 1841 was 61,617. The number of illegitimate births in 1846 was 358. In the same year, out of 933 marriages, 481 men and 632 women—heavy proportions—signed with their marks.

There is little difference between the species of ware manufactured by the different pottery towns. In all of them, all the branches of the art are more or less carried on. Longton, locally called Lane-end, was, until lately, to some degree an exception to this rule; the coarser sorts of earthen and stone-wear, manufactured in a great degree for the use of hawkers, and sold to them for ready money, having long been almost exclusively produced there; but of late years the finer branches of the trade have been carried on there, as well as the coarser departments. The tone of the population of Lane-end is somewhat behind that of the other pottery towns. The wages of the people are not materially lower, but the strongest local *patois*, the coarsest and toughest manners, and the lowest and most brutalizing amusements, such as dog and cock fighting, still linger in Lane-end to a greater degree, and with a firmer hold, than in the other districts. The locality is also more tinged with colliery population than any other in the Potteries, a circumstance amply sufficient, considering what Staffordshire coal mining and Staffordshire coal mines are, to account for the phenomenon in question.

The Industrial Process and Wages

I shall now proceed to give an account in some detail of the various stages of the most interesting and beautiful manufacture carried on within them. The labour is essentially cleanly, and, in by far the greater portion of its processes, a healthy one. There is a quiet comfortable look about the majority of the rooms in which the work is carried on. The air smells fresh and pure, and even the furnaces are so constructed and managed, as to give out far less heat than the workmen in such kindred establishments as glasshouses are exposed to.

I now proceed to the first process, which consists of grinding and mixing the clayey and flinty ingredients which are to be worked up into stone ware. The clay is of several qualities, suited for coarse or fine pottery—for China or for common ware. The inferior clay is found in Somersetshire and Devonshire, and is known generally as blue clay. The finer or China clay comes principally from Cornwall. In its dry state when piled up for grinding and mixing, it exactly resembles whiting. The price of this article of raw material carries with it its exact quality, but it is now much cheaper than formerly. A ton of average purity may cost in the Potteries about £4 4s. Double the money used to be a common price. The task of mixing the different clays so as to produce ware of the exact degree of fineness requisite, is the first skilled labour performed. A personage, called from his grinding duties a miller, is entrusted with the work. The clays are flung under his directions in proper quantities into great round tubs containing more or less water.

In each of these tubs, a wheel—somewhat like a paddle working horizontally with floats, which in their revolutions graze the sides of the vessel, and are turned by steam—continually works, driving the clay and water round and round, and gradually reducing the mixture, to an exquisitely fine pulp. More clay of proper degrees of coarseness is added generally once in about two hours. The miller is paid 1s 8d per ton, and he can generally prepare about 7 tons a day. Out of these wages he pays the labourer requiste to assist him. With the clay, it is necessary that calcined flint and Cornwall stone—the latter a soft greyish friable mineral—should be mixed. The flint—a great deal of which comes from the Kentish coast, near the mouth of the Thames—is first calcined by means of slack coals. It is then pounded and finally ground. This last process is similar to the pulping operation undergone by the clay, and the same miller superintends both. The pounded fragments of flint are flung into capacious circular tubs, round which, as in the former case, revolve great horizontal paddle-wheels—what we may call the floats; consisting, however, in this instance, of ponderous square lumps of stone. The process of flint-grinding takes about twenty-four hours, at the expiration of which the stone is reduced to powder as fine as snuff. The bottoms of the flint tubs are paved with stone. The miller makes the necessary changes in the quantity of water or mineral twice a day. The ordinary time which the steam-engine is kept going, is from seven o'clock in the morning until six o'clock at night. Sometimes a day and a fourth, and sometimes a day and a third are worked; the hours being prolonged respectively until eight p.m. or nine p.m. The meal times are half an hour for breakfast and half an hour for dinner. The appearance of the tubs is very much as though the arms of the revolving wheel were splashing through great cauldrons of blancmange and cream. Of course the steam-engine does the actual work, the tubs being left unattended for an hour together.

The flint and clay, having each been reduced to a fine pulp, have now to be run through like sieves, so as to intercept the slightest impurities, the creamy mixtures, after straining through the silk filters, mingling in a common tank. The process is superintended by a man with a boy to help him. The wages of the former are about 2s 2d per day; hours from seven o'clock a.m. until eight o'clock p.m. The lad has about 4s a week and each receives extra pay for the extra time which they are sometimes called upon to work.

The raw mineral dough has now to undergo its first slack-baking process. The old method—still occasionally practised in the manufacture of coarse ware—was to run it into tanks called air-kilns, where, after being well-stirred up and agitated, it was left to silth into the requisite consistency. This process is generally accomplished in about two days. During the operation, reeking clouds of steam constantly ascend from the simmering tanks, keeping the attendants in some potteries in a constant vapour bath. In the better ordered establishments, however, the roofs are raised so high, and are so well provided with the means of ventilation, that the great body of steam floats above the level of the attendants. There are generally two men to each slip kiln, each relieving the other, in charge of the furnaces and the hot fluid. They are paid severally 1s 8d per ton for the clay paste which they produce, the quantity being generally about seven tons per week.

The next process is the squeezing of the paste or dough, in machines something like gigantic coffee mills, so as to compress out of it any lurking bubbles of air, and finally to crush the mixture into one soft lumpless gritless mass. Each set of presses are fed and attended to by a man and a boy, who fling huge lumps of clay into the cone-shaped hollow cylinders. Powerful screws, fashioned somewhat on the Archimedian principle, revolve inside, and with a slow and steady certainty crush down the yielding clay, each branch of the screw receiving the substance from that above, and forcibly squeezing it further and further down towards the narrowest part of the cone, from which it emerges in a continuous square-shaped flow, of the exact consistence and appearance of putty. The workman, provided with a small brass wire which passes through the solid clay almost as through water, cuts it into oblong blocks, each weighing about one hundredweight, and carries every block into an adjoining warehouse, from whence it is fetched to the workmen whose duty it is to mould the plastic material into shape. The presser makes from 20s to 22s per week.

We now come to the first of the plastic processes—that of making round cups or pots, and a beautiful one it is. Each "thrower" as the operator is called, is attended by a woman. He sits upon a stool placed on a table, with his legs stretched out; and between them, fixed upon the top of a perpendicular spindle, there whirls rapidly round in vertical fashion, a circular platter of wood called a "throw block". This whirling platter is, of course, put in motion either by the hand, or by the steam-engine. The principle of the apparatus is exquisitely simple, and as old as pots themselves.

The attendant female having broken off from the lump a little round ball of clay dough, hands it to the thrower who places it upon the centre of the revolving platter, urging with gentle and skilful pressure his thumb into the mass, which, impelled by the centrifugal force and moulded at the same time by the guiding fingers of the operative, straitway assumes the form of a circular vessel within his grasp. If the phrase of an article rising up under the maker's hand can ever be literally applied, it is in this beautiful process of throwing pottery ware. Beneath the skilful fingers of the workman vessels of any shape, so long as the general form be circular, appear as if by magic from the little round dab of clay. The interior of the cup or pot is moulded by a thin piece of metal, the outline of which shapes the vessel into its required form, while the exact diameter necessary between the opposite rims is obtained by allowing the pot to whirl round until its extreme edge all but touches a guiding wand placed for the purpose. The operator keeps his hands constantly wet, so as to mould the clay with the least possible friction. He is skilful in giving the rims or edges of the basin either an overlapping or bell-shaped form, as may be required; and by a rapid easy motion of the fingers produces the requisite indentations for the reception of spouts and handles. A good thrower in constant work earns considerable wages—the average may be between 30s and 40s per week. The woman who hands him the clay is called a "baller". She is paid about 8s per week. In this, as in all the other skilled branches of the pottery trade, beginners serve an apprenticeship of seven years. The first year they are paid about 2s per week, the second from 2s 6d to 3s and then they are set to piece work—a consummation which both they and their employers are generally anxious should arrive. Thenceforth until the expiration of their apprenticeship, they are paid half of the regular journeyman's prices. All the pottery which they spoil ere the attainment of requisite skill, they are obliged to work up again without any payment.

The thrower having detached the basin or cup from the wooden platter by means of a very thin iron hoop, it is carried away to the drying oven, there to acquire a certain degree of toughness, amounting to hardness, before the turner operates upon it. The ware comes into the hands of the latter functionary in what potters call a "green" state. The lathe of the

7. Putting manufactured articles into saggars

8. Placing the saggars in the biscuit-kiln

9. Printing blue-ware

10. Transferring the print

11. View in a lace-dressing room

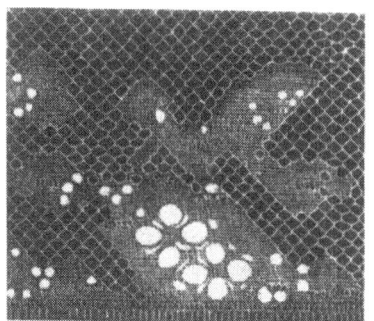

12. Specimen of machine lace

13. Specimen of run lace

15. Throwing or spinning by hand

14. Lace-runners or embroiderers at work

turner works much in the same way as the throwing block as described in the last operation. The cup or basin is placed again upon a vertically revolving surface, fastened thereto by a few drops of adhesive liquid, and then the turner applies his chisels just as his brethren do when operating upon wood. The requisite outside mouldings and scoopings are thus quickly and easily given to the vessel. Pottery turners work in large rooms down which there run rows of lathes. Girls and boys are occupied in carrying the vessels from workman to workman. Turners are paid by the piece. A good hand can make his 5s per day.

It will be obvious as yet that the pots are destitute of handles, or, supposing them to be required, of spouts. The making and fixing one of these appurtenances constitute a separate branch of the trade. Both handles and spouts are formed in moulds. Each of the handles is made in one mould. The operator first rolls out and kneads the clay, gives it the required shape, and fixes it neatly to the cup with no other tools than his wet fingers, a crop of adhesive liquid, and a moist sponge. Spouts are cast in two pieces, joined and stuck on in exactly the same way. The apprentices in this branch are frequently employed in the fabrication of handles for little toy jugs. Journeymen will not find it difficult to earn a pound a week. The rooms, I may add, in which these processes are carried on, are uniformly warm, airy and cheerful and the work is light and clean.

Leaving the basins, cups, and tea-pot ready for the first burning, we will now turn for a moment to the plate and dish-makers. The plate is formed upon a mould, which whirls round as in the throwing process. The dish being oblong, and frequently constructed with peculiarly rounded corners, requires a greater degree of skill to fashion it. The clay in the first place has to be batted and mashed so as to render it as plastic as possible when it reaches the hands of the workmen. Two men and a boy frequently work at dish-making together. The boy kneads and mashes the clay, the first workman rolls it out exactly as a housewife would a cover of a pie, and hands it to his comrade, who proceeds to give the smooth layer of clay paste its requisite form. To accomplish this, he places the plastic substance upon a mould made of plaster of Paris, which forms the inside of the dish, and then, giving the mould, which revolves upon a pivot, a series of twirls round, and working the clay at the same time by corresponding jerks of the wrist, he brings the ductile material into a smooth layer exactly corresponding in every respect to the mould beneath. Both are then removed to the drying oven, half an hour's exposure in which causes the clay to separate readily from the plaster. A good hand at dish-making will earn from 30s to 35s per week.

The apprentices are usually set, at the commencement of their labours, to the easier task of plate-making. After the expiration of about three years, as in other branches of the trade, they are employed by the piece, receiving half the amount of the journeyman's wages.

No jugs and vessels, not round, can of course come under the hands of either thrower or turner. They are therefore cast in moulds in different pieces, and put together with adhesive liquid so delicately that the mark of the junction can hardly be perceived. A great number of ornamental jugs and vases are thus constructed, the handles, when wanted, being attached to them in the manner already described. The moulders earn from 25s to 30s per week.

The next process is the hardening one—of the first or biscuit firing. I have described the outward appearance of the pottery furnaces as that of huge brick beehives. Their internal construction is peculiar. The hive-shaped structure is merely a sort of case built round the red furnace, leaving some four or five feet between them. This case is called an "ovel". It serves to protect the furnace from irregular draughts, which would cause varying degrees of heat, and so spoil the "baking". The ware to be burnt is put into round earthenware tubs, somewhat in the shape of foot-pans, called "saggars"—a word said to be a corruption of "safeguards". These saggars are piled up one above the other in great pillars, reaching to the mouth of the furnace, and smeared with clay at the joints, so as to keep the smoke and soot from the wares inside. The fuel is then kindled beneath them, and the "baking" commences. The furnace is attended to by a principal fireman, who is responsible for the proper burning of the ware, and who employs his own assistants. When in good work, the former can get upwards of £2 per week. Two men can attend to a furnace in operation, but five or six are employed to set and draw it. The ware continues exposed to a white heat for about 48 or 50 hours. The first night one man only is required to feed the furnace—the fireman and his assistant are both on duty during the second. While the baking is going on, the men generally sleep at the works, and in their clothes, lying down in the most comfortable corners they can find. From time to time the fireman draws a pot to see how the oven is getting on. Of course the entire pile of crockery is at a bright white heat. The fireman's assistant or stoker earns 12s or 14s per week.

As soon as the ware is burnt sufficiently hard, the fires are allowed to die out, and the furnace is drawn. The crockery is then in the state of biscuit-ware—perfectly white and hard, but still rough and unglazed. It is then transferred to the hands of the "dipper", a workman who performs by far the most unhealthy duty of any connected with pottery labours. To give crockery its glaze it is dipped in a solution, the ingredients of which are various, but the basis of which is white lead. The dipper stands over a tubful of this deleterious wash. He is attended by two boys, the business of one of whom is to take up each article singly as it comes cooled from the furnace and toss it into the tub. Here the dipper catches it, gives it a plunge into the mixture, and flings it to the second boy, whose duty it is to stack up the dipped utensils in readiness for the glossing over, which fixes and dries the wash. Sometimes the dipper works with his mouth covered, so as to prevent him inhaling the vapour arising from the constantly agitated mixture. In some potteries, too, the proprietors furnish a species of smock-frock, which envelopes the whole person, and prevents the clothes from being splashed by the deleterious mixture. The diseases, if they take a constitutional form, arising from this work, are similar to those common with house painters, but the dippers in general are locally affected. The hands which are almost constantly immersed in the wash, suffer; the fingers being often distorted and paralysed, and the forearm becoming more or less affected. This state of things is sometimes produced in two or three years. Sometimes a man will work at the dip-tub all his life with apparent impunity. The poison affects different constitutions in different ways; but a great deal depends upon strict cleanliness, upon careful washing of the hands, and using means to remove any deposit which may gather under the nails as soon as a man's work is over. Many of the dippers, I am told, are very careless in this respect, and suffer accordingly. The fumes of the white lead, if they act constitutionally, are peculiarly apt to disorder the digestive system, and produce a long train of dyspeptic symptoms. The wages earned by the dipper run as high as £2 2s per week. The boys are paid 4s per week.

The glazing qualities imparted by the white lead have now to be fixed by the agency of fire, and the ware, for this purpose, is removed to the glossing oven. Here it remains for about twenty-four hours, subjected to a more moderate heat than that which it has already undergone. Each set of these furnaces and ovens is attended by a fireman and his assistant, who earn about the same amount of wages as those paid for superintending the previous baking.

The ware is now—supposing it to be the finer sort, china or porcelain—ready for the hands of the painters, who trace upon it those bright and beautiful blazonings, the execution of which requires a trained and steady hand and an artistic eye. The painters are both men and women. They work in large ateliers, usually oppressive with the strong smell of spirits of turpentine and spirits of tar, with which the pigments are mixed. These artist-operatives find their own brushes and pencils, the paint is provided. They work at long benches. The article to be painted is held in the left hand, and steadied against the bench and upon the edge of a flat piece of wood propelling at right angles from it. Along this the painter lays his right arm, the support rendering it perfectly steady while he uses the brush, turning at the same time with his left hand the article which he is ornamenting, so as to subject every part to the process. Sometimes the pattern is already traced in relief upon the cup or vase, in which case the task of colouring it is simple; but frequently the painter is required to form the outline as well as to supply the filling up of the design. The patterns principally painted are flowers and leaves, disposed in many flourishes round the moulded forms of the vessels. Artistic skill, in the higher sense of the term, is, of course, rarely required. The operative requires knack rather than art. To make a good china painter, however, a man must be endowed with an eye susceptible of the grace of form and the harmony of colour, and he must possess a hand skilled in the necessary manipulation and perfectly steady. The circles formed outside and round the rims of vessels, are traced with beautiful steadiness of finger and brush. The apprentices in this branch of the business are frequently employed in painting toy, tea, and dinner sets for children. Painting is at present in a somewhat slack condition in the Potteries, the public taste having, as I was informed for some time back, run upon articles distinguished by beauty of form, rather than by brilliancy of coloured adornment. As a general rule, the most skilled work of this kind is performed by men, who earn wages ranging from 20s to 50s per week. Very few, however, are employed at the latter rate—I was informed that the average might be about 30s. The women earn from 9s to 12s weekly. The emblazonment of china and porcelain, is an occupation well-suited to develop anything like artistic talent amongst those who pursue it. I have accordingly not been surprised to see sundry very fair copies of well-known paintings, produced by persons earning their living by tracing glittering adornments on cups and vases. Several of our principal steel engravers were, I believe, brought up as china and porcelain painters.

The ware, gorgeous from the hands of the colourist, has now to undergo a third baking called the "enamel firing", the effect of which is to fix the paint in the substance of the vessels. The enamel-oven remains lighted only about eight hours, at the expiration of which, if there be gold, as there generally is, traced in the design, the ware is handed over to the burnishers. When they receive it, the gold lines are dim and pale and blurred-looking. It is therefore their duty by friction with agate and blood-stone, to burnish up and bring out in all their glittering richness, the gilded blazonries. The burnishers frequently work in the same room as the painters. They are mostly young women. When the china comes from their hands, it is ready for the warehouse. The burnishers earn about as much as the female painters.

The three last processes described pertain only to the fine and most expensive species of pottery. The vast mass of ware, after coming from the biscuit furnace, undergoes quite a different set of operations, the designs wherewith it is adorned being printed or stamped instead of painted. The printing process is an ingenious and interesting one. Each set of workpeople consists of one man (the copper-plate printer), two women and a little girl. Part of the operation is similar to ordinary copper-plate or steel-plate working. The printer stands between his press and a little stove. On the former, he heats the plate engraved with the design or pattern, then spreads his colours upon it, these last being made up with a strong spirits of tar—wipes clean the level surface of the plate, and in the usual way takes off an impression upon thin tissue paper, previously dipped in a strong adhesive solution. The design is then handed to the little girl, who dexterously cuts away the superfluous paper—not trenching, however, upon the blanks in the interstices of the pattern—and then hands the latter to one of the women, who immediately applies it to the cup or vessel to be ornamented. The adhesive mixture causes the paper to stick, and it is briskly rubbed and smoothed with a hard roll of flannel, to one end of which the operator presses her shoulder. After being allowed to remain for a few minutes, the cup is flung into a vessel of hot water. The paper instantly peels off, leaving the impression with which it was engraved stamped clearly upon the ware. The work of "transferring" as it is called, is the hardest which devolves upon women in the range of pottery manufacture. The set of operatives whom I have described, generally work in a sort of partnership. The articles printed are usually paid for at the rate of 6d a dozen. Of this the copper-plate printers have 5¼d, and the transferring girls ¾d. One printer with his coadjutors will produce from 80 to 100 dozens per week. The little girl who cuts earns about 2s per week. After the biscuit-ware has been printed, it is transferred to the dipper, and from him to the glossing oven, from whence it emerges hard and glass-like, the colours shining through a coat of transparent glaze.

Besides the operations which I have described, there is another which gives employment in most potteries to a number of women and children. This is the manufacture of variously shaped circlets, triangles etc., formed of the commoner clay, and afterwards baked, for the purpose of placing between the different articles when they are piled up for firing in the saggars, so as to prevent them from injuring each other. The operators are women and boys. They roll the clay cakes out thin, cut them into long strips, sever these across and mould them into all manner of skeleton shapes called "stilts", "triangles", "cockspurs" and so forth, so as to suit the requirements of any species of crockery. The boys are usually paid one halfpenny a gross for these little pieces of clay framework, in other words, they make a twelve dozen for a single halfpenny, and can generally earn about sixpence a day.

The ornamented vases and pieces of porcelain and china, enriched with figures and flowers and star-work in relief, are, if not cast altogether in a mould, supplied with their adornments by manual labour—the projecting ornaments being cast in separate moulds, and fixed on bit by bit by means of strong adhesive composition. The operatives are men who make from £1 to 30s per week. A vast number of small ornamental articles are got up in this way.

The production of small pieces of statuary is another semi-artistic kind of labour, practised to a great extent in the Potteries. The method adopted is exclusively that of moulds, and the operatives earn from £1 to 36s per week. The work bears about the same relation to sculpture, as china-colouring or pattern-drawing does to painting. But it struck me very forcibly that the influence of the humanizing and elevating art spirit, even in its faintest development, as distinguished from proficiency in mere manual labour could be very plainly traced in the looks, bearing and species of intelligence of the operatives, even although their money wages were in many cases not higher than, nor even as high as, cup-throwers and dish-makers.

The modeller who is attached to the larger pottery establishments, has claims to be considered as an artist, in the fair meaning of the word. He prepares the shapes by means of which the mould-makers construct their useful fabrics. He is competent to model clay from drawings, and works with sculptor's tools. In fact, he is a copying sculptor. One modeller to whom I was introduced was engaged in preparing a very beautiful Mercury, from a design by Flaxman. A new bust of Shakespeare from his hand was in readiness for publication. Amongst other artistic matters in the room, were the pretty statuettes of Locke and Newton, evidently modelled from the portraits in Hampton-court. These figures I have since repeatedly seen in many houses in the district. We talked of popular works of the kind. Two nude figures of children, one of them reading, the other writing, with his legs crossed were, I was told, among the most popular which were issued from the Potteries. The "Praying Samuel", another very well-known cast, was and is in immense vogue; tens of thousands of these were sold, as was also the case with another morceau of statuary described to me as, "Good night, a companion to Samuel".

"But here—see here!" said my companion, observing my looks wandering back to Flaxman's Mercury, "see this," and he produced a well-known figure—exhibiting in full canonicles the not very graceful form, and the long peculiar countenance of John Wesley. "Here is the man that sells. Here is the statuette they buy down here. Flaxman is all very well, but, in a commercial point of view, one Wesley is worth a dozen Mercurys!"

Little china-ware ornaments are, as may be conceived, profusely scattered through the cottages in the pottery districts. A curious use to which I observed small busts of the Queen and Prince Albert put, was placing them under the legs of sofas, like caryatides, so as to raise the article of furniture from a damp brick-paved floor. A vast number of copies of the Portland vase, the clay fired so as to exhibit the exact colours of the original, are yearly manufactured in the Potteries. You meet them, although rarely, in the homes of the workpeople. The first facsimile of this famous vase, made in Staffordshire, was managed in a true spirit of monopoly. Fifty copies were cast, and then the mould was destroyed. Nowadays the vase is reproduced by thousands, carrying into as many homes a memorial and an example of that sincere and perfect art spirit, conceived and developed by the exquisite mental organization of the antique races of southern Europe. In the case of the potteries of Staffordshire, however, as in the calico-printing districts of Lancashire, the art creative faculty seems all but torpid. "The French," said the modeller already alluded to, "do all these things far better than we can. For good well-made serviceable pottery, we can compete with the world; but when we come to art manufacture, we are compelled to acknowledge our inferiority. Our statuettes, for instance, with some few exceptions are far inferior in grace, and in freedom of handling and design, to those of the French."

For the greater part of information embodied here, I am indebted to the facilities most courteously afforded me by the Messrs. Wedgwood for inspecting their extensive works at Etruria—works in which every process appertaining to the pottery manufacture is carried on.

Housing in the Potteries

The exact local population in each of the Pottery towns appears by the last census to be as follows:

Stoke-on-Trent, and the immediately surrounding villages	8,391
Hanley	10,185
Shelton	11,836
Longton	12,407
Fenton	4,923
Burslem and District	16,090
Tunstall	6,945
Total	70,777

I have said that the Longton district is that most behind in the tone of its population. The house accommodation there is also inferior to the standard of most others. Filthy and crowded courts—ill-arranged, undrained and irregular streets—and expanses of half waste-land, covered with rubbish and cinder-heaps, patched with neglected gardens, piled up with broken saggars and smashed fragments of pottery, all bear testimony to a hastily ill-built, and ill-laid-out town.

Perhaps the best specimen of a pottery village is to be found in Etruria. This characteristically named hamlet, which is indebted for its classic appellation to the founder of the great pottery firm of Wedgwood, is situated in the township of Shelton, upon the banks of the canal which connects the waters of the Trent and Mersey. The village is entirely the property of the Messrs. Wedgwood, and is almost wholly occupied by the working people in their employment. The manufactory faces the canal—indeed a branch of the latter runs through it—so that barges float beneath gateways into inner quadrangles, and deliver their cargoes at the threshold of the storehouses; and the regularly built streets of the village extend behind the pottery. The houses are of several classes, affording more or less accommodation at different rents. I visited and minutely inspected several of each grade, and never was I more pleased with the appearance of operatives' dwellings. The abundance of furniture, the hearty air of comfort which reigned in them, one and all, was pleasant to see.

The first house which I entered was one of the largest class. It contained no less than six rooms—a comfortable living chamber, a small back kitchen, and a parlour upon the ground floor; upstairs were three bedrooms. The lower apartments were paved with bricks, the upper were floored with boarding. The living room, I could see, was generally used for cooking, the kitchen being appropriated to the purposes of the scullery. There was a capital range, containing boilers, ovens, and apparatus for roasting, all as clean as hard brushes and blacklead could make them. I may mention also that in the case of a great number of these cottages the doorstep was brightly blackleaded. In almost every house in the village a handsome eight-day clock ticked in the corner, and one side of the living room was occupied by a sofa, perhaps not very elegantly shaped but ample and covered with glazed calico. In the kitchen was a good store of pots, pans, and tea and dinner ware; and behind the house was a garden about twenty yards by six or seven. The rent of the dwelling, garden included, was £7 10s. The local rates formed a separate burden.

The next house into which I proceeded was even more comfortable than that which I had just left. In the latter there was a large family of young children, turning everything topsy-turvy. In the other there was no such juvenile demonstrations, and the appearance of plain, substantial, unpretending comfort was complete. A carpet was spread over the brick floor, a roaring fire danced and flickered upon the perfectly polished range and fire-irons; there was a clock and a large and handsome chest of drawers in the room, a central table, and several smaller ones, a sofa, and a comfortable easy chair, in which the man of the house was snugly ensconced, while his wife prepared tea. Upon the several ledges and ridges of the old-fashioned chimney-piece were set a profusion of little chinaware ornaments—dogs, vases, and shepherdesses tending their flocks beneath very green crockery trees. There was also a bookcase, very fairly stocked, and newspapers and cheap serial publications lay in the broad window-sill. The occupant of this abode, one of the workmen in Messrs. Wedgwood's employment, told me that he had been born in the house; and hoped never to leave it. Indeed the place was in many respects just what an operative's house ought to be: warm, comfortable, and almost crammed with substantial furniture.

In the next house I visited there were two rooms on each floor. The rent was £6. Here also the floor was at least partially carpeted, and a horse covered with good white crisp linen was airing before the fire. Among a number of portraits and engravings hanging upon the walls was a very fair copy, executed in oil of David's picture (I think it is) of Napoleon crossing the Alps. The brass candlesticks which were arranged upon cupboard and shelf were as bright as a Dutch housewife could wish them; and at the end of the garden was a small greenhouse. These gardens were one and all provided with proper private accommodations. The fences were formed of old "saggars"; and a fair quantity of kitchen vegetables were, as I was informed, produced by each patch of land. Indeed,

I heartily wished as I was going over these nice, warm, substantial houses, peeping into their bedrooms and their generally well-stocked pantries, that all the manufacturing operatives, or, indeed, all the pottery operatives, were as well off—for the houses in Etruria are, unhappily, not by any means to be considered as typical of the entire district, although in Stoke, Hanley, Shelton and Burslem, there are many streets inhabited by the working population, in which the houses are just as well-built and as well-furnished as those belonging to the Messrs. Wedgwood.

I examined with some attention the worst parts of Hanley and Shelton. The houses are very seldom built back-to-back, and there are scarcely any cellar dwellings. With very few exceptions, each tenement has its means of thorough ventilation. Courts, however, abound. The older houses are sometimes built on all sides of a small airless square, with a narrow passage leading to the street. Occasionally the common ash-pits and the conveniences are erected in this delectable quadrangle. More generally, each house has its backyard — these places being too often, however, in a filthy state of dirt and neglect — frequently piled up with broken saggars, articles which the people seem wonderfully prone to collect and treasure. The occupants of the worst class of houses, I often found to be widows, with miserable, dirty, unkempt-looking children, picking up a livelihood by washing and depending upon it being eked out by parish relief. Even in the poorest class of dwellings, it was curious to observe how the fashion in furniture prevailing in the district was perceptible; wretched imitations of sofas — all rickety boards, and torn and dirty calico — were often drawn near the fire. In more than one instance these served as day beds, and probably night beds too for sick children.

I examined several of the houses in Hanley in which deaths from cholera had taken place. The disease, when it broke out, produced an absolute panic amongst the poor people. In the first house which I inspected in which a cholera case had taken place, the patient, a labouring man, had been left to die unattended. It was a damp squalid place, with a mere strip of a back-yard, shared with the adjacent tenements. The privies which had been placed close to the backdoors, were removed to a more suitable situation by the Poor Law and sanitary authorities of Stoke. The house in question consisted of three poor rooms, and the rent paid was 2s per week. In a small yard close to another house, I found a ragged patient-looking donkey, standing listlessly to be snowed upon. The woman whom I found within — the occupant of a cold, damp and squalid room, with little furniture, and that of the most crazy description — said that the donkey slept in the yard all night. I suspected, however, by the very marked odour of the apartment, that Dobbin formed one of the domestic circle, at all events during the long, cold winter nights — an opinion which was shared by my companion and guide, a gentleman connected with the Poor Law administration at Stoke. The husband in this case was a labouring man out of work. The place, I was informed, had been a perfect miracle of dirt until, before the advent of the cholera, the Poor Law authorities took it in hand. It is, indeed, probably to the active and timely measures adopted by the officers of the Stoke Union that the district owed its comparative escape from cholera, which was excessively severe a couple of miles off, at Newcastle-under-Lyme. Since October 1848, an energetic system of house to house visitation for the discovery and removal of sanitary nuisances had been carried on, and although no official records have been preserved of the actual number of foul places cleansed or improved, I am assured that the change effected is a very considerable and important one.

As in South Staffordshire, although by no means to the same extent, the earth in some districts of the Potteries has partially collapsed over deserted mine workings, and played the usual havoc with the houses above. I saw in Hanley and Shelton many crushed and deserted dwellings; in some cases contiguous houses leaning away from each other, and in others smashed down lintels and riven walls. I was told that in more instances than one these movements of the earth had been productive of most afflicting consequences to honest and industrious workmen, who had invested their hard-earned savings in small building speculations, and whose property was thus virtually destroyed.

The possession of house property is much coveted by the better class of operatives in the Pottery districts. There are several flourishing building societies, and I was gratified to learn that instances were very common of working men living in their own houses. Rows of newly erected cottages, upon a plan infinitely superior to the old class of houses, are very common in many districts. In some of these the stone facings, well-kept door steps, and smart window blinds, give the streets quite a jaunty appearance. The old and wide-spread fault of making the entrance door the living-room door is, however, still generally persevered in.

Public bakeries are common throughout the potteries, and are mostly open at fixed hours every day. A great proportion of the bread consumed is home-made, and baked at these ovens. The charge for baking is generally 1d a lot — the lot to consist of not more than four quartern loaves. I was told that it was only the most improvident among the working classes who purchased their bread at the baker's. Home baking insures a cheaper and a more unadulterated article.

The Water Supply

The water supply of Hanley and the surrounding districts is partly derived from wells, partly from the North Staffordshire Waterworks Company, which conducts the water in its pipes from springs welling out in the high moorland ranges near Leek. Stand taps are common in the poorer localities, the charge to each cottage benefiting by them being generally 2d a week. I presume that the inhabitants are not very punctual with their rates for in several instances in the course of my wanderings through back courts and unpaved alleys, I found the supply "cut off". In many cases, however, the ingenious defaulters, fertile in expedients, had managed to perforate the leaden pipe, or partially to wrench open the metal lips at the place where the sides of the tube had been crushed together, and so to ensure a small but continuous dribble. In one instance the pipe had either burst or been broken below ground, and so furnished the supply of a small well which came bubbling up, not in the clearest condition, in the centre of a muddy unpaved court. The regular wells seemed to me for the most part forbidding receptacles for mere surface water. Those sunk deeper and provided with pumps yielded a somewhat purer supply.

Before leaving the subject of house and street architecture I may be permitted to observe upon the constant recurrence of a phenomenon which I have remarked in many industrial districts of England. In the houses of the worst class — in those the inhabitants of which are obviously at once slatternly and poor — the seldom-failing pictorial decoration upon the walls is derived, with significant frequency, from the illustrations of some penny highwayman novel. In more comfortable dwellings, although occupied, perhaps, by individuals of the same nominal rank in the social scale, you may find a stiff family portrait or two — probably a crown or half-crown's worth — from some vagrant artist; or perchance there are engravings of some Chartist or Radical leader belonging to the political school of the paterfamilias. But enter the dirty, untidy dwelling, where the hearth is unswept, the bed unmade, and everything betokens want and squalor — and almost to a certainty you find, stuck by pins or wafers to the wall, a coarse woodcut showing Claude du Val with his face masked, prancing in a laced coat beneath a gallows, or Dick Turpin on Black Bess, with a cocked pistol in either hand, clearing the turnpike-gate on his famous ride to York.

The Coal-Pits in the Pottery District

The coal-pits about the Potteries are managed very much after the fashion of those in the Wolverhampton and Bilston district of the same county. A few pits are worked by gins and horse-power. The buttie system flourishes as in South Staffordshire, but I think upon the whole that the aboveground apparatus is more efficient and less rude. A great many of the coal mines hereabout are rented by the Earl Granville from the Duchy of Cornwall, to whom it seems the royalty belongs. The principal seam worked — as I was told at a shaft mouth — is one six or seven feet high. The men work from six in the morning until different hours in the afternoon. There is none or very little "tommying" in this part of the county, but the wages of the colliers are seldom paid as working men's wages ought to be—weekly.

The Social Condition of the Population

The accusations of improvidence and of a tendency to waste an over proportion of their money upon eating and drinking, which I heard so often urged against the working men in the South of Staffordshire, I find re-echoed and applied to the potters of the north. Upon a point of this sort, all I say must rest on the authority of informants who, living in the district and intimately acquainted with the habits of the people, can base their statements upon far-extended and long-continued observation. A gentleman connected with the Poor Law administration of Stoke observed that in many cases there was "nothing but roasting, and broiling, and frizzing in the houses on the Saturday nights, the Mondays and the Tuesdays, after which time the families had too often to pinch for it till pay-day came round again". The favourite beverage is ale — the newer and sweeter the better. With the exception of a little cricketing, the people are not much in the habit of engaging in manly games. "The public house is in general," I was told, "the greatest attraction when the day's work is over." The principal supporters of the Mechanics' Institutes among the pottery population are the painters and the figure moulders, who may be supposed to belong to a higher class than the ordinary run of workmen; but in North Staffordshire, as almost everywhere else, the institutions in question are practically for the benefit of shopmen and clerks. Dog-fighting and cock-fighting are both dying out. You see, however, a great number of ferocious-looking bull-terriers still lurking about. In many instances I was informed, that when a dog or cock-fight is got up, its patrons and supporters are not working men, but individuals moving in a better rank of life. The vigilance of the police however has all but suppressed these miserable exhibitions. Very little outdoor relief is granted by the Poor Law administrators in the district, except in cases of widows and old and disabled men. Almost all relief to able-bodied persons, given out of doors, is in the form of food or necessaries. The workhouse test is sometimes put in force, by requiring able-bodied paupers to pick oakum, or break stones within doors all day, and then permitting them to return to their homes with food, or perhaps a trifle of money, at night.

The Manufacture of Boys' Marbles

There is no employment connected with the pottery trade carried on at the homes of the people, with the exception of an instance here and there, in which small ornaments may be fabricated after the regular work hours — and excepting, too, the cases of a few individuals who make and paint boy's marbles. In Burslem a considerable number of these are made, and in a little back street in Shelton I came upon a household in which the painting of "alleys" and "commoneys" formed the staple industry. The operators were a young woman and a girl. The mother of the elder — an old infirm woman — was sitting by the fire-side, propped up in an armchair. She told me that she had been a marble painter for sixty years, and that her daughter now carried on the trade. At my request, the latter — an intelligent woman — explained the process from first to last. The maker first rolls the lump of clay into a tolerably round form, in his hands. By the help of a common thimble, he then brings it into a perfectly globular shape, and smooths away all surface asperities. The marbles have then to be baked, to be brought into the biscuit-ware condition, just like any other description of pottery. They are burnt in large dishfuls, at an ordinary furnace, the maker paying 1½d per dish. He then sells them to the manufacturer who pays him 8d, 10d, or 1s per thousand, according to the size and quality of the clay. The women who paint and beautify the articles purchase at the same rates, and after finishing them off with the brush and the glazing dish sell them again at 2s, 2s 6d, and 3s per thousand. Large marbles, the size of plums, are paid for by the hundred. The process of painting these clay pellets is neat and expeditious. A flat platter of wood, revolving vertically on a spindle, just as in the case of the throwing block, carries round the marble, which is placed upon its centre. The "painting" generally consists of a succession of rings, something like equators, and arctic and antarctic circles upon globes. The operator holds his camel-hair pencil to the clay, and the revolving marble in some sort paints itself. It is then placed to dry in a little oven or dish by the fireside; and is next dipped into a bowl of the same composition with the lead used for glazing the ordinary biscuit-ware. The woman was quite sensible of the deleterious nature of the mixture; but she was not, she said, long over the bowl at a time, and she was very careful in thoroughly washing and cleaning her hands. For the subjection of the dipped marbles to a glossing furnace she paid 1½d a dish. This, of course, came out of her profits, as above stated. She was not able to tell me how much she thought she earned, because she worked irregularly. The painting process soon fatigued the eye, so that she could not make the circles true, and then she had to rest.

The Potters' Joint Stock Emigration Society and Savings Fund

About six years ago the working men of the Potteries set on foot a scheme which presented some features of novelty, and which has, so far as I can ascertain the facts, been to a certain degree successful. This was no other than the establishment of a "Potters' Joint-Stock Emigration Society and Savings Fund". Although apparently instituted for a twofold purpose, the grand and predominating object of the scheme was to provide a home beyond the Atlantic for members of the trade. The Society has since been opened to persons following other occupations; but to the energy and the enterprise of the potters, the original idea and its practical working are due. The rules, progress and condition of this Emigration Society, I shall detail as fully as the data furnished to me will permit.

The Association was established in May 1844, and was duly enrolled under act of Parliament. Its operations were at first strictly confined to potters and their families. The entrance fee was, and is, £1 1s 6d, with an extra 1s for rules, certificate and card of membership. The weekly regular contribution was, and is, 1s 6d. The society was thrown open about eight months ago. Before that period it had purchased and peopled an estate of 1,600 acres, called "Pottersville", situated at Columbia, in the State of Wisconsin, in North America — a portion of the district called "The Oak Openings" — a region, by the way, which supplied Cooper with the name of his recent novels. The present number of the inhabitants of Pottersville is stated at 134. The association, having extended its means, is now in treaty for a tract of 50,000 acres, situated upon the Fox River, near Fort Winnebago. The preliminary arrangements for the purchase have indeed, I believe been completed. The land will be formally made over in October 1850, and in the meantime it is held by what is called "squatters' right". Two hundred and fifty families are either already located upon this land, or are on their way thither. The association has erected on its 50,000 acres estate "two good stores, seven miles apart, stocked with every variety of food, clothing, domestic utensils, farming implements and live stock — the whole" (I am quoting from a printed document furnished to me by one of the secretaries) — "to be purchased by the colonists for a little moderate labour on the reserved land of the society. Of the reserved land in question, 300 acres are stated to be in cultivation; a ferry with a proper boat has been established; a blacksmith's shop is at work; and subscriptions are being raised in order to send out a grist-mill.

The beauties and advantages of the transatlantic Paradise are, of course, very glowingly set forth in all the manifestoes of the society; and it is to be hoped that the picture is as faithful as it is flattering. The soil is pronounced "surpassingly rich", and minerals, "it is expected", abound beneath the surface. The average crop of wheat is stated to be thirty bushels to the acre, and the average price of the bushel 3s. Indian corn, we are told, yields sixty or seventy bushels per acre. Grapes grow wild in the woods, and such game as deer and prairie hens are alleged to be abundant. The advantagous situation of Pottersville and the larger estate are then insisted upon. Milwauki, a "most flourishing town" on Lake Michigan, is 90 miles distant from Pottersville. Fort Winnebago is on the Portage between the Fox and Wisconsin rivers, "on a great route between the Lakes and the Mississippi" and "sixteen oxen conveyances of new emigrants pass through Pottersville daily, in the spring, summer, and autumn of the year". The prospectus goes on to state the cost at which an emigrant may be provided with house accommodation. A log dwelling of two rooms may be erected for about £10; a frame dwelling, with oaken floors, cement plaster to make the walls wind- and water-tight — each room fourteen feet by twelve, with locks, doors, and latches complete — may be had for £12 10s. The cost of breaking up and sowing five acres — in the "openings" I presume — is stated at £5, and the average passage money of an adult from an English port to Pottersville is about £8.

The mode in which the society works has now to be explained. It comprises an unlimited number of shares, the price of each being £1 1s 6d, with the weekly payment of 6d. The possessor of a share has a right to the occupancy of 20 acres of land, but not to the permanent possession, until he has paid £5 10s to the society — thus fixing the absolute cost of the allotments at 5s 2½d per acre. A person having become a shareholder, may immediately emigrate at his own expense, carrying with him his certificates. Upon each estate, or each department of the larger tract, estate stewards are resident, who are bound, upon the production of a certificate, to supply the bearer with a land allotment. The unappropriated allotments are balloted for, each emigrant drawing the number of his farm from a bag. So far as it is possible, the allotments are so parcelled as to contain each a "fair share of clear and wooded land". The emigrant, being put in possession, has right to the store provisions of the society, and to the use of agricultural implements. These, I presume, include oxen for ploughing — the document from which I quote stating that a team of five oxen and a strong plough are requisite to break up the virgin prairie sod. "The frost of one winter turns the broken land into the richest soil." Until the emigrant clears accounts with the society, he holds his land only by a deed of lease duly signed. He may, if he be willing and able, pay the entire amount down before leaving home, in which case he is furnished with proper title deeds, conferring on him the freehold of the land; and he may also become entitled, by paying at the same time an additional £23, to a free passage, to a log hut when he arrives, and to the cultivation and fencing of one-fourth of his twenty acre allotment; in short, the society professes to take up a working man, and upon the receipt of about £30, to settle him comfortably on his own land in Wisconsin. Emigrants not in command of the ready money may proceed on the terms which I have before described, and they are allowed six years after taking possession to repay the society for all advances made on their behoof. For the money, no interest is charged; the exact sum expended is alone required to be returned, and the repayments may be made in wheat. In general the land is expected to be paid for by the weekly "levy" of sixpence. Thus a man who has been a member for a year has already paid nearly one-half of the purchase money of the twenty acres. A failure in the weekly instalment does not preclude the defaulter from the advantages of the money he has already paid in. He may at any subsequent period renew his contributions, as if no lapse had taken place; but in the interim he will lose his right to ballot — an important privilege in the list of those which the society offers.

This balloting is in fact a sort of lottery—success in which entitles the winner to claim his land, outfit and passage from the society, becoming bound to repay the whole within ten years. The process of balloting takes place at stated times, and every individual holding a share has a chance of being chosen. The ballot may be held at any place—in the rooms of any branch of the parent society—but its effect is always general. The mechanical plan adopted is peculiar. Each shareholder is distinguished by a number—those numbers being enrolled in duplicate in the central and branch books. They are also inscribed round the edge of the ballot table—a circular apparatus four feet in diameter every number being divided by "raised brass-work as sharp as the edge of a knife". By means of a large wheel moving on a pivot, and some other mechanical contrivances, a chance number is indicated, the possessor of which can claim the whole emigrating expense of himself, wife, and all the members of his family under eighteen years of age, as well as the other advantages purchasable, as already stated, by less lucky members, at about £23. Two acres of his land he receives sown with Indian corn, and three with wheat. He is provided with agricultural implements and provisions for the first year of his settlement. The latter advantages he pays for in labour on the reserved land of the society, and the money actually laid out for him is repaid in ten yearly instalments of wheat. A winner at the ballot, if he is not prepared to proceed across the Atlantic, may sell his privilege to whom he pleases. I was informed that "ballots" have fetched as much as £18 and £20 a piece, the value of the claim to the original shareholder depending very much on the number of his family. Loss of right to benefit by the chances of the ballot occurs when a member is four weeks in arrear with his sixpences, but he recovers his claim if he can prove that the deficiency in payments was caused either by sickness or unavoidable loss of work. For every additional £1 1s 6d paid into the society, a member obtains a right to an additional chance of the ballot, without, however, incurring any further weekly responsibility than the original sixpences.

As to the land purchased by the society, the scheme proposes its ultimate division into separate estates of 2,000 acres each. Each of these will comprehend 100 allotments of 20 acres each. One half of these allotments are reserved for sale purposes, their cultivation being effected by the labour due to the society in payment for provisions and the use of agricultural implements. At any future time which may seem most advisable for the interests of the society, these cleared allotments will be offered for sale, the colonists having the preference. Should the latter not purchase, the land will be sold to strangers. Things are so managed that the reserved patches alternate, in position, with the allotted ones. The acre, I should mention, is reckoned at 4,840 square yards. One of the allegations put forth by the society is that in Wisconsin all kinds of farming stock—live stock is meant, I presume—are 400 per cent cheaper than in England; and among the inducements to working men to emigrate, the political franchise of the United States, acquired on the easy terms of six months' residence in the territory is not forgotten. A somewhat singular undertaking which the society professes to accomplish is, in case of the death of the head of a family incapacitating its surviving members from continuing the yearly instalments of repayment, to "take such family under its care, and protect it in its adversity until the said family be equal to the honest discharge of its liabilities". In all the estates save that of Pottersville, the salaries of the land-stewards are to be paid by means of a commission on the sale of store goods. It is expressly stipulated that no particular allotment will be reserved for a shareholder who does not choose to take possession at once. The land-steward, or local manager, is bound to find land for a member presenting his certificate, and, if no allotment remains unoccupied, "a new purchase must be made". No money paid into the coffers of the society is to be returned, except in case of a dissolution of the association", or when a member is emigrating on his own resources, in which event the money he has paid up is, of course, expended upon him.

In the document from which I have mainly gathered the foregoing facts, an appeal is made to trades to connect themselves en masse with the society. It is urged that they would thus secure a quick and cheap means of providing for their unemployed brethren, and, of course, lessening the burden of competition upon themselves. They are reminded that for the money advanced from the trade funds for the purchase of membership, the payment of passage, and the erection of a log hut, there will be landed security—the sum being entered in the deed of lease, and the annual repayments being made to the estate-steward, and finally to the trade through the parent society. The exponents of the Potters' Emigration scheme, in developing their views in this respect, venture a little on delicate ground. How superior they plead, would the adoption of some such means of rapid emigration be to the "common plan of strikes and turn-outs—to the supporting of willing labourers in a state of pernicious idleness"; and then the writer proceeds to put this query—"Could not a new system of strikes be established, by clearing a work at once—by making farmers of the turn-outs—and then dictating terms for a new complement of hands?" The spirit of this proposition does not seem peculiarly conciliating. "Dictating" is a harsh word on either side; but absurd in some respects as the scheme may be, the idea is worth noting as one of the moving straws in the atmosphere of our social and industrial system.

In the last published report of the affairs of the society I see it stated that about £1,690 has actually been remitted to America for the purchase of land, stores etc. The estate of Pottersville is represented as being worth four times its original purchase money; but it is regretted that "a great portion of the money and provisions advanced to the colonists on that estate still remains unsettled". Payment, it is announced, however, "can and will be" enforced. It seems that matters had fallen into some confusion at the time that the society was thrown open to all trades, but the accounts have been audited, and things are now stated to be advancing prosperously. The number of land certificates sent out has been 250—each, in almost every case, representing a family. The number of members now connected with the society is 3,500. The treasurer and the committee seem to be recompensed on a scale of laudable economy; the amount paid to the former being 5s weekly, and to each member of the latter, 1s for each meeting. The Potters' Trade Union was dissolved in June last, when the scheme was made general. In one of the documents before me, there is a list of the branch clubs or associations scattered throughout the chief towns of Great Britain, in connection with the parent body. The number of those enumerated is 105, and the amount of money received from them, from the 8th of June, 1840 to the 8th of September, 1849, is about £2,871. The names of some of these local clubs is not without their significance. I transcribe a few. "The Home in the West", Crewe; "The Emigrant's Castle", Newcastle; "The Land of the Free", Preston; "The Washington", Manchester; "The Labourer's refuge", Oldham; "The Hope of Indpendence", Manchester; "The New Paradise", Ashton; "The Poor Man's Hope", Duckinfield; "The Spinner's Home", Preston; "The Republican", Halifax; "The Rights of Labour", Kilburnie; "The United Labour", Oldham; "The Hope of Freedom", Bury; "The Tree of Liberty", Birmingham. "The Salve's Hope", Hull; "The Stripes and Stars", London; "The Prairie", Manchester; "The American Prospect", Dundee; "The New Ark", Dale Hill. There is one foreign branch:"The Abbeville", in the town of the same name.

A feature in the constitution of this association is that they have established a small weekly newspaper, the *Potters' Examiner*, published in Shelton, and exclusively devoted to promoting the objects and gaining the necessary publicity for the schemes in view. The printing apparatus and premises are the property of the association, and much of the typographical work of the various working men's societies throughout the district is performed at their office. The paper itself is published at one penny, and is usually filled with reports of the proceedings of branch clubs, and with copious extracts of letters received from the emigrants. Some of them have also been published in a separate shape. In the numbers of the *Potter's Examiner* which I had an opportunity of seeing, the letters published from the settlers in Wisconsin appeared to me to have been fairly enough selected. The general tone was by no means that of men suddenly finding themselves in an earthly paradise. There was nothing, in short, of a clap-trap character about the documents. The various obstacles and hardships encountered were set down candidly enough. Many cases of the quarrel and split-up of parties were narrated, and the grand chorus was "Let no one come out here who is afraid of rough living and hard work." In a few instances, "home sickness" was ominously alluded to, and apropos of one of these, the writer adds, "The London men are the worst of all."

I have now given as detailed and minute account as possible of the

"Potters' Emigration Society," not because of any intrinsic importance possessed by the institution, but because it was the first—and is, so far as I can learn—the only—association of working men for the avowed purpose of facilitating emigration. Respecting the ability of the body to accomplish the work it professes to undertake, I know nothing. I have described its plan of operations, not as the grand scheme of an all-potent corporation, but simply as a phenomenon constituting an instructive sign of the times. To a certain extent the principle of the Building Societies would seem, in this instance, to have been applied to emigration. And so far as I can see, there is nothing unreasonable in the supposition that, if association and small weekly payment can provide a man with a home in England, the same agency may be employed in securing for him a freehold in the United States.

Newcastle-under-Lyme

About a couple of miles from Hanley, lying to the west of the line of Pottery towns, is the ancient borough of Newcastle-under-Lyme. The latter portion of the name refers to what was once a tract of forestland, skirting the eminences above the town. A brook, called the Lyme, not many degrees removed from the status of a common sewer, runs through the place. The population in 1841 amounted to 19,489; and the number of living persons to one death during the seven years from 1838 to 1844, was rather more than 40. Newcastle-under-Lyme, although lying on the outskirts of the Pottery district, has nothing in common with it. The town is ancient and quaint—the houses frequently exhibiting high peaked gables, and the by-streets being narrow, old fashioned and tortuous. The massive square tower surmounting the church is of vast and obvious antiquity. A casual glimpse of the borough reveals little to distinguish it from scores of commonplace English country towns. The visitor from the Potteries will look in vain for any sign of the industry which he has just left. No piles of smashed pottery-ware lie mouldering in yards and corners. A few tall chimneys are visible, but the chances are that they will be smokeless; and the spectator may, perhaps, in connection with this ominous symptom observe men with aprons, having the appearance of operatives in some textile branch of industry, lounging listlessly about the street corners.

Newcastle-under-Lyme is, in fact, the seat of a dying—almost a dead trade—that of the manufacture of beaver hats. Factories which once gave constant employment to hundreds of hands now provide fitful jobs for perhaps a dozen or a score; and workmen who were once engaged in the production of the most expensive hats, now think themselves lucky if they can earn a pittance by the manufacture of coarse felt "wide-awakes", locally called "caps". The introduction of silk hats has been, as I understand, the cause of this revulsion in the trade. The old beavers have all but gone out of use. The cheap silk hats manufactured in London, in Lancashire, and abroad, have completely supplanted the more expensive article, and ruined the staple trade of Newcastle.

Without much difficulty, I found out an intelligent operative hatter—one of the few still lingering about the scene of their former prosperity, and striving, by the profits of uncertain and ill-paid labour, to make both ends meet. His account of the state of the hatting trade in Newcastle-under-Lyme was nearly as follows:

"Out of the multitude of people engaged in the hatting business twenty years ago there are now, I should say, hardly a hundred left in Newcastle. The trade is gone away and ruined. Since the cheap silk hats came in, hardly anything else is made. If an order does come, the wages are a mere nothing to what they used to be. The men struggle for the job and so bring wages down. I mean the few of us who are left. The great body of the Newcastle hatters are gone long since. There was not a living for them here. They had to take to all manner of trades—to do anything for a living. Some of them went to work in the clay pits; others went to the brick-field. Some got to be potters; lots went to be cotton-spinners in Lancashire; others turned railway navvies; and a good many went to London to work at silk-hatting if they could, or to do anything which might turn up. In fact they are all broken up and away. A good many of those who had the means went off to America, and some had to go to the workhouse. Of the hundred or so who are still here, the most are making felt caps, and some few have turned their hands to silk hats; but the silk is quite a different trade from the beaver; and it is hard for a grown-up man who has served an apprenticeship, to set to and learn another craft.

"In the good days of the beaver trade, the hatters used to work, the most of them, in factory, and a small number at their own homes, or in shops attached to them. These shops were principally at the backs of the houses. The owners of them were generally piece-masters, as they were called, and they had the privilege of taking apprentices. I am a piece-master; but of course there are no apprentices now. That is all over. The piece-masters worked for a factory. They got the material from the manufacturer, and took back the finished goods. Besides the beavers there was a common sort of hat manufactured to a very great extent in Newcastle. They were called 'stuff hats'. I have known a single firm here have upwards of 32,000 dozen of these hats on stock. They were exported to America and the West Indies for the slaves. Thirty years ago the prices paid for making the bodies of stuff hats were 8s, 9s, and 10s per dozen. The same work is done nowadays for 2s 9d. The old prices for making the body of a beaver hat were 2s 6d, and 3s a-piece; they are now made for 14d and 15d and sometimes for even less than that.

"When the hat trade was fairly broken up, and the people gone, a great swarm of Irish came, and took possession of the houses. In a district called the Blue-buildings, three-fourths of the people used to be English hatters, and now three-fourths, and more than that are Irish. A few, but only a very few, of these Irish try to work at hatting; the great bulk of them go strolling about begging, and collecting bones, rags, bottles, and the like. The few who work at hatting have been regularly brought up in the trade. The wages that a man can earn at cap-making are very low; he might almost as well be idle. The bulk of that trade is in Lancashire. I have said that a body-maker is now paid 2s 9d per dozen. It takes a good week's work to make four dozen, and a very hard week's work to make four and a half dozen. But there is little work even at this price. I have had only two dozen for the last fifteen weeks, and there are many as ill-off as I am. A 'rougher' would be paid about 5s 6d per dozen, and he would 'rough' from three dozen to four dozen a week. A finisher would have about 3s per dozen, and he might turn out about several dozen, or rather more, a week. These are about the prices when there is work. We hope that there will be some potteries started here soon. They talk about it, as soon as a new branch railway is opened. Then perhaps we should have a chance of turning our hands to something new, for there's no use in talking about making a living in the hat trade any longer."

I proceeded to several small shops where the caps or wide-awakes were manufactured but found only one open. It was merely a miserable, crazy shed crusted over with dirt from long neglect. Four or five men were at work within it. They made any sorts of hats for which they could get an order; but the wide-awakes formed their staple trade. Working twelve hours a day, when they could get work, they assured me that they hardly earned 10s a week. The hours some of the men laboured, when an order came in, were excessive—sometimes from three in the morning until ten at night. "But as I might well conceive," they added, "it is not from over-work we suffer."

III

THE MIDLANDS

Nottingham

Introduction

The industrial staples of the three Midland Counties of England, Nottinghamshire, Derbyshire, and Leicestershire, consist in a general way, of the manufacture of lace, of silk, and of hosiery, in all its very numerous branches. Of these, the hosiery or framework knitting trade is the oldest, and the most impartially scattered over the three counties. The town of Nottingham is, however, beyond doubt, the metropolis of the Midland lace trade, and as such I give it the first place in describing the district.

Nottingham lies in the very centre of England. It is built on high ground, occupying part of the southern declivity of a long range of hills, running from the north, and which hereabouts fade away into the open champagne country beneath. The town extends over an area of about 2,610 acres. In 1831 it contained 10,642 houses. In 1841 the number increased to 11,612. In the former year the population was 50,680; in the latter 53,091. Nottingham presents characteristic features commercially and socially. To a superficial observer, it appears a handsome, old-fashioned town, full of quaint and quaintly-named streets, narrow and winding, but frequently affording glimpses full of architectural picturesqueness, while so long as the visitor confines himself to the principal thoroughfares, his impression will also be decidedly in favour of the town, as respects the important essentials of good substantial paving and of cleanliness. Both soil and situation facilitate the latter quality. A great portion of the town is built upon the face of such steep declivities as afford natural surface drainage, and the soil, generally of sandstone, is almost as absorbent as a sponge.

Notwithstanding these advantages, however, Nottingham is in one respect, one of the worst built towns in England. Its area is the most crowded in the kingdom. According to Mr. Hawksley's report, there is in Nottingham one individual to "every square of four and a half yards on the side", the calculation including the very large open space of the market place, while in one particular part of the town, it has been ascertained by the Poor Law authorities that upwards of 4,200 people dwell in a space not measuring 220 yards square. The inhabitants are thus crowded because, of course, the houses are crowded. "In Nottingham, sir," said a framework knitter to me, "the poor live on each other's backs." Out of the 11,000 houses of which the town is composed, more than 8,000 are inhabited by the working classes, and more than 7,000 are built back-to-back and side-to-side. Of course, a great majority of these open into narrow courts and cul-de-sacs, very frequently approached by openings which are rather tunnels than passages, many of them being under eight feet high and three feet wide. "These courts," says Mr. Hawksley, "are almost uniformly closed at both ends." In some of the better-class which I have seen, the blocks of buildings are far enough apart to admit of miniature plots of garden ground, each about a couple of yards square, and enclosed by toy palings, a foot or so high. But in many instances the courts in Nottingham are mere grimy slits in the masonry, with broken pavements, and abounding in unsavoury sights and smells. Great quantities of yellowish linen are habitually hung up to dry in these places, stopping the current of what little air might otherwise circulate; and in the lower parts of the town, a similar display is often stretched from window to window across the public thoroughfare.

The peculiarly crowded state of Nottingham arose from the land in its vicinity being very extensively held by a peculiar tenure, which permitted the freemen or burgesses to turn out a certain number of cows to pasture upon it annually. The town thus grew up as though girdled by walls, beyond which the mason could not penetrate. The consequence has been that the surplus population, instead of spreading forth into suburbs, has overflowed into many distinct villages and hamlets, such as Carrington and Ison-green. The absurd restriction upon building is now on the eve of being removed. Had it been demolished a score of years ago, it is calculated that Nottingham would have been at least a third larger at the present day.

Of course, in a town composed of buildings so closely huddled upon each other, the principles of ventilation and efficient drainage could not have been originally attended to. Since 1832, however, the successive parochial highway boards have been carrying on a vigorous system of sanitary and structural reform. Previously to that period—and indeed, as improvements of this sort can proceed but slowly, the description still to a certain extent applies—multitudes of thickly-populated streets were utterly unpaved and undrained, pools of stagnant water, and ridges of dung, ashes, and refuse running down their entire length. The privies, where they existed at all, were generally constructed in clusters beneath the houses, and neglected and offensive in the extreme. So late, indeed, as two or three years ago, there existed groups of thirty and forty houses, the occupants of which, since the dwellings were built fifty years ago, had never enjoyed any accommodation of the kind whatever, and "hundreds" of the places actually existing were pronounced by the recently appointed local sanitary commission to be "unfit for the use of any human being". The supply of water to the town was, at the period in question, scanty and defective. The sewerage which had been formed was also "very defective and unsystematic"—indeed, Mr. Hawksley in his report enumerates more than 61 streets which were undrained as late as 1844. In 1832 the cholera attacked Nottingham, and raged with great severity. There were upwards of 1,100 attacks, of which 289 proved fatal. As usual, the principal ravages of the scourge took place in those wards where the rate of mortality was highest under ordinary circumstances.

In the late cholera visitation, however, Nottingham got off almost scot-free. There occurred but eight cases of which six resulted in death. One of the causes of this comparative immunity may no doubt be found in the sanitary improvements effected since 1832. The water supply subsequent to that year has been, and is, most abundant; and the work of sewer-making and pavement-making has been steadily progressive. In 1836 a proprietary cemetery of twelve acres in extent was formed in the outskirts, and upwards of 6,600 burials have, up to the present time, taken place there. Another open burial space of seven acres was allotted during the cholera time, and many interments have been effected within it. Still further to stay the plague of intramural sepulture, two public cemeteries have lately been opened without the town, the one connected with the church, the other with dissent. The local authorities, however, not satisfied with the gradual progress of sanitary reform, bestirred themselves, and nearly three years ago the sanitary committee above referred to was appointed. This body seems to have done its duty vigorously. At the instance of the committee, thirty-four dwellings erected over the privies and ash-pits have been removed, the change in many instances throwing open hitherto unventilated courts and noisome alleys. A great number of foul nuisances of a similar class, including 21 pig-sties and 24 cess-pools containing "dangerous collections of manure", have been got rid of, and many courts and small streets paved and drained.

These improvements will, it is to be hoped, gradually dethrone Nottingham from the head pre-eminence which it occupies in the bills of mortality. By the last returns of the Registrar-General, the proportion of males living to one death was 34.3, of females 39.4, showing a mean rate of about 36 persons living to one death. This is a higher rate of mortality than prevails in any of the cotton towns excepting Manchester, and higher than that existing in any of the woollen towns—not even excepting Leeds. The comparatively great mortality of Nottingham the town owes to a few of its lower districts. There is a difference of nearly 100 per cent in the value of life in the high and surburban, as compared with the low and crowded wards of Nottingham. In Park-ward the mean age at death is 37. In a district close to it, composed of courts and back-to-back houses, the mean age at death is less than 18. On the elevated plateau of the Common, the mean age at death rises to 40. In one part of Castle-ward it sinks to 14.3, and in an adjacent district, an average constructed on 63 deaths, gave a mean age of 14.9 years. In Castle-gate, "open, elevated and well-drained", with 38½ yards of space for each inhabitant, the mean age at death is 39.6. In Mortimer-street, "crowded, low, and indifferently drained", with only 16 yards of space for each inhabitant, the mean age at death is 17.1. Taken altogether, the mortality of Nottingham is 26 per cent greater than the mortality of England and Wales, and the mean age at death in Nottingham 22.3 years—just seven years below the average age of death in England and Wales. Some of these results are taken from Mr. Hawksley's report in 1844; but that the general rate of mortality has not diminished is proved by the last tables of the Registrar-General.

Housing in Nottingham

About three-fourths of the housing in Nottingham are constructed for and occupied by the working classes, and as a rule they are built in courts and back-to-back. The general plan of construction divides them into three clear stories, of one room each—a singularly inconvenient and defective arrangement. The staircases are very steep, dark and narrow, and under them are frequently situated black choky holes of pantries. In many cases coals and provisions are kept in the same recess. The houses have seldom a sub-story, and cellar dwellings are consequently unfrequent. I believe that there are not above 200 in Nottingham. The lower room is in general the living apartment. It is almost always floored with brick, or, if boarded, as it may be in rare cases, sand supplies the place of carpeting. The street door is invariably the room door. In point of furniture, I should say that the living apartments of the Nottingham operatives, particularly those of the framework knitters, are decidedly inferior to the dwellings of the mass of workpeople in the cotton, woollen, and northern coal districts. I have been very frequently struck with the bare appearance of the rooms, and this even in the houses of middlemen in the hosiery trade, who had perhaps a dozen or score of knitting frames at work. An inferior sort of sofa, however, and a clock are common. The lace-workers' houses are somewhat better furnished. A few of the latter belonging to operatives earning the higher class of wages, boast a substantial and occasionally crowded *ameublement*. The apartment on the first floor is invariably a bedroom; that above it either a bedroom or a workshop, in which the knitting machines and occasionally warp-lace frames are set. The central bedroom opens upon the staircase, and is usually patent to the view of the workmen ascending or descending from the shop. In some cases there is a garret above the working room, used occasionally as a lumber receptacle, occasionally as a bedroom, occasionally as both. These places are got at by means of a trap-door and a ladder, and are miserable dark dog-holes. In houses not constructed in the regular three-storied and three-roomed fashion, the apartments are usually very small, and the bed-closets, off the living rooms, are perfectly unlighted and unventilated.

The floors of the higher flats in Nottingham are almost universally composed of a layer of coarse plaster of Paris, mixed with ground ashes, and laid about two inches thick. The floors absorb moisture rapidly, and are excessively cold to the feet. I have frequently found them rough, and worn into dusty and flaky cavities. The whole construction of the houses is generally slight, and the roofing particularly so. In crowded cities there must be crowded houses, and in crowded houses crowded rooms. I have frequently found families of five and six living and sleeping in close chambers not more than 12 feet square. The average weekly rent including parochial taxes, of houses of two stories, containing one living room and one bedroom, is about 1s 9d; of those containing a garret in addition, 1s 11d; and of those containing a garret and cellar, 2s 1d. The average weekly rent of a three-storied house, containing a living room, bedroom, and workshop, is about 2s 2d; if a garret be added, 2s 6d; and if there be two bedrooms, as well as the other accommodations, about 2s 11d.

The Water Supply

I have already referred to the water supply of Nottingham, but its abundance, excellence and cheapness merit further and more detailed notice. Up to within a few years, Nottingham was principally served by two companies. The smallest of these, called the Nottingham Old Water Company, has existed upwards of 150 years, but it was not incorporated until 1826. In 1844 it supplied water derived from springs, welling forth at a higher level than that of the town, and about a mile and a half north of it, to from 12,000 to 14,000 population. The other company—The Trent Water-works Company—was incorporated in the year 1823. It derived its supply from the Trent, taking the water about a mile south of the town, and filtering it through beds of sand. The company supplied about 36,000 of the inhabitants. Certain minor concerns, deriving the water from wells, accommodated an additional 7,000. In 1845 the two companies amalgamated. The works of both are now kept in action under the general and very economic system of management, with the following result. Out of the total number of houses, amounting to near 12,000, about 11,500 are supplied in different ways. Of these, more than 3,000 are independent tenements, paying the water rates individually, and about 8,500 are small houses, compounded for in groups not less than three by the landlords, the tenants of course paying the diminished rate as portion of their rents.

The dwellings of the poor are supplied at an average charge of about 5s per annum, or not quite 1¼d per house per week. The highest charge is calculated at five per cent, and the lowest at three per cent on the rent. Houses of £5 are thus charged 5s 3d, and so up to £13, when the rate diminishes to 12s. Houses of £30 are charged 24s; houses of £50 are charged 35s; and houses of £100 are supplied for 60s. When landlords compound for their property they are allowed 25 per cent if they pay poor rates and parochial charges, and 20 per cent if they do not. Water closets in private houses are supplied for 10s per annum and private baths at the same charge. Gardens are supplied for 2s 6d; and mills for drinking and washing, per individual employed, at 3d yearly. When a landlord compounds for a block of tenements, the company conduct the water to the boundary of his property. He may then erect merely stand-pipes, or lay pipes into every one of his houses at his own pleasure.

In Nottingham, the water, by day and by night, is perpetually "on", and thus all the expensive and cumbrous machinery of tanks and cisterns is avoided. One of the reservoirs being situated at a higher level than the highest houses, there is seldom, in cases of fire, occasion for the engines. Plugs are placed at every hundred yards along the streets, and the hose has only to be screwed on at these apertures to the main. The quantity of water supplied in Nottingham is calculated as amounting to about 450 million of gallons per annum, or from 13 to 20 gallons per head per day. Previously to the adoption of the present system, a great portion of the poorer part of Nottingham was supplied by carriers. They sometimes charged ¼d or ½d per bucket, according to the situation of the house. The general price was stated to have been three gallons for a farthing. The price is now ¼d for about 79 gallons, or at a cheaper rate by more than twenty-six times than the charges of yore, the supply, too, being constantly at hand day and night. The medical men of Nottingham are unanimous in bearing testimony to the excellent sanitary effects of this abundant water supply.

The State of Education and Morality

So far as the state of education and sexual morality can be got at through the Registrar-General's returns, I find the condition of matters to be as follows: in 1846 the number of illegitimate births in Nottingham was 179, or about one to every hundred of the female population. In 1846, out of every 642 marriages, 532 were celebrated according to the rites of the Establishment, and 110 in other modes. In 38 cases, the man, and in 88 cases the woman, were under age. In 157 cases, or about one-fourth of the whole, the man signed with his mark. In 300 cases, or about one-half of the whole, the woman signed with her mark.

The Lace Industry of Nottingham

The branch of industry generally known as the lace trade includes two principal departments—the warp process, in which the mechanism is still generally moved by hand labour, and the twist or bobbin-net process, in which the mechanism is nowadays commonly, although not uniformly, driven by steam. Subordinate to these two principal branches there exist an infinity of minor trade sub-divisions in the manufacture—by twist and warp machines, constructed after different fashions—of an endless variety of kinds and qualities of goods. The lace trade, in all its ramifications, however, sprung originally from the hosiery manufacture. The first approach to lace weaving by machinery was the fabrication of ornamental stockings, with eyelet holes running up the ankles. Then the stocking frames were used to knot purses, and afterwards, by a peculiar arrangement of their mechanism, to construct point lace. The first great step in advance was the invention of the warp machine which involved to a certain extent the principle of the stocking-frame. The warps were for some time the principal mechanical producers of lace. The jacquard was applied to them and they were found capable of turning out patterns of a complicated nature. Meantime, however, an apparatus upon a new and improved principle for the fabrication for the most delicate and elaborately wrought lace made its appearance in the twist and bobbin-net machine—the principal and characteristic feature of the new invention being adopted, it is said, from a contrivance put in use by some ingenious person for the better weaving of cabbage-nets.

Statistical Background of the Lace Industry

The bobbin-net manufacture dates its origin from the year 1811. At that time the population of Nottingham, and of the surrounding districts and villages of Lenton, Beeston, Radford, Basford, Arnold, and Snenton was 47,300. In 1831 it was calculated that the hosiery trade employed fewer people than it did in 1811; and as the population in question then increased to 79,000, the augmentation is principally to be ascribed to the rapid growth of the bobbin-net manufacture. By the last census, the population of the area I have mentioned amounted to more than 130,000. In 1831 there were at work in the town of Nottingham upwards of 1,240 lace-making machines, and in the surrounding villages about as many more.

The number of machines then in operation in the kingdom was estimated at 4,500, of which Nottinghamshire, of course, possessed more than half. In 1836 another careful inquiry was set on foot from which it appeared that the total number of machines had decreased to 3,800. A severe and long-continued depression in the trade had been the cause of upwards of 600 of them being broken up, and sold as old iron. The machinery had also been in a transition state. In many of the cases, two of the old narrow frames had been joined to make one broader engine, and a few had been exported. The number of machine hands employed had, of course, decreased with the decrease of the engines upon which they wrought, the number being about 6,000, or less than two to every machine. The number of owners of these machines was stated at about 800. In 1831, there were 1,982 owners. The decrease took place almost entirely in the owners of one or two machines a-piece. In 1836, the number of machines in the town of Nottingham was 576; in the subsidiary towns and surrounding district it was about 1,470; showing that the tendency of the manufacture had been to flow from the central point of Nottingham, and to spread itself over the surrounding area. The total number of machines in England actually at work in 1836, was 3,547, of which again the county of Nottingham possessed 2,162, or more than one half. At the period in question,

1836, the number of machines making fancy-net in the Midland district was increasing, and great improvements were also in the course of being introduced into the mechanism. Indeed it was then estimated that 1,000 machines had been raised from the value of £2 to £10 each, to the value of from £50 to £100 each; while from 1,500 to 2,000 men were employed in making fancy goods, over and above the number to whom work could be given in the manufacture of plain nets.

Since 1836 no census of the number of machines employed in the lace trade has been taken, but I am informed upon the highest authority in the manufacture that the numerical account of the machines in use remains pretty stationary, but that their productive power has, by the introduction of mechanical improvements, greatly increased. Indeed, the improvement in the machinery employed in lace-making may be conceived from the following extraordinary fact: in 1810 and 1811, a square yard of a particular kind of lace fetched £5. In 1824 its price was 15s. In 1847 it might have been purchased for 5d. Part of this astounding reduction is owing to the cheapening of the raw material, but of course the great cheapening agent was improved machinery.

The lace of Nottingham is manufactured from cotton and silk threads. These yarns are spun in Manchester and Coventry. For the manufacture of lace it is requisite that they should be loosely doubled. This doubling process is partly performed in Lancashire and Warwickshire, partly in and around the town of Nottingham. The doubling mills are worked principally by women and children, superintended by male overlookers. The processes are simple. The yarn is received from the fine spinning mills of the North in bundles called "cops", and placed on the doubling frame. Spindles are passed longitudinally through these cops, two of the latter being transfixed on each of the former, and the threads are then by power machinery rapidly run off the whirling cops and on to bobbins, each couple of threads being doubled and loosely twisted round each other in the winding process. Women superintend the operation, assisted by children to change and replace the bobbins and cops. The thread is next taken to the clearing frame, where it is run through delicate metal interstices. The occurrence of any lump or inequality breaks the thread, which is the workman's business to knot again so daintily and delicately as to permit it to run through the testing aperture. If thread of a particularly fine quality be wanted, the filament is next passed several times through the flame of gas, so as to burn off all downy fibre attaching to it. The fourth process consists in unwinding from the bobbins, and reeling the thread into hanks or "slips"; and the final operation is that of the "preparing frame", where the thread is squeezed through cylinders exerting a pressure of from 80 to 100 lbs weight, in order to smooth and give it gloss. The doubling factories come under the regulations of the Ten Hours Bill, and work daily for that period. They employ about four children for every ten women. The wages of the former range from 3s to 4s per week, those of the latter from 6s 6d to 7s 6d per week.

The Lace-Making Process

I proceed to the description of the simplest species of lace-making—that known as the warp trade. The warp machine—as I have stated—sprung directly from the knitting frame. In its uses the former is an extremely flexible apparatus. It is capable of making plain nets, fancy nets, and blonds, with all the tribe of lace "borderlings", known as "tattins", "pearlings", "quillings", and so forth. Purses and braces of silk or any other material can be wrought upon the warp frame. It is used also for the fabrication of strong fleecy hosiery, gloves, stockings, and under-garments; and latterly it has been made to weave very good cloth. The jacquard has been applied to the warp, but I understand that the class of fancy goods constructed by its help is now being almost uniformly made by the twist or bobbin-net machines. The warp is, as I have said, generally wrought by hand.

Formerly the manufacture was principally domestic; now the machines are very generally being gathered into factories; but as yet factory regulations are by no means uniformly applied to these concentrations of machinery. The system of obliging the workman to pay rents for their warp-frames is a vestige of the knitting trade, from which the warp manufacture has sprung. The system, however, in this branch of manufacture is not universal. There are in fact two scales of wages in use, the journeymen's and the "independent" workmen's rates. In the case of the former, the goods manufactured are paid for according to a certain scale and no frame rent is exacted. In the case of the latter, the scale is fixed at higher rates, and a certain stipulated rent is paid weekly. This rent differs with the width and capabilities of the machine, but I am informed that a fair average is about 3s 6d. A few of the warp frames are charged as high as 5s weekly.

When the mechanism is not collected in factories, the work is generally received from the manufacturer and given out by middlemen. This is another relic of the framework knitting trade. If a workman be the proprietor of a warp machine, he will frequently purchase the requisite yarns from the large manufacturer and sell the lace in the best market on his own account, but the constant tendency of the trade is to concentrate the machinery in factories, or at all events to concentrate the management of it in the hands of middlemen, each of whom may superintend a dozen frames. The warp machines are wrought either by jerking a pair of levers, or by a rotatory motion like turning the handle of a winch. The men frequently have their children to assist them in operating upon the latter class of machines. In the lever frames the feet are used to work treadles, as in a loom. Although the machinery looks heavy, and the frames are sometimes fully twelve feet broad, the mechanism is so nicely balanced, that the toil of putting it into motion cannot be said to be severe. In this respect, however, different frames vary materially.

A not unimportant branch of the employment consists in warping, or placing the warp thread in due order for different patterns upon the beam. When a workman labours at home, the middleman furnishes him with the beam ready warped. In factories there are men engaged upon warping who do nothing else, and are generally paid regular wages, averaging from 16s to 18s per week. The girls who do the requisite winding from the skeins on to bobbins—always one of the initial processes in textile manufacture—work in the factories generally about eleven hours a day, and are paid about 7s a week. The warp factory rooms are seldom large. Six or eight frames is an ordinary number to find working together. No artificial heat is required. In some factories the men are charged for candle or gas light; this is when the machines are worked by relays. When only a single hand is employed at a frame, as he labours principally by daylight, no such exaction is usually imposed. The relay system is one which obtains to a very considerable degree, and forms one of the characteristic features of the lace trade. I am informed that, particularly in the case of the bobbin-net machines, the value of the mechanism is so great, as compared with the fabric manufactured by it, that to obtain a due return for the capital sunk, it is necessary that the machinery should be kept in motion for a greater number of hours per day than in the instance of any other species of textile mechanism with which I am acquainted. Both bobbin-net and warp machines are sometimes wrought twenty hours out of the twenty-four. Two men belong to each machine, and relieve each other every four or six hours. The shifts alternate their task-times every week, so as to come in for the bulk of the night work in turns.

One of the principal drawbacks in the warp trade arises from the necessity of occasionally changing the class and pattern of fabrics produced. The process of disposing the myriad threads so as to fit them for being wrought into new combinations, is not only toilsome but tedious. Very often an alteration will keep two men working during a week, and for this they receive no remuneration whatever. They are paid by the piece, and the week which sees no piece produced sees no wages earned. In the branch of warp-lace-making, the operatives suffer much during the winter season from slackness of work. I have heard many complaints from the men labouring by shifts of the pressure of the night-toil. "After a week of it", said one of them to me, "I'm fit for nothing on the Sunday. I may go and take a little walk perhaps after breakfast, and then I go to bed, and sleep the rest of the day." When making alterations, some proprietors allow the men to draw a portion of their wages on account, others will not advance a farthing. The trade, it is right to say, is at present to a great extent in a transition state. The twist machines have taken a considerable portion of the fancy work formerly wrought by the warps; but I understand that some new branches of lace manufacture are likely to infuse fresh life into the warp trade. The bordering fabrics commonly manufactured are wrought upon the warps in broad webs, and the disentanglement of each particular stripe of tattin, or pearling, forms one of the manual employments which occupy children in the lace districts, and to which I shall come speedily. The wages earned by the warp-frame workers vary widely, ranging from 23s and 25s down to beneath 10s. A number of workmen to whom I referred the question, after a long consultation told me that in their deliberate and candid opinion, the average wages earned by warp-work knitters, clear of all deductions, were from 12s to 14s per week.

I now come to the bobbin-net or twist branch of the lace trade. Here the most complex and expensive machinery is employed in the production of the most delicate and elaborately patterned lace. I have not, the reader will perceive, attempted to explain the mechanism of the warp-frame. I shall still less endeavour to describe that of the twist machine, which of itself is by far the most profoundly complex apparatus existing in the range of textile mechanism; while in many cases ingenious adaptations of the jacquard give the machinery an additional degree of elaborate complication. To build a twist machine requires an outlay of at least £500. As I have already stated, steam power is now being generally applied to the working of these splendid pieces of mechanism—the number of those wrought by hand being daily decreasing. As in the case of the warp-trade, the factories are not generally of great size. In fact, nothing like the vast, grimy, bricken box with which we naturally associate the word "factory", is to be seen in Nottingham. The twist factory rooms there are generally moderate-sized apartments.

Besides the work of placing the warp upon the beam, which I have already alluded to, there is another set of preliminary processes characteristic of the branch of lace manufacture in question. These are involved in the use of the "bobbins and carriages", which, to employ a very rough and in some respects inaccurate analogy, perform one function of the shuttle, and supply the weft to the warp—the machine by its own operations gradually emptying the bobbins of their contents. The charging with the thread, and final preparation of these bobbins, are processes partly performed by women, and partly, notwithstanding the dexterous and delicate manipulation requisite, by little imps of boys, often under ten years of age.

The first thing to be done is the ordinary process of winding the thread from the hank upon common pirns or bobbins. Women or children perform the work, the former getting from 6s to 8s a week, the latter from 2s to 3s. From the bobbins the thread is again wound upon large cylinders called drums, a great many threads from many bobbins being rolled on simultaneously. This operation, requiring more care, is paid for at rather a higher rate, the boys who perform it earning from 4s to 4s 6d weekly.

The next process is the first belonging exclusively to the twist trade, and is usually performed by a woman. It consists of putting the thread upon the bobbins used in the machinery. These bobbins are flat circular pieces of brass, each about the size of a small Geneva watch, and so deeply grooved, as only to be connected in the centre by a small piece of metal. Round this the thread is wound, sheathed, of course, on each side by its brass case. The way in which the bobbins are filled is ingenious. The operator takes up a number corresponding to the number of threads upon the drum, passes the bobbins by means of a central perforation upon a revolving cylinder, and then, stretching the threads over them, slips each into its respective groove. A few rapid turns to the handle of the winding mechanism and the bobbins, revolving at great speed, fill themselves from the ample supply of the drum. The operator then slips them off the cylinder, puts on a fresh set, adjusts the threads by passing the full bobbins delicately over the empty ones, then snips the threads in question with her scissors, lays the full bobbins aside, and proceeds again to fill the new batch. The wages earned at this species of work are about 10s a week.

The bobbins, being filled, have now to be inserted in the "carriages"— the latter slight steel frameworks, forming the cases in which the former wheel round. Through a minute hole in one part of the frame or carriage, the other end of the thread upon the bobbin has to be passed. The inserting of the bobbins and the threading of the carriages are performed by boys with a rapidity and neatness of manipulation which makes the process almost appear like legerdemain. The wages of these boys are about 3s 6d per week. In other respects their condition is by no means a satisfactory one, from the irregularity and frequent length of their hours. Their services are, of course, only required when the bobbins want refilling; but those periods are very uncertain and continually vary. A dozen twist machines may start together making the same pattern, driven by the same steam-engines, and with the same quantity of thread on their bobbins; yet as accidental delays in greater or less number continually occur, it generally happens that a dozen sets of bobbins become exhausted at different times. Whenever that exhaustion occurs, however, by day or by night, the bobbin-fillers and threaders must be set to work. Sometimes these children are required to be if not working at least in attendance from four o'clock in the morning until after midnight. Part of this hardship might be avoided by using a double set of bobbins and carriages, and in some factories this is actually the case. These delicately-fashioned articles are, however, very expensive.

The beams being duly in place, and the bobbins and carriages set in order, the machine is ready for work. In 1835 the average hours of labour in the west of England were 13; in Nottingham, Derby and Leicester they were, and still are, 20 hours a day. The relay system is, of course, requisite. In the first factory I visited the machinery was wrought 18 hours. The first man commenced operations at six a.m., working until 9 a.m. The second took his place from 9 a.m. till one p.m. The first man again resumed his post from one p.m. until six p.m., and the second superintended the frame from six p.m. until midnight. The shifts equalised their respective working hours by changing turns every week. In another factory working 20 hours the following arrangements were adopted: A wrought from 4 a.m. until 9 a.m.; B from 9 a.m. till until one p.m. A resumed his post again from one p.m. until six p.m., and B from six p.m. until midnight—an arrangement fairly dividing the 20 hours. So long as the machinery works steadily and without hitch and there is no breakage in the multitudinous array of threads, the workman may be a mere spectator, but he must always be a vigilant one. His eye must be continually fixed upon the hundred threads, wires, hooks, and wheels which throb and quiver before him. The breaking of a single filament, of course, involving the necessity of stopping the machine, and carefully and delicately repairing the damage. So exquisitely delicate, indeed, is the mechanism, that a few moments' inattention to a single ruptured thread may lead to a smash both amid fabric and machinery which it will cost the workman days and the master pounds to repair.

A regular source of delay and consequently of loss to the workman is involved in the refitting and shifting of the bobbins, particularly when, as sometimes happens, half-a-dozen machines are exhausted nearly at the same time, and there is but one set of bobbin threaders to supply them. But a still more formidable cause of loss of time is the periodical alterations of the warp, for the purpose of placing on the machine new patterns. These alterations are seldom effected under three days, and sometimes they occupy a fortnight—the average may be something under a week. In some factories the workmen are paid an allowance while "standing for alteration" of from 12s to 15s per week. In others they only get an advance, which is repaid by half-crown instalments, deducted from their subsequent weekly wages. This system of advances and forced repayments is considered by some of the highest authorities in the trade as objectionable, commercially and socially speaking. If any holes or similar imperfections be found in the lace after it has been taken off the machines, the men have to pay for the mending by needlework. Sometimes a regular sum is deducted from their wages for mending; in other cases they are mulcted from week to week in proportion to the actual amount of breakage. The former plan is more popular among the men, as they say under it they at least know what to expect on Saturday night. Lace workers in factories usually pay for lights. If the men work by relays, the sum exacted is 1s 6d per week each. If one man only works a machine, he pays 1s. The operatives employed upon hand machines have generally to hire a boy to help them to turn, and who is paid by them about 4s per week. The net amount of wages paid to good hands in the twist trade is considerable. There are some men at bobbin-net machines who can earn 35s to 40s per week.

Making allowances for stoppages, a tolerably skilful hand working at fancy goods will make from 25s to 30s per week. The average amount may be taken as 18s or from that to 20s; and the lowest earned by the youngest hands is about 10s. In the first factory which I visited—one producing exquisitely beautiful fancy goods—the first workman whom I questioned stated that he was earning 27s or 28s per week; another superintending the production of an imitation of Mechlin lace said he was making 22s 6d; and a third, engaged upon a filmy species of silk lace, was receiving about a £1. The general run of wages, however is below these. There is no regular apprenticeship served to the twist trade. Failing eyesight is the great bane of a workman in all branches not only of the lace but of the hosiery trade. The vision too often becomes early impaired from the strain to which it is subjected, and men are often compelled to give up the most profitable branches of lace-making while enjoying to its fullest powers every other faculty, bodily and mental.

The lace we shall now suppose to be finished and taken from the frame whether a warp or a twist machine. It has next to undergo the processes which it receives at the hands of the dresser and gasser, and those of the bleacher. The work in a dressing and gassing establishment is carried on almost entirely by women, and is exceedingly simple. The gassing process is similar to one which I have described amid the operations of calico-printing. The net or lace, when taken from the machine, is full of downy fibres, which gave the mesh work a dull semi-opaque appearance. To get rid of these, the fabric is passed quickly along cylinders and athwart a thin sheet of gas flames extending along the entire width of the piece. Four girls or women tend the machines; two feeding the revolving cylinders with the lace, two receiving it after the flame has purged off all its superfluous filaments, and extinguishing many sparks which may appear still alive upon the material. These girls are paid 8s a week, working ten hours a day. They receive 2d per hour if called upon to work overtime. This rate of 2d per hour is that very commonly paid for overtime in female labour in many departments of lace-making. Having been gassed, the fabric is handed over to the bleacher, who submits it to those processes common to the blanching of all textile materials, and which therefore need not be more particularly alluded to here. The fabric is then returned to the dresser's establishment to be stiffened. This operation is performed by passing the bleached and purified pieces through a hot mixture of gum and starch boiled together, and then submitted the reeking lace to the action of revolving cylinders, which squeeze out the surplus stiffening fluid. The labour requisite is here all but unskilled. It is generally performed by a man and two or three boys, the former earning 18s, the latter from 6s to 8s per week.

The dank masses of lace with their folds sticking to each other through the agency of the clammy mixture, are now hurried away to the stretching rooms. These consist of vast extending corridors, down which runs a framework, something like a long skeleton table, the edges bristling with close-set wire points or teeth. The girls employed, each of them armed with a little bamboo cane, range themselves at the upper end of the room, on either side of the framework, while a boy carrying the clammy wreaths of lace in a basket walks down the centre. The upper corners of the piece having been already fastened to the upper corners of the framework, the girls, following the boy down the skeleton table, fasten with nimble fingers the sides of the extending web to the rows of wire teeth, at the same time switching it with their canes or "bats", so as to get rid of all the extra starch, and to dislodge any little impurity which may have clung to the meshes. When the whole web is fixed, one of the women turns the handle of the winch. The beams of the framework instantly recede from each other, and the lace is extended out as rigidly as though the threads were iron wires. The material is now left to dry, while the girls proceed to repeat the process in another gallery. Matters are sought to be so arranged that by the time the lace is stretched in the last corridor, it is dry in the first. Should this not be the case, however, the girls fan it with light spade-shaped implements, very broad in the blade, the sweeps of which, wielded by skilful hands, produce powerful currents of air. When thoroughly dry, the lace is disengaged, and folded in readiness to be sent off to the warehouse. In the stretching and dressing rooms the women employed are paid 1s 6d per day, with 2d an hour for over-work. The regular hours are generally from eight o'clock until one, and from two o'clock until six. The temperature in which the labour is carried on is extremely high, the thermometer in a stretching room being seldom below 80. In some establishments the heat is more complained of than in others, and in almost all the girls have a thin, pale look.

I now proceed to describe shortly the different processes in lace manufacture carried on by manual labour of women and children. Of these, the two most important are mending and tambour, or embroidery work. The minor operations are "running", "catching up", and "drawing". I shall first refer to tambour work. It consists of embroidering plain net with flowers or fancy figures by means of a delicate hook called a crochet needle. Comparatively little tambour work is done at Nottingham. The manufacturers find it cheaper to disperse the labour throughout the neighbouring counties. There is hardly a hamlet in the Midland shires of England where the wives and daughters of cottagers do not eke out the general income by help of the tambour frame. Indeed, the Nottingham lace manufacturers look still further for female labour. The partners of one of the first lace embroidery houses in the town informed me that much of their very best work was performed in Essex. The inferior sorts of tambouring, however, are uniformly executed in the villages around Nottingham, Leicester, and Derby. "I can get," said a warp manufacturer to me, "I can get lace embroidered in the county for 2s and 3s, for which I would have to pay 4s or 6s in Nottingham; and in the country cottages they keep it cleaner too. All round the town, however, the crochet needle is plied in almost every second house. The lace is stretched upon a frame large enough to enable several persons to work upon it at the same time. The occupation, although in one respect graceful and feminine, is of course severe upon the eyes; and from its perfectly sedentary nature, and the stooping position which it demands, is apt to create pulmonary and digestive complaints. The great mass of the embroidery performed round and near Nottingham is managed by middlewomen or "missusses", who receive the work from a warehouse at a fixed rate, and give it out to whom they please, and take it back when finished. Sometimes the "missusses" give the lace to women to be tamboured at home; sometimes they assemble at their (the "missusses") own houses as many girls and children as they can accommodate—the latter thus plying their tasks in the various departments of the trade under their patronesses' immediate superintendence.

The wages of the most skilful and most industrious lace tambourer, employed upon the best work, very rarely amount to 10s a week, and still more rarely exceed that sum. The average may be from 6s to 7s a week, but many, especially in the country, do not earn so much. The middlewomen, of course, pocket a goodly percentage of the wages, amounting, as I am informed, to something like 3d out of the shilling; and they always endeavour to keep up their influence and their profits by preventing any communication between their employees and the manufacturers—keeping the former in ignorance, if possible, of the warehouse for which they are working. A tambourer whom I visited in Nottingham was a married woman, with a family, which prevented her from earning above 3s a week. If she had no domestic duties to perform, and stuck to the work closely, she might make from 5s 6d to 6s. To gain that sum would take twelve hours labour the very least. She had her work second-hand, and did not know for what warehouse it was intended. Could she have the lace direct from the manufacturer, she calculated that she could earn at least 7s per week, but few or none of the warehouses would have anything to do with single hands. The middlewoman saved the former a great deal of trouble and the workpeople paid for it. This was the substance of the account given by several tambourers visited, of their situation and earnings. They alternated to a greater or less extent their needle with their household labours. Those girls who met and worked together I generally found assembled in clean and tidy rooms. They gave their earnings at from 10d to 1s 3d per day.

The remaining kinds of lace needlework which I have enumerated are performed partly at the warehouses and partly at the homes of the workpeople. The chief of these employments is "mending", an operation requiring a quick eye and a practised hand. The menders fill up any accidental holes in the lace with such neatness that the injured part can hardly, if at all, be recognised. Those who work in the warehouses are paid by the week at rates varying from 6s to 10s, and extra for overhours. The regular period of labour is from 8 a.m. to 6 p.m., with an hour for dinner, and half an hour for tea. At some warehouses from 80 to 100 girls are employed in this species of labour. Menders generally begin very young, at five or six years of age. One girl told me that she could not remember the time when she had not been mending. They are frequently short sighted. Black lace is especially prejudicial to the eyes. The statement of a lace-mender, visited at her home—a very squalid place, consisting of a single room—was as follows. She was paid 8d or 1s per piece, according to the size and number of holes to be repaired. One week with another she earned about 6s or 6s 6d. She had her house to attend to. Her little girl, eight years old, gave her some trifling help. If she were working in a warehouse she could earn about 8s. Her hours as a regular thing were very long—from six in the morning until nine o'clock, and sometimes ten o'clock at night. She had been mending lace since she was six years old. Another lace-mender stated that she was working at Mechlin lace. The price of the piece was 1s 6d. To do her piece took her over two days—sometimes more, sometimes less. If she worked at a warehouse she would have about 7s 6d per week. She had been a mender since she was five years old. The wages had fallen greatly within her own recollection. She remembered receiving six shillings a piece for mending for which she would now get only 1s 6d. Her hours were from eight o'clock in the morning until ten o'clock or eleven o'clock at night. Her earnings one week with another, were about 5s.

"Running" consists in circumscribing with a thread the outline of patterns wrought in the net by the machine. The lace is stretched upon a frame as in tambour work. Four or five "runners" working together estimated their average earnings at 1s per day each. They worked 14 and sometimes 15 hours. The best hands on the best work could not make more than 1s 4d per day, and many, particularly in the country, did not clear above 6d. For the last two years good runners had had plenty of employment. At night they lighted three candles to every four workers. Two runners—a mother and a daughter, in another house—calculated that they each made 4s 6d per week. They worked in the winter from daylight in the morning until ten at night. They got their work from a middlewoman, and were paid according to the number of figures in the pattern. These poor people were at dinner when I called. The meal consisted of bread and tea, with dripping for butter.

The remaining species of work—"drawing" and "catching up"—are generally performed either at the warehouses or at the houses of the mistresses. The wages are excessively low, and the labour—being perfectly easy, particularly that of drawing, which consists merely in pulling out the thread which unites the stripes of edging material—is chiefly performed by children, who make from 3d to 6d a day. These juvenile labourers are set to work at ages sadly early. A gentleman informed me that he has seen a baby, twenty months old, sit in a high chair at a table, and gravely employed in drawing lace.

The missuses, or middlewomen, have generally themselves been embroiderers or menders. They very often have money-lending transactions with their employees, and instances are not unfrequent of their carrying on the truck system in a small and modified way, supplying bread, groceries, and candles, and deducting the amount, of course with an additional percentage, from the wages paid at the end of the week. The missuses always, however, profess to supply the articles at market price, and to look to reimbursement and profit from the discounts allowed by the tradespeople.

The Hosiery Trade in Nottingham

The manufacture of hosiery is a trade almost exclusively confined to the three Midland counties of Nottingham, Leicester, and Derby. It extends over about 230 parishes—that being the number in each of which, as was ascertained by the industrial census set on foot in 1844 by Mr. Felkin, of Nottingham, not less than six framework knitting machines were in that year actually at work. The articles of hosiery manufactured—that is to say knitted upon the frames, and afterwards either seamed or stitched by women—are gloves, stockings, drawers, under-waistcoats, and a variety of small miscellaneous pieces of dress; amongst which may be reckoned the outside woollen jackets sometimes worn by women and children, and for which Leicester of late has acquired some celebrity. The materials used by the framework knitter are cotton, silk, wool, and various combinations of them. The trade, which may be called a semi-domestic one, is marked by not a few peculiar characteristics. It has been for at least half a century an occupation in which a miserable degree of chronic distress has prevailed, and framework knitting has long been treated as one of the very lowest of textile manufactures.

The Rise and Progress of the Hosiery Trade

The knitting frame, it is commonly known, originated in the county of Nottingham. The somewhat curious account of the invention ordinarily received is that it was the contrivance of William Lee, a scholar, and the incumbent of Woodborough, early in the time of Elizabeth. The reverend gentleman, finding a lady to whom he was attached generally more intent on her knitting needles than interested in his protestations, vowed that he would construct a machine which should revenge him upon the fair one's primitive occupation. The result was the first stocking-frame. It was set up in London in a house in Bunhill fields. Queen Elizabeth in person visited the ingenious artist, and accepted a present of hose wrought by the new mechanism. At the outset, Lee met with fame and encouragement; but the tide soon turned. Elizabeth died and James neglected the claims of the inventor, who in consequence accepted the invitation of Sully, and established his manufacture in Rouen. But Henri IV was assassinated, his minister disgraced, and Lee, sickened with hope deferred, died poor and an alien. His brother returned to England and established the manufacture in London, where it long flourished, and where the Framework Knitters Company, a powerful and important guild, still maintains a shadowy existence. Its arms commemorate the inventor of its craft. They display a stocking-frame, supported on one hand by a clergyman, on the other by a woman displaying her useless knitting needle.

Lee's engine, simplified and improved, spread over many countries of continental Europe, and still plays a conspicuous part in the industry of Saxony. In 1669, there were 660 frames in England—400 of them in London. At that time there were only two frames in the town of Nottingham, and not one hundred in the county. In 1714, there were 2,500 frames in London, 600 in Leicester, and 400 in Nottingham. After this era the trade began to flow steadily from the capital to the central counties, one of the alleged causes being the vexatious tyranny of the Company of London. In 1753, there were only 1,000 frames in London, while the number was as great in Leicester, and half as great again in Nottingham. Up to the end of the first quarter of the last century, silk was the principal material upon the stocking-frames. In 1730, cotton hose was first produced. A succession of mechanical improvements and adaptations of the knitting machine followed, rendering the mechanism capable of producing imitations of the pillow-lace then manufactured. Knitting machinery, in fact, was the parent of lace machinery, the one trade grew out of the other, and the elder and younger branches of industry have long continued close neighbours. In 1782, the number of frames in England was about 20,000, and of these more than 17,000 worked in the Midland counties. In 1812 the number in Notts, Leicester and Derby was more than 29,000.

Wages in the Hosiery Trade

The hosiery trade has frequently been a suffering one. The wages being paid for lace working were amongst the highest—as those earned by hose-knitting were amongst the lowest—of all the branches of textile industry. The general causes of this last phenomenon were stated by Mr. Muggeridge, in his report upon the hosiery trade, to be the frequent surplus of labour in the market, sometimes occasioned by the very irregular demand for the goods produced, but the perpetual and chronic source of which was the comparative facility with which the process of manufacture could be acquired, and which constantly tempted women and unemployed workpeople of other trades to engage in it; the long-continued custom of compelling the operatives, on various pretexts, to heavy deductions from their ordinary wages—deductions which made it the interest of employers to spread their work over a larger amount of frames than was necessary to its performance; and finally the exorbitant rents paid by the operatives for their frames—rents which led to the construction of a vast amount of these machines, not by manufacturers engaged in the trade, but as a profitable investment for the capital of private individuals. Mr. Muggeridge concluded his report by stating that the trade can only be maintained by a very marked improvement not only in the mode of conducting the manufacture, but in the quality of the goods produced.

At the present time, the wages of the framework knitters—partly in consequence of the recent continental turmoil, which has dislocated the foreign-made supply, partly in consequence of an improved and improving demand in the home and United States markets—are higher than the average amount throughout a long period of years. But the hours of toil are still excessively long, and the remuneration excessively scanty. In the industrial census taken in 1844 already referred to, there are very ample returns of the hosiery wages throughout all the districts in which the trade is carried on. A few of these interesting results I threw into tabular form—and that the more readily, as I shall presently have to state the prices now paid for framework knitting in the chief seats of industry throughout the three counties.

LEICESTERSHIRE IN 1844	
Rothley: Ribbed hose, clear weekly earnings per frame	4s 6d
Burbage: Cotton hose, ditto	5s 6d
Kidworth: Wrought worsted hose, ditto	5s 6d
Hinckley: Cotton and Worsted, ditto	5s 3d
Leicester: Ditto	6s 6d
DERBYSHIRE	
Egglestone: Plain fashioned hose, clear weekly earnings per frame	5s 6d
Alfreton: Plain cotton and silk	5s 6d
Belper: { Hose, ditto	6s 0d
Belper: { Gloves, ditto	8s 6d
Chesterfield: Hose, ditto	5s 6d
Derby: Silk hose, ditto	6s 6d
NOTTINGHAMSHIRE	
Kirkly: Socks and half hose, clear weekly earnings per frame	6s 6d
Eastwood: Fashioned hose, ditto	5s 0d
Newark: Plain cotton hose, ditto	5s 6d
Bulwell: Gloves, ditto	7s 6d
Nottingham: Hose, ditto	7s 6d

The general summing up of wages is given as follows: "The average net earnings for sixty hours clear labour throughout the counties of Nottinghamshire and Derbyshire in the following sub-divisions of employment are—wrought cotton hose 6s; silk hose 7s 3d; silk knitted hose, 8s; plain silk gloves 7s 9d; wrought cotton gloves, narrow frames, 6s 6d; cut up cotton gloves 7s 6d; cut up cotton hose 8s 0d; drawer and pantaloon branches 7s 6d." Appended to the statement, some results of which I have given, are annexed various cases arranged in a tabular form, detailing the exact amount of wages earned by individuals and families, with the primary and necessary deductions, such as trade expenses and house rent—and showing the actual amount of money weekly available in each family, per head for food and clothing. From these curious and valuable tables I select the following results:

	s	d
In Belgrave 57 persons had weekly, out of which to food and clothe themselves, per head	0	10
In Barlestone 35 persons, ditto	1	3¼
In Sheepshead from 2s to 8¼d—average	1	0
In Loughborough, 21 persons	0	10

From the notes appended it would appear that in many instances the knitters had not had new coats for periods ranging from ten to twenty years—that the clothing purchased was very often obtained from second-hand stalls—and that the families were usually in a state of wretched raggedness.

Location of the Hosiery Industry

The district which is understood to be the area of the hosiery manufacture contains, as I have stated, 230 parishes—the boundary towns being in a general way, Chesterfield on the north, Newark on the east, Ashby-de-la-Zouche on the west, and Market Harborough on the south. These topographical limits would indicate a space about 70 miles in length and 45 in breadth. Within this area the twist machine and the knitting frame reign pre-eminent. To proceed to a more detailed topographic allotment of the hosiery trade. There were in 1844, in the county of Notts, 60 parishes, in each of which there were more than 6 frames at work. The number of separate shops or working places in the county was ascertained to be 4,621, and the total number of frames 16,382, of which 14,879 were, at the time of the inquiry, in operation. In the county of Leicester there were 100 parishes in each of which more than six frames were at work, and the total number of frames was 20,861, of which 18,558 were in operation. In the county of Derby there were 60 parishes in which more than six frames were at work, and the total number of frames was 6,797, of which 6,005 were in operation. The total number of frames, therefore, in the three counties, may be stated as about 44,000. This was the number in 1844, and as the number of new frames constructed in the three counties, between the years 1833 and 1844, was not above 1,000, it may be assumed that the estimate of 1844 is a tolerably close approximation to the statistics of the trade of the present day. In the last census, the number of individuals employed in framework knitting was reckoned as about 53,000. This estimate however gives a false idea. When we reckon not only the men and women—the number of the latter, I may state, is fast diminishing—who actually ply the machines, but the number of women and children directly connected with the trade, and who are occupied in winding the thread, and seaming and stitching the goods after they are removed from the frame, it may be fairly estimated that the number of people closely connected with and dependent upon the hosiery manufacture considerably exceeds 100,000. This mass of population is to a great extent scattered over the three counties, in great numbers of small villages and hamlets, the names of which are only locally known. In the three principal towns of Leicester, Nottingham, and Derby, there were in 1844 only 8,000 frames, forming less than one-fifth of the whole number.

The different branches of the hosiery trade are pretty equally divided throughout the several localities in which they abound. In the town of Nottingham, however, only a small quantity of silk hose is manufactured, the staple in that material being gloves. Cotton drawers and hose are produced to a very considerable extent. In Derby the main hosiery articles manufactured are silk. In Leicester a vast quantity of spun-thread gloves, of the kind ordinarily called "Lisle", are knitted, and there is also an important production of woollen and fleecy hosiery. The minute subdivisions into which the manufacture of hosiery is split are almost endless. But one great distinction runs through the whole trade, separating the production of all articles of all materials into two general classes called "fashioned" and "cut up" goods. Although the definition may not in all cases be technically correct, the phrases may be explained by saying that "fashioned" articles are those which receive their shape during the manufacture of their fabric—which are in fact knitted in the form they are intended to assume. "Cut-up" pieces, on the contrary, are made in square breadths, often extending across the entire width of the knitting-frame, and afterwards cut into shape with the scissors. In "fashioned" pieces the operative forms a "selvage" along either edge, so as to permit the opposite sides or halves of a garment to be seamed together. In "cut-out", on the contrary, the sides are joined by the more clumsy, and to the wearer, less comfortable, fashion of stitching. Of the two modes of manufacture the "fashioned" is of course the best, requires the most skilful workmen, and commands the highest wages; but a spurious article is sometimes manufactured—a "cut-out" in reality, but a "fashioned" piece in appearance—and of course intended to command the price of the latter in the market, while the knitter only receives the earnings commonly given for the former. This is one of the grievances of the framework knitting trade, and for the removal of which the men contend that all goods prepared upon frames should be sent into market officially stamped with their real quality.

The Organisation of the Knitting-Frame Trade

A very great proportion—more than two-thirds—of the frames belong to the hosiers or manufacturers, who give them out to undertakers or middlemen, these last letting them in turn to the workmen. A middleman may have only two or three, or he may have as many as twenty or thirty frames. These he sets up in his own house—always, in Nottingham, in the highest story, so far as he has room for them. The others if there be any, he sub-lets to knitters, who establish them in their own homes. The proportion of frames which do not belong to hosiers are often the property of frame-smiths, or of individuals unconnected with the trade. These machines are called "independent frames", although those who work them are generally the most thoroughly dependent class of individuals in the trade. Very few of the regular knitters possess frames of their own. The work comes so habitually through the channels of the undertakers, that property in machines would be of small use to operatives, who of course could never look for a supply of labour so long as one frame belonging to a hosier, or under the patronage of a middleman, was standing idle. Indeed, I have heard of repeated instances in which a knitter who was the proprietor of a frame had to submit to the usual rent and charges payable by those who use the machinery of others, before he could secure a day's employment.

The middleman then receives the yarn to be wrought from the hosier, with the necessary instructions, undertakes the due performance of the labour, and then sets his subordinates to work. He is responsible for the material and for the machines entrusted to his care. In respect to the hosier, he acts as a sort of foreman and manager; in respect to the men, he acts as a sort of agent and work collector. Rightly performed and upon a fair footing, there would be evident convenience in the ministration of such a functionary; and I do not find that the framework-knitters object to the middleman so strongly as they do certain of the exactions which, by custom of the trade, he has a right to enforce. The hosiers or warehousemen, on the one hand, state that it would be impossible for them and inconsistent with their other business, to control and manage the separate accounts of perhaps a hundred knitters, working in localities scattered throughout the town and district; while the operatives acknowledge that it is better than one agent should obtain and fetch work for perhaps a dozen men at a time, than that each individual should be obliged to repair to the warehouse on his own account as often as the yarn entrusted to him was worked up. The great grievance alleged by the workman lies in the rent and frame charges. These charges are full of minute shades of difference, indeed, the great difficulty in dealing with this as well as the lace trade is the prevalence of the most puzzling diversities of detail—each slight variation frequently involving a totally different class of trade customs and usages. But after paying some attention to the subject, I believe I may state that 3s is a tolerably close approximation to the average sum weekly paid by each framework knitter under the name of frame rent and charges. This amount is made up by the following items:—

Frame rent	1s 3d
Taking-in	0 9
Standing room	0 3
Winding	0 9
	3 0

The frame rent goes of course to the proprietor of the machine. The "taking-in" is the commission paid to the middleman for his trouble in receiving the yarns and orders, taking back the manufactured goods, and keeping the accounts. The "standing room" is the rent paid to the same person for the space taken up by the frame in his house. The winding—that is, of the thread from the hank to the bobbin—is likewise generally, but not always, paid to the middleman, who of course makes a profit upon that also. In the rarer case of a knitter having a frame at his own house, he may keep the charge for winding in his family; but it often happens that even in these instances the workman must pay the middleman for "standing room" quite irrespectively of where the frame may really be. This is especially the case when the middleman allows the knitter as a favour to have his frame in his own house. "If I let you have the frame at your home as a convenience to you, you must pay standing room all the same, as a convenience to me." This is the nature of the understanding usual in such instances. The rent of the frame varies, of course, with the breadth and capability of the instrument, but none that I heard of were let under 1s weekly. Half a dozen frames are a common number for a middleman to set up in his house.

Although virtually a factory in miniature, no sort of factory regulations are enforced in such establishments, the men come and go when they please, and labour as hard or as easily as they like. The middleman commonly, however, stipulates that the work shall be performed within certain reasonable hours—say from five or six in the morning until eleven or twelve at night. Towards the latter end of the week, however, I am informed that the knitters often labour all the night through in order to get the work for the Saturday delivery to the warehouse; and as a general thing, their hours of labour are exceedingly long. In the first frame-shop which I entered, the people stated that they usually worked from six o'clock a.m. until ten or eleven o'clock p.m. These are described as very ordinary hours in the trade. The manufacture being carried on was that of drawers and under-waistcoats. In the second shop I visited, a silk-glove factory, the hours were described as being from seven in the morning until ten o'clock at night, with an hour for dinner, and a half-hour for tea. As is more or less the case, however, in all kinds of labour not brought under regular discipline, framework knitters are sometimes given to work by fits and starts. This is especially the case with the quickest hands in the trade; and I have been again and again informed that in many instances they are among the most intemperate. They will work with unnatural perseverance for two and three days, and then go and drink for the other two and three days, and boast of the money they have earned. "When a master," said a very intelligent workman to me, "talks of our wages, and how much we could earn if we had a mind, it is very often to cases like those that he points."

The frame rent, the standing room, and the taking-in, are none of them exacted, if the machine has been idle throughout the week. This is the rule, whether the frame belong to a hosier who ordinarily supplies the work, or to a person not in the trade. But if more than one day's work has been performed the full rent and charges are payable and exacted. This is one of the most palpable anomalies in the frame rent system, and one naturally and directly leading to the construction of more frames than there is occasion for—not as implements of work, but as implements for bringing in rents. The system occasionally assumes this flagrant form: a middleman will obtain, say, six frames from a hosier, in addition to six others under the control of, or belonging to, himself. The work which he obtains from the hosier to keep the latter six frames going he will spread over the twelve, and thus pocket a double set of full perquisites, wrung from persons to whom he only gives half work. This, I am assured, is a case of no unfrequent occurrence; and modified in various ways, it is undoubtedly the tendency of the whole frame rent system to give rise to similar or analogous evils. Frames are thus often built by persons who never intend to be parties to the production of one inch of knitted stuff. The original cost of a machine of this kind is on the average from £16 to £20, and with ordinary care it will last, without being repaired, for a dozen years. One workman had assured me that he had worked a frame for nearly twenty-five years ere any repair became necessary. A very small amount of calculation is requisite to prove what a profitable investment was the capital sunk in such an apparatus, quite apart from the more legitimate profits which it must have realised in the way of fair production.

This frame rent system has, as may be easily understood, always had the effect of leaving a large margin of machinery, the owners of which, except during times of brisk demand, were seldom or never able to obtain regular work for the men whom they nominally employed. It is, of course, always in the interest of a manufacturer owning machinery to keep that machinery as fully employed as possible; but the proprietor of an independent frame has his purpose served if the operative can earn only so much as suffices to pay the rent. Various efforts have been unsuccessfully made by the framework-knitters to rid themselves of the rent and charges system. First, the point was raised whether the exaction of frame rent was not illegal under the Truck Act, inasmuch as the workman was compelled to accept the machine, and to pay his employer for the use of it, out of his wages. Westminster Hall decided in favour of the frame rents. A bill was afterwards introduced by Sir Henry Halford to do away with the grievance, but it was thrown out. Measures are, however, at present, as I learn, being taken with a view to the re-opening of the question. A number of remedies have been proposed for the evil—many of them going upon the principle of fixing the minimum of wages. Another proposition is to gather the machines into factories, and to work them under ordinary factory regulation. The workmen, so far as I am acquainted with their sentiments, are, however, averse to this plan. They admit that it would be advantageous in many respects but they state their apprehensions that its tendency would be to prevent work from being obtained by the older and less keen-sighted men (clearness of vision is indispensable to the best paid sorts of framework knitting)—a result which they contend, is at all events prevented by the present rent system. The method most in favour appears to be the payment by the workman to the owner of the frame of a percentage upon the work actually performed.

I have said that the principle on which the frame charges are calculated varies as respects different classes of goods. This is specially the case in certain branches of the silk-glove manufacture, in which the deductions are calculated by the dozen of gloves produced. A statement of the items in detail will give a fair notion of the drawbacks to which the wages of the men are subject, and of one of the modes of levying them. For the production of a dozen pairs of a common class of gloves, of the cut up species, 3s 9d is the regular price paid by the warehouseman to the undertaker. From the 3s 9d are deducted the following charges:

Stitching	0s 8d
Winding	0s 1½d
Rent of frame	0s 2d
Standing room	0s 0¾d
Taking in	0s 2¾d
	1s 3d

Leaving for the knitter as his actual earnings, 2s 6d. Take another class of gloves—one of which great quantities are made, and for the production of a dozen of which the warehouse pays the middleman 4s 11d. In this department of the manufacture two men are employed with two frames upon each dozen of gloves; one making the hands, the other the fingers. The proportion paid to the latter will be the greatest, seeing that about eight dozen of hands can be made to six dozen of fingers. The knitter's share of the 4s 11d will be lessened by the following deductions:

Seaming	0s 10d
Winding	0s 1½d
Rent of frame	0s 4d
Standing room	0s 2d
Taking-in	0s 5½d
	1s 11d

Leaving for knitters as their actual earnings 3s, thus divided: 1s 1½d for the hand-maker, 1s 10½d for the finger-maker; total 4s 11d. It will be seen that in the first estimate, the frame-owner's rent was 2d, and in the second 4d in the respective dozens, while the net profit of the middleman— the taking-in and the standing room—in the first transaction was 3½d, and in the second 7½d. I shall now, still keeping in the glove trade, lay before the reader some statements of figures, from which I believe that a fair average of the present rate of wages can be arrived at. That average, taking one season of the year with another, is under 10s a week; the glove trade representing so far pretty accurately the general manufacture—some branches of the former being paid at a higher, and others at a lower rate, than the hose, drawers, and waistcoat departments.

I take again the common glove at 3s 9d. Of this sum as I have shown, 2s 6d actually goes to the workman. A fair week's work will, I am assured, produce from four to four and a half dozen. The outside of the workman's earnings will therefore be 11s 3d per week. Of thread gloves there are seven or eight different qualities. I take the sort called "sixties", for which there is a great demand. The warehouse price for a dozen of these is 2s 8d and six dozen can be made in a week. In the manufacture of these gloves, frame rent and standing room are rated at a certain fixed weekly amount, generally 3s 3d. The cast then stands thus:

Six dozen at 2s 8d		16s 0d
Deduct frame charges	3s 3d	
stitching @ 7d per dozen	3s 6d	
Total deductions		6s 9d
Net earnings		9s 3d

The warehouse prices for "cotton slights" are 1s 11½d per dozen, and eight dozen can be made in a week. The following will be the actual remuneration:

Eight dozen @ 1s 11½d		15s 8d
Deduct frame charges	3s 3d	
stitching at 5½d	3s 8d	
Total deductions		6s 11d
Net earnings		8s 9d

The warehouse price for spun silk gloves—of the kind called "38 gauze slights"—is 2s 4d per dozen, and about seven dozen is allowed to constitute a fair week's work. The account for the manufacture will stand thus:

Seven dozen @ 2s 4d		16s 4d
Deduct frame rent	3s 3d	
stitching at 6½d	3s 9½d	
Total deductions		7s 0½d
Net earnings		9s 3½d

There are, of course, many kinds of gloves and other hosiery goods, by the manufacture of which considerably higher wages can be realised; but taking one man with another, and one season with another, I am assured that the figures given above may be taken as fairly representing the wages of at least the glove-makers in the three counties. In the hosiery, and in the lace trade as well, a man soon becomes too old for the best-paying part of the business. The keen eyesight required often fails long before grey hairs come, and the best workman so far as manipulation goes must then sink back into a secondary position. Spectacles of a high magnifying power are often used; but some of the men, more careful than others, employ artificial aid only during the performance of the most delicate portion of the work. Here and there I have heard isolated complaints of a lingering truck system, carried on sometimes by the masters, but more often by the middlemen. The instances reported to me all existed in villages around Nottingham. In one of them the brother of the middleman kept a general shop, and the men were always paid there in a small inner office. After they had received their wages the middleman used to observe in an off-hand way, "I suppose you'll be going to have some bacon"—or sugar, or coffee, as the case might be—"my brother has some very good; perhaps you would find it suit you." Of course there was no resisting so considerate an intimation. In instances in which the truck system prevails, the workmen rate the price which the goods are charged as about 10 per cent higher than the market rates. Two small habitual sources of expense to the framework knitter, which I have not yet mentioned, are candles and needles. For the former, the usual price, which the middleman charges during the winter months, is a penny a day. The "needles" in question are tiny steel hooks, a great number of which are used in a frame, and which are brittle and easily broken. A knitter will estimate his needle expenses at from 2d to 3d per week. The repairs requisite for the frame are performed at the expense of the proprietor.

The Domestic Workshop

The houses in which framework-knitting is carried on in Nottingham are—as I have already explained, in reference to the town generally—constructed on the principle of a ground-story living room paved with red brick, a bedroom on the first floor, the workshop on the second, and sometimes a hole of a sleeping garret above it. The windows of the workshop are frequently long glassed strips, such as those used in weavers' houses, and the frames are ranged close to it. In the lower room it is usual to find the wives or children of the knitters engaged in winding. Sometimes old men, whose eyesight has failed them, are obliged to fall back upon this poor resource. With one of the broad knitting frames employed upon a stout fabric, the physical exertion requisite on the part of the workman is by no means inconsiderable. The machine, which, although simple compared with lace mechanism, is still too complicated to be easily explained, is moved by jerking iron levers to which both hands are applied, and the production of every new row of loops is accompanied by a loud grating noise. There is no apprenticeship served to the knitting-frame. Lads of fourteen and fifteen are frequently found working it. At one time, women as well as men found employment in the trade; but of late years they have been confined almost exclusively to the needlework branch.

Female Labour

There are two classes of needlewomen employed upon goods wrought at the frames; the seamers, whose business is with the fashioned pieces—and the stitchers, who deal with the cuts-up. These women very commonly are the wives and daughters of the knitters; but among them are to be found young girls and widows, who struggle to obtain a livelihood at a toil which is certainly the most miserable that I have seen carried on in connexion with any manufacturing process whatever. The needlework, like the knitting, is chiefly managed through the intervention of a third party—very often the middleman's wife, who naturally undertakes this part of the business. The work is always performed at the residences of the needlewomen. In answer to the first inquiries I made upon the subject, an undertaker in the silk glove branch estimated the earnings of the seamers in that department as from 3s 6d to 4s per week, and to realise this he admitted that they must work, at the very least, twelve hours per day. A "missus"—that is a female undertaker or middlewoman—in the stocking line, reckoned that 3s a week was as much as the seamers could well earn, one week with another. The prices which she paid were:

Seaming fashioned goods according to size, 6d and 7d per dozen.
Seaming half-fashioned goods, ditto, 4d, 4½d, and 5d.
Stitching cuts-up, 3d, 3½d, 4d.

The amount of work which a good hand could turn out, she reckoned, was in seaming fashioned goods, about a dozen pair a day; in seaming half-fashioned goods, about a dozen or rather more; and in stitching about two dozen; the three classes of earnings being thus 6d a day for stitching; 5d or perhaps a fraction more, for half-fashioned seaming; and 7d per day for full fashioned seaming. To earn these amounts, a day's unremitting labour of at least twelve hours was absolutely necessary. During our conversation a woman who stitched for the "missus" entered the room. She stated that she counted herself a fair hand, and that labour as she might, she could not earn above half-a-crown a week. She was receiving parish relief. She could not live otherwise.

From the "missuses", I proceeded to see some of the seamers and stitchers in their own homes. The first person of the kind upon whom I lighted was a young married woman, occupying with her husband a small choky room paved with the sort of gritty plaster common in Nottingham, and flanked by a miserable sleeping apartment, cut in two, as it were, by the slope of the roof, and perfectly lightless and airless. This species of bedroom, I may here observe, is unhappily too common in the poorer parts of Nottingham, and so notorious are its effects upon health, that the Poor Law authorities, as a general rule, refuse outdoor relief to persons occupying such dwellings. In the present case the living room, though very small was clean and tidy. The occupant stated that her husband was a bill-sticker. She stitched cuts-up. She was paid 3½d per dozen, and her general earnings were from 1s 6d to 1s 9d per week. She could finish a dozen a day if she stuck to it; but then she had her household work to attend to. On Monday she did her own and her husband's washing. The other days she worked as long as she could, and on Friday nights she generally sat up till midnight, and very often later. She thought that if she had nothing at all to attend to, she might manage 1½ dozen, and she did not count herself one of the quickest hands. The stitching was very easy to do. She could manage it almost without looking at her work. She had employment generally but not quite regularly. The rent of their rooms was 9d per week.

The next woman I saw was an elderly person living in a similar abode to the last. The room was miserably blank—the bed stretched upon the plaster floor. Two chairs and a tiny round table constituted the furniture. This woman worked at seaming cotton socks. She was paid 6d per dozen. To complete a dozen took her fourteen or fifteen hours of hard work. She was weak and not well, and she could not manage above three dozen in a week. If she were strong, she thought that she could do another dozen. As it was, 1s 6d was as much as she could make per week. Her thread was found her. (The thread is always found both in stitching and seaming.) For the seaming of some sorts of socks 6½d was paid, and she did not think that they took more time or trouble than the sixpenny ones. When she first came to Nottingham in 1810 she used to be paid 1s a dozen for seaming. She had the goods direct from the warehouse—her son, who worked there, fetching them. The woman was receiving parish relief.

The next room into which I found my way was occupied by two elderly women. One was seaming and the other stitching. The seamer said that her eyesight was failing her, and that she could not get through near so much work as she used to do. The price paid her was sevenpence per dozen. Half a dozen was as much as she could accomplish, but she knew many hands who could manage the dozen per day. She used to be able to seam nine pair, but not more. The stitcher stated that she was paid 3d per dozen. Some hands would make two dozen a day but "more would make less". She had seen a quicker stitcher than she was work very hard to make out her 1½ dozen. The seamer added that thirty years ago she had had 3d per pair for seaming. She could do many sorts of needlework connected with the hosiery trade, and she had been offered a job at "chenening" gloves, very recently. There were three patterns to be "chenened" in each glove for 3d a dozen, and she would have nothing to do with it, poor as she was.

"Chenening" is a species of embroidery, consisting in the production of the flower patterns common on the backs of spun silk gloves, and upon the ankles of superior kinds of stockings. A very considerable number of females make their living in Nottingham by chenening, and to a house where this sort of industry was going on I repaired. The cheneners I found to be two sisters. They were working at spun silk gloves. The labour requires considerable skill, and is severe for the eyes. One of the girls, although quite young, wore a pair of huge iron-mounted spectacles. They received 10d a dozen for the gloves they were chenening, and they could do about a dozen pairs a day. The prices paid in the trade ranged from 2½d per dozen to 3s. The latter sort, however, required so much work, that the rate of earnings realized by them was not more than could be got by the gloves at 10d. They generally worked ten hours a day, thus earning 1d per hour. The silk they used was found them. The best time for chenener work was the winter months. In summer, trade was generally slack, and work very short and uncertain. Chenening was an employment which a woman required great practice in before she could hope to maintain herself. The profit of chenening stockings came to about the same as chenening gloves. My informants had their work from a "missus". They would be better paid if they had it direct from the warehouse, but that was impossible, because a single hand would give as much trouble and require as long an account as a middlewoman employing fifty workpeople.

The next person I visited was also in the silk-spun glove trade. She was both a seamer and stitcher, seaming hands and stitching fingers. The gloves she worked at were "full women's size", and the warehouse for which she laboured paid less for them than any other in Nottingham. The general price was 1s per dozen, but she only received 9½d. After she had finished the batch in hand she intended to look out for some other work. She had two children and their father had deserted her. She was sure that these children had not a sufficiency of food. She could not procure it for them. The eldest (a pale little girl of seven years old) helped her with the stitching. Last week the poor little creature had earned 1s 6d. This child had been stitching since she was four years of age. She had never been to school. The mother said that she was too poor to send her. If the child went to school she must go without food. Were she an unencumbered woman, she, the mother, could earn about 8s a week. As it was she generally made from 4s to 5s a week. She paid a 1s for rent and 9d weekly for coals. This left them only 2s 6d to live on—2s 6d among three. Their food was generally bread and coffee, and sometimes bread without the coffee, and occasionally they had a herring for a treat. The room was miserably poor; the bed clothes of that rag-like texture and that dingy brownish hue which always make their material a matter of some doubt, and which I have been taught by experience invariably to associate with grinding poverty—but things looked in other respects tidy and clean, and some humble plants were arranged in pots upon the window sill.

Allotments for Workers

Gardening is a favourite amusement with the workpeople, both in the lace and hosiery trades. On the northern outskirts of the town, at a place called the "Stone Waterings" there are many small allotments of garden ground, let to the labouring classes at 1d or 1¼d per square yard. It is hoped that one of the consequences of enclosing the land, so long kept common on the outskirts of the town, will be to give facilities for the extension of a taste so rational, and often fraught with so many excellent social results.

Derby

Introduction

The town of Derby affords no bad specimen of those third-rate English cities which are at once the seats of an anciently-established population, and of a more recently-founded industrial importance. It is pleasant to see a town manifestly old and manifestly thriving—a town at once of the present and the past, pervaded by the quaint air of antiquity, and yet instinct with the living energy of an actual and a bustling prosperity. Derby neither looks as if its existence dated from the birth of the steam-engine, nor as if it had lived out its real life in by-gone days, and now lay upon the land a little better than a brick and mortar skeleton. On the contrary, the fair old Midland town has kept bravely up with the industrial march of the times. As it was the first nursery of the silk manufacture in its infancy, so it has remained one of the principal seats of this branch of industry in its prime. At the same time the industrial resources of the place are fortunately so varied, that although one branch of its trade may occasionally be in a languishing condition, the town as a whole enjoys to a high degree a general and continuous degree of prosperity.

Derby lies upon the river Derwent, a stream rising amidst the rocks of the Peak. It was a wool-stapling place in the time of the Plantagenets, the burgesses possessing repeated charters conferring on them exclusive privileges in the matters of weaving and dyeing woollen cloth. In the sixteenth century numerous fulling mills stood by the waters of the Derwent, and a thriving trade for ages was carried on in malting and the brewing of humming ale, great quantities of which were drunk in London. It was almost a century and a half ago that Derby suddenly began to rise into importance as a seat of textile industry. The knitting-frame trade, ebbing from London, took up its head-quarters in the three Midland counties, and in the year 1717, John Lombe, an ingenious and adventurous artisan, returned to his native country from Italy. Carrying with him the secret of the silk-throwing trade, as it was then practised in Piedmont, Lombe settled in Derby. The corporation leased to him, at a low rate, a swampy island in the Derwent. Then he established in the Town-Hall certain provisional machinery, and with the profits accruing from its working he erected upon his swampy island a building which still stands there, and which is now, as it was then, designated par excellence "The Silk Mill". Within its walls was produced the first silk thread spun by other than hand labour in England. Lombe, the daring and skilful adventurer, died by poison but he left the germ of a great trade behind him. The products of the silk-spinning machines soon began to be made largely available for the knitting-frames; and improvement after improvement was effected in the latter, each successive step enabling the workmen to grapple with the difficulties of producing new and more elaborate fabrics.

Aided by these useful and profitable means of employment, Derby throve apace. Before "The Silk Mill" was erected, the town boasted of 700 free burgesses and 4,000 inhabitants. It had fair public walks planted with goodly trees, a well-supplied market place, many churches, almshouses, fulling mills, and bleaching grounds. With the growth of improvement in silk-throwing and hosiery knitting, Derby rose steadily into something like its present importance, trebling its population within thirty-five years. In 1801, the town numbered only about 10,000 inhabitants; in 1811 it had increased to 13,000; in 1821 to 17,500; in 1831 to 23,000; and in 1841, to 35,019. About twenty years ago mechanism for the weaving of piece or broad silk was introduced into Derby, and about the same time the bobbin-net trade was established.

At present, then, the principal branches of textile industry pursued are the throwing of silk; the weaving of it into ribbons and trimmings by steam power, and into dress pieces by hand; the twisting of boot laces and sewing silk; and the knitting upon frames of all manner of silk hosiery. The lace trade of the town is not extensive. It is confined to a single factory, producing for the greatest part plain lace. There are about 35 silk manufactories engaged in the various branches of the trade in Derby, and in the different factories it is estimated that about 5,000 people find employment. The town possesses minor resources in its iron-founding establishments. This branch of industry has subsisted for half a century, and there exist at present nine foundries, several of them of great extent. I have stated that the population of the town in 1841 was 35,019. The number of living persons to one annual death appears by the last returns to be: males 38.4; females 41.6—giving a mean of somewhat under 40. The total number of marriages in 1840 was 450. Of these, 382 were celebrated according to the rites of the Church, and 74 in other modes. Of the 456 couples married, 103 men and 189 women signed with their marks. The number of illegitimate births during 1846 was 111. The replies returned by Derby to the questions put by the Sanitary Commission are abstracted in one of the reports of that body, much to the following effect: the local act regulating the construction of new buildings and streets is not attended to; the courts and yards are neglected; the sewers and drains are very defective; refuse accumulates in house drains to a great extent; there are no local regulations for systematic drainage, nor for the amendment and cleansing of drains actually in a foul and offensive condition; there is a regular service of scavengers. The town is supplied with water, principally from pumps and wells.

The sanitary and structural state of matters hinted at in the above replies does not seem particularly favourable. Nevertheless, in point of building arrangements the working population of Derby are very decidedly better off than their neighbours at Nottingham. Derby, in fact, has always had more elbow room. Its suburbs spread freely forth, and the town exhibits none of that structural piling and huddling, characteristic of the capital of the lace trade. Back-to-back dwellings exist, but they by no means constitute the rule; and towards the suburbs, and in most of the more recently constructed blocks of dwellings, the presence of back doors gives facilities for full and free house ventilation. The smallest class of houses contains two apartments, one above another, and the average rent is 2s, although they sometimes fetch 2s 3d, or, according to situation, 2s 6d. Tenements of a better order, with two rooms on each floor, are let at rents ranging from 3s to 3s 6d. In numerous instances these last houses are occupied by the power-loom ribbon weavers and the hands employed in the foundries. The ground floors are almost invariably paved with brick. As to the generally filthy state of the backyard, I can corroborate the replies returned to the Sanitary Commissioners. It is very common for the workshops of the framework knitters to be established in little detached buildings erected over privies and ash-pits. Courts are very common in the crowded parts of the town. The labouring classes draw their chief supply of water from pumps and wells. The fluid so obtained is clear and tasteless. The present existing waterworks company is indebted to the river Derwent, water from which is forced up into a great tank, situated in a curious locality—namely at the summit of St. Michael's Church—whence the fluid is conveyed by mains and service pipes throughout the town.

A sketch of Derby would be incomplete were all mention omitted of the well laid-out public gardens or park called the Arboretum, the free gift to the town of Mr. Joseph Strutt, the first mayor after the Reform Bill. As a pleasant place of public summer resort—half a garden, half a park—so planted and arranged as to possess a botanical interest and value, while it furnishes pleasant glimpses of parterre, shrubbery, and woodland—the Arboretum is probably unmatched in its way by the pleasure grounds of any other provincial town in England. It is freely open on Wednesdays and Sundays, and considerate arrangements have been made in ornamental lodges for the accommodation of those townsfolk who may propose to pass a day upon the green sward and bring their own provisions with them. Since its original opening, the Arboretum has been considerably enlarged by the purchase of an adjoining field. There is, I may add, a strong, and I think, reasonable desire in the public mind of Derby that these pleasure grounds should be always instead of periodically accessible.

Derby possesses one extensive cemetery beyond the walls and arrangements are on foot for the establishment of another. A new waterworks company have nearly completed their arrangements, and will commence operations some time this summer. They propose to deliver water in a filtered and perfectly pure state at the top of the highest houses—to establish four reservoirs—to guarantee a supply of 20 gallons per head per day—to keep the pressure continuously on, and to open at least 300 fireplugs in the streets. Between 1842 and 1848 about 6,600 yards of sewerage have been constructed in Derby by private individuals and about as many yards more were formed under a local act. Since the latter period, several additional drains have also been constructed but the majority of those already formed have, says Mr. Cresy, the Superintendent Inspector, been laid down "more with reference to carrying off the street waters than draining the numerous alleys and courts, and freeing them from their pollutions". Adequately to purify the 352 courts and alleys and small streets within the borough, Mr. Cresy calculates that 40,000 yards of tubular drainage, at a cost of about £20,000 will be requisite.

There are in Derby eight Churches of the Establishment, one Unitarian chapel, one Friends' Meeting House, one Roman Catholic chapel, one Independent chapel, one Congregational, four Baptist, three Wesleyan, one Methodist New Connection, two Primitive Methodist, and one Swedenborgian. With the single exception of the Friends' Meeting House, Sunday Schools are attached to all the above places of worship. The Church schools are attended by about 1,160 boys and 1,430 girls; the Catholic Sunday School by 150 boys and 150 girls; and about 2,845 children attending the different Dissenting Sunday Schools, making altogether a total of 5,735. The National and Infant schools in the borough are attended by about 1,600 children.

Silk Manufacture in Derby

I have already described, in the section on Macclesfield, a silk mill, and detailed the principal processes in the manufacture. The machinery in general use in Derby, however, is of improved and far more modern construction, as compared with the mechanism employed in the Cheshire town; and the mills in the former place are the largest, and are accounted the most perfectly organised and disciplined of any in the manufacture. Amid the Derby silk-throwing and weaving factories, the principal is the splendid establishment of Messrs. Thomas Bridgett and Co, a mill employing upwards of 1,100 hands. Without professing to give a regularly detailed account of the various departments of the manufacture of silk, as carried on in this great factory, I may advantageously introduce some notices of the process, illustrative of the earnings and the social and industrial position of the workpeople. Mr. Lewis, the managing partner of the firm, introduced the Ten Hours system into Nottingham several years before the passing of Lord Ashley's factory bill; and he informed me that the consequence was that he had, for a considerable period on that account alone, the pick and choice of the best hands in Derby. In the multitudinous operations of a throwing—that is, a silk-spinning—mill, young women and boys do the work almost exclusively under the superintendance of male and female adults. In Messrs. Bridgett's establishment the boys and girls are, as far as possible, kept apart. The several winding processes are principally performed by healthy and happy-looking little girls, earning according to their age and capacity, from 1s 6d to 3s. The number working at the former trifling wage, is however, very small—merely a few of the beginners. In the cleaning rooms older girls and young women are employed at wages averaging 7s. The spinning-frames are managed entirely by boys, under the superintendence of an overlooker. The spindles in these superb machines make upwards of 4,000 revolutions per minute, and each frame contains 306 spindles. The biggest boys are competent to manage a frame a-piece. The wages in the spinning rooms range from 4s, the lowest point, to 5s 6d, the highest. In the "staff room", in which girls of various ages perform a variety of finishing operations on the silk thread, the wages run from 5s to 6s. In the department in which the sewing silk is divided into skeins, the wages may average about 7s 6d. The soft silk winders, i.e., the young women who wind the silk after it has been dyed, so as to prepare it for the weavers, make, according to age and capability, from 2s 8d to 9s 3d. In the dye-works to which the silk is consigned after leaving the spinning frame, and before being placed upon the loom, men are of course the operators. The dyers who mix and prepare the colouring compositions receive from 28s to 30s per week. The labourers who help them, and whose work is little if at all skilled, are paid 15s, 16s, 18s.

A peculiar department in most of the silk factories in Derby, and one which exists also to a great extent at Leeds, is the manufacture of sewing silk. I was about to say that the operation is entirely carried on by hand, but I ought rather to describe it as being conducted by foot. The sewing silk rooms are long sheds or corridors, each 24 yards from end to end. At either extremity—their number depending on the breadth of the room—are placed wheel machines with hooks, exactly on the same principle as those used in a rope-walk. Opposite these wheels stand frameworks, containing large bobbins, upon which the silk thread has been wound, so as to be easily disengaged by clusters of two, three, or four filaments, as the stoutness of the sewing silk to be spun may require. The operators consist of a man stationed at each wheel, and two or more boys, his co-adjutors. It is the business of these little fellows first to seize the ends of each group of threads upon the bobbins, and run with them to the wheel at the other end of the room. The man then fastens the groups of thread, each of which form the strands to be twisted together, to the hooks on the circumference of the wheel, the boys making successive journeys with the thread until every hook around the wheel is supplied. The man then sets the machine in rapid motion—each hook, of course, firmly twisting together its own contingent of threads. When the process is complete, he breaks the latter off close by the hooks, and attaches the newly-twisted threads to a winding machine, so as to ensure their being tightly and equably rolled up.

I have described in detail a sufficiently commonplace process, because it is one in which there is more muscular motion requisite than in almost any other in the range of textile operations. The actual amount of ground covered at a sharp trot by the boys engaged is calculated at an average of from 20 to 21 miles per day. Mr. Lewis has devoted some attention to the subject and this is his estimate. The length of the thread twisted is 24 yards, giving the length of every run. There are two or three boys employed at each wheel, and each one has several runs in succession when the threads are being attached to the hooks, and a breathing time when the hoops are being whirled round. The speed at which the little fellows proceeded appeared to me to be nearer six than five miles an hour. The duration of their toil is ten hours per day. Admitting, then, Mr. Lewis's estimate of the extent of ground daily gone over, it would follow that about one-third of the entire time is passed running and two-thirds resting. The boys, however, running or not, always keep on foot. I watched this novel species of industry for some time and with some interest; and I am bound to say that the boys appeared to go through it with perfect ease. They were evidently, and no wonder, in fine running order. There was not the slighest perspiration on their faces nor did there appear anything like a difficulty in breathing. I should add that the day was intensely cold. In warm weather the case is probably different. I tried in vain to distinguish any characteristic peculiarity in the appearance of the boys. Two or three of them had no superfluous flesh on their bones; others, on the contrary, were decidedly stout. A few performed their work barefooted, with handkerchiefs lightly tied round their heads, and in their shirtsleeves. The others wore shoes, caps and jackets. The floor, I ought to mention, was composed of bricks. None of the boys whom I questioned would admit that the work tired them. They did not go home and go to bed as soon as it was over—they went to play with other lads in the street. Mr. Lewis informed me that the silk-twisting boys had the reputation of being about the most troublesome set of urchins in all Derby. In point of activity and agility they beat all the other boys hollow. This was a point on which similar testimony was given before Lord Ashley's committee by Mr. Douglas Fox, a medical gentleman of the town. Mr. Fox was asked how he accounted for the phenomenon. The reply was that he only professed to speak for the fact. These lads are gradually broken in to their running duties, beginners being only set to do about half the work of the regular hands, or rather feet.

Curiously enough they are not necessarily included in the Factory Act, the provisions of which only apply to buildings in which the labour is regulated by a steam-engine. In Leeds there are a great many silk-twisting establishments into which steam-power is not introduced at all, and in which the boys are, therefore, liable to be worked any number of hours that may be thought expedient by their employers. These last are always the men who turn the wheels, each of whom engages and pays as many boys as he thinks proper. Their wages—generally about 3s 6d or 4s per week—the wheelman pays over to their parents. The actual amount is estimated by the quantity of work done; but it is the custom to give the boys, as pocket money for themselves, the produce of any labour above a usual fixed amount. The boys thus make from 3d to 6d a week on their own account. The wheelman, if he has a family, generally employs his own children. One of the overlookers in Messrs. Bridgett's establishment told me that he had begun by being a running boy. He was then only eight years of age. Boys do not now begin until they are eleven. He did not remember to have ever found the work fatiguing. He was soon too hardened and inured to it for that. In an experience of 33 years, he had never known an instance of a boy breaking down under the fatigue and giving up the business. In the summer evenings, after work hours he sometimes walks through the fields as far as Quarner (three or four miles from Derby) and there he often recognizes some of his own "flock" running and jumping, and beating all the other boys at both exercises.

The ribbon-weaving department is the only branch of the silk trade in which the mass of the operatives employed are men. Their earnings are considerable, but often irregular—an irregularity in the great part the fault of the men themselves, who are some of them apt to keep their frames longer flung out of gear than is necessary. Mr. Lewis kindly laid before me the wage book of the firm for this department. I selected the week previous to my visit. It was that before Christmas, and one in which the men commonly exert themselves to get through a good amount of work. On examination I found that 131 powerloom weavers had been paid £144 6s 3d, or on an average about £1 1s 11½d each. The highest amount earned was £2 1s 10½d, and I was informed that this individual weaver sometimes earned £2 7s 6d for weeks together. He was, of course, a skilful and exceedingly careful and industrious workman. I was requested to observe—the steam-engine being the real motive labourer—that the earnings of the higher amounts of wages depended not upon any increased manual exertion on the part of the workman, but on unremitting attention in keeping his loom as much as possible in gear. In weaving narrow ribbons, the operatives are paid so much per cut. Every man is bound to produce a cut weekly or he will get nothing at all. A great number of hands work out just the minimum and no more. Others produce a cut and a half, and a few weave nearly two cuts per week. Broad ribbons are paid for by the half cut. The prices of the cuts and the half cuts vary with the breadth of the goods manufactured. I inquired what would be the amount of wages earned if it were possible to keep the engine applied to the loom throughout the whole of the daily ten hours of toil. From the calculation made, at my instance, it appeared that, were the loom kept in gear during the whole of the time the engine is at work, the average produce of the factory would be about doubled. A great many stoppages are, however, requisite for many purposes. In the power ribbon-weaving looms, the warp is stitched perpendicularly, in many strips—each of them, of course, the breadth of the ribbon to be woven, and each of them traversed backwards and forwards by a tiny shuttle. After being taken from the loom the ribbons require to be picked, in order to free them from any little inequalities and thickenings previously existing in the thread. This operation is performed by girls, one of whom picks for about ten weavers—the latter uniting to pay her wages, which are about 8s per week. The quill winders, who prepare the shuttles, receive about an equal amount of earnings.

There is a feature in Messrs. Bridgett and Co's silk mills too interesting to pass over unnoticed. It is a most useful and kindly-meant experiment, which Mr. Lewis is engaged in conducting. Fully recognizing the truth that one of the great drawbacks of the factory system is the ignorance in which girls employed in mills invariably grow up, in reference to anything like domestic duties—and knowing by long experience that nothing is more common than for a factory girl to marry, without being able even to darn a stocking, make a pudding, or boil a potato—Mr. Lewis is engaged in trying whether he cannot give some of the female children in the mill a domestic as well as a factory education. For this purpose he has selected a number of girls, either orphans or deserted by their parents, from various unions in the neighbourhood of Derby. These girls he boards, clothes and lodges. They live in a large house suitably fitted up and under the charge of a schoolmaster, a schoolmistress, and a matron. In the mill they are upon precisely the footing as the other children, working the same hours, and nominally earning the same wages; and in their leisure hours at home they are taught the elements of a sound education, and instructed in the domestic duties which they will afterwards have to perform. The characteristic peculiarity of this domestic school is that the girls are instructed naturally and in the regular course of things, in the work in which they will gain their livelihood, and trained to the habits which will make their future homes comfortable and happy. At the mill they are kept as much as possible together. Mr. Lewis, with a very wise consideration, is careful that the colour and the fashion of their dresses may differ, so as to prevent their being marked out and known by anything approaching to a badge of charity. As yet the experiment is too recent to admit of any practical results showing themselves, the institution not having been established more than three years. So far as regards the pecuniary aspect of the affair, I am informed that the children eat more than they work for—and certainly a plumper, chubbier, more perfectly healthy-looking group of girls I never saw. The guardians of the parish whence they were taken often come to see how they are getting on. I may add that Mr. Lewis's protegees go to school one hour and a half in the evening, that they wash and mend their own clothes, and perform part of the ordinary duties of the establishment.

A very careful estimated average of the wages paid in a Derby silk-mill, has been handed to me by Mr. Lewis. It is as follows:

WINDING, CLEANING, REELING, DOUBLING, AND SPINNING

Women employed in winding	6s 6d to 7s 6d per week
Women employed in doubling	6s 6d to 7s 6d
Girls in doubling	5s
Girls in winding—the youngest beginning as learners at 11 years of age	1s
Then advancing every three months until they earn between 13 and 16 years of age	3s 6d to 5s
Boys—employed in cleaning—the youngest beginning as learners at 11 years of age	1s
Advancing every three months until they earn between 12 and 15 years of age	3s to 4s
Ditto, in spinning room	3s to 5s
Reelers—girls	5s
Reelers—young men	6s 6d to 7s

RIBBON WEAVERS

Men	20s to 21s per week
Average of a summer month with no gas to pay for and good light	23s 9d
Average of a winter month, clear earnings	19s
Young Women—soft silk winders for weavers	7s 6d to 9s 3d
Girls—ditto, about 13 years of age	3s 6d
Warpers—young women	7s 6d to 8s 6d
Fillers—ditto, of quills for the shuttles	7s 6d to 9s
Pickers and Trimmers	6s 6d to 8s

DYE-HOUSE

Labourers	16s 0d to 18s
Dyers	25s 0d to 30s

Overtime paid in proportion. Hours of work—ten

Silk Glove and Hose-makers

In Derby the silk-hosiery knitters generally work in shops belonging to middlemen or second masters. These shops are usually low two storied buildings often situated amid dust-heaps and ash-pits in back yards; sometimes, when in the outskirts of the town, more pleasantly located in little gardens. The middleman system is universal. As a rule the frame rent paid is 1s per week but some of their masters permit their hands, when work is short, to pay 3d per dozen on the quantities of articles turned out. This statement, be it remarked, applies only to the glove trade. Standing room is always charged 3d. Cases in which the knitter works at home, and is yet charged by the second master with standing room as though he laboured in the shop, are exceptions to the general rule, but they are exceptions which do occur. Sometimes, if a master has all his frames going, he will employ an independent frame without exacting rent; but it is only when trade is very brisk that the independent machines have any chance in this way. The knitters assured me they had frequently to complain of being served with old rickety frames, which they were afraid to work vigorously. They were often, they said, obliged to pay 1s per week for a piece of mechanism for the fee-simple of which no one would give a pound. To some frames additional works, called "carriers", are added, and for these carriers a separate and additional rent of 2d is demanded. In answer to my inquiries as to whether the men would in general prefer the factory system to the present irregular and uncertain mode of working, I was informed that the subject was one on which great difference of opinion existed, but that the framework knitters were unanimous in wishing for the substitution of a rent calculated according to the work actually done, instead of the present fixed weekly sum. The estimates of wages with which I was furnished agree precisely with those already published, so far as the glove branch goes. In a large silk-hose knitting shop, the men informed me that their charges were 1s for frame rent, 8d for standing room, 9d for winding, 3d for needles, and about 6d for fat to burn in lamps. They estimated their wages at about 8s or 8s 6d for a week's full work. On Mondays and Saturdays they generally worked for twelve hours, on other days for fourteen. The amount of rent they had to pay for broken meshes of work entirely depended upon the character of the second master.

A Lace Factory

I have stated that there is in Derby but one lace factory—that of Messrs. Morley and Bouden. As the style of work and the fabric produced differ considerably from those which I have principally had opportunities of seeing in Nottingham, I may advantageously give some account of the establishment in question. It is a power factory, weaving, by means of bobbins and carriages, plain net. There being no patterns or difficult complications of threads primarily to arrange, the machines go on almost continuously. The number of hours wrought per day is eighteen, and to each machine there is a man and a boy. The relay system, in the strict meaning of the phrase, is not practised; the work being so arranged that while one hand alone is engaged at the machine during the first hours in the morning, both are employed together for the bulk of the day, and the second hand is left to work out the last two hours at night. Thus A commences work at 4 a.m. and tends the machine until 8 a.m. At that hour B relieves him, while A has an hour for breakfast. After 9 a.m. both are employed together—with the exception, of course, of the dinner hour—until 5 p.m., when A leaves off for the night, and B, who has also in the meantime had an hour for tea, continues operations until 10 p.m. The two colleagues were, as I have said, a man and a boy. During the time that only one is at the frame, he has of course to tent the mechanism; when both are together the boy always tents, and the man prepares his carriages and bobbins, so as to have them ready for the frame when the supply of shute actually in use is exhausted. In the factory in question, there is a double set of carriages and brass bobbins, so that the threaders and winders are not required those irregular and often distressingly long hours which I have alluded to in the account of Nottingham. It was, indeed, the strong representations made as to the possibility of dispensing with overlong hours of infant labour by means of using double sets of bobbins and carriages, that prevented the provisions of the Ten Hours Bill being applied to lace factories. As I have said, however, the double mechanism is rather the exception than the rule. The women who fill the brass bobbins perform their work in this factory by a very simple but very neat apparatus, something like a comb, set with teeth exactly corresponding to the clefts in the bobbins. By this means the threads are combed into their respective grooves with the greatest exactness. The women in question work twelve hours a day, and can earn from 9s to 13s. The wooden bobbin winders make from 5s 6d to 9s. The threaders, boys generally from 12 to 14 years of age, make from 3s 6d to 6s.

As regards the pay of the higher classes of workmen who tent the machines, the wages book was submitted to my inspection. I found that the last class of workmen received upon an average, about 30s per week; the inferior class of hands from 21s to 25s. The boys, whose ages vary from 15 upwards, earn from 10s to 14s per week. These gradations are the result of different degrees of care and skill bestowed upon different qualities of work. Mr. Bouden informed me that a graduated scale of wages was found of great practical importance, as an inducement to the men to exert themselves, so as to be deemed fit for the best quality of work. The net-weaving rooms I found rather hot—the effect of the working people having a greater aversion to draught than relish for air. I was informed that it was difficult to induce them to allow any of the windows to remain open. In this species of plain lace-weaving, the task of the workman is easy, the thread being of so strong a texture as seldom to break with the action of the machine. The man and boy, I ought to mention, change hours every week. The trifling amount of embroidered goods wrought in the Messrs. Morley factory is of an inferior quality, technically known as "rubbishing" fancy lace. It consists of very cheap stripes used for borders. The wages in this department are the same as in that of the perfectly plain net.

"Mending"

The "mending" is never performed upon the premises. The firm do not encourage the middlewoman system. They prefer to give out work to individual menders. At the same time they are aware that, to a greater or less extent, a mender will frequently get a number of little girls around her, at her own house, and employ them upon the more slightly damaged pieces—work which children are quite capable of performing, and which it would not in all cases pay an expert needlewoman to undertake. To this extent it is thought that the middlewoman system is almost inseparable from the lace manufacture. Any running or tambouring practised in Derby is in connection with Nottingham houses. The number of male hands employed in Messrs. Morley and Bouden's factory is about 240.

Broad Silk Weaving

The broad or piece silk-weaving trade is of comparatively recent introduction. The goods woven are of a similar class to those produced at Macclesfield, Middleton and Spitalfields. Indeed, many of the Middleton weavers, including more than one whose residence I have already described, work, I find, for Derby houses. The partners of one of the establishments informed me that their best weavers in Derby were Lancashire men, and that the Middleton people were on the whole better and more industrious workmen than the native midland county weavers. There are a few Irishmen weaving silk in Derby. They have, however, in the majority of cases, been previously employed, either in Macclesfield or in London. The broad silk weaving firms in Derby employ their hands in either regularly-fitted shops or at their own houses. In the majority of the latter cases, the workmen are scattered through the country in the numerous hamlets within a dozen miles of Derby. The number of looms in shops is about equal to those in the weavers' houses, and the number of jacquards is about equal to that of the plain looms. A few women work in the shops, but the number is decreasing. These shops may each contain a dozen or so of figured and plain looms upon each floor. The looms belong almost invariably to the manufacturers. The ordinary charges paid by the weaver for their use are 6d weekly for loom rent, 6d for shop rent, and in the winter time 6d for gas. If a man has a loom at his own house, he of course pays merely the rent of the mechanism. The hours commonly worked in the shops are, in summer from 6 o'clock until dusk, in the winter from seven o'clock until eight o'clock in the evening. The men are not compelled rigidly to attend these hours, but within these limits the shops remain open, and practically they are tolerably closely observed. The domestic weavers work more irregularly, but in the summer they have frequently very long hours, sometimes from three o'clock and four o'clock in the morning until dusk. Contrary to the practice in Middleton, manufacturers here are in the habit of advancing money to their hands before the completion of the pieces on which they are working. And I am informed that it is often difficult to persuade the men not to anticipate almost the whole of their earnings. The weavers who apply the shuttle at their own houses in Derby suffer great inconvenience from the structure of the dwellings, these last being totally unsuitable to the trade. The men are thus obliged to erect the looms either in the principal room or in a bed-chamber. I have repeatedly found the best portion of a house thus occupied. Very often, too, the weavers find it difficult to induce the landlord to allow of the erection of a loom at all, and in some cases the ceiling is too low to admit of the lofty structure of the jacquard. These causes tend to the concentration of the trade in shops, where it can be carried on with greater convenience to all parties. The rural weavers bring in their own work when it is completed, and are frequently visited by the manufacturers or their agents.

The following statement of wages paid to handloom weavers has been handed to me from the firm of Messrs. Stone and Kemp. It is intended to give an idea of the maximum, medium, and minimum wages earned by weavers in their employment during the last six or eight months:

WAGES OF SILK WEAVERS IN AND AROUND DERBY

	Weekly Earnings
Man on a jacquard loom	19s 0d
Do. do. do.	20s 6d
Do. do. do.	20s 0d
Do. do. do.	15s 0d
Do. do. do.	11s 3d
Lad do. do.	14s 9d
Woman do. do.	15s 0d
Do. do. do.	7s 0d
Man on plain work	7s 0d
Do. do.	12s 0d
Do. do.	10s 0d
Woman do.	5s 0d
Man on velvet	13s 4d
Do. do.	15s 0d
Do. do.	11s 3d
Woman do.	5s 6d

Strutts Cotton Mill at Belper

About seven miles from Derby, situated in a pleasant spot by the waters of the Derwent, is one of the largest and longest-established rural factories in England, and one which for several reasons, I was anxious to visit. The establishment in question is a cotton-mill belonging to the Messrs. Strutt. Under its shadow the best part of the village of Belper has grown up. For considerably more than half a century the factory has given employment to successive generations while almost all the workpeople live in houses and on ground belonging to the firm.

This mill, which employs more than 1,200 hands, is driven entirely by water. There are no tall chimneys, and no pouring smoke, to disfigure one of the most charming rural spots in England. Just above the factory, which is embowered in shrubbery, and has masses of ivy clinging to its walls, the dammed-back waters of the Derwent expand into a shining lakelet—the surplusage tumbling in sparkling volumes over a weir. All round it rise steep, grassy hills, clumped here and there with groups of stately trees, or roughened by brakes of tangled underwood. Cottage and villa buildings are studded here and there. Along the steep high road, amid gardens and sheltering boughs, run broken and irregular rows of old-fashioned houses—a wayside tavern, with its bough-hung sign and horse-trough, many quaint old tenements grouped in picturesque irregularity, with grey ridgy roofs, and cottage lattices opening in the midst of woodbine and ivy. I chanced to be at Belper during one of the few and precious glimpses of the sun which the winter solstice is blest with and as the red light came sprinkling down on the knoll and brake, on the sparkling frost-bound grass, and the broad shining river—as the smoke from many dwellings swelled perpendicularly up into the still air, and robins and other small birds twittered joyfully from thatched roofs and crisp unstirring branches—I thought I had seldom looked upon a scene more thoroughly and pleasantly rural and peaceful. And yet, from where I stood, I could distinguish the plash of the waterwheels and the murmur of the whirling mechanism of one of the greatest cotton-mills in England.

The people in Messrs. Strutt's factory gave, some years ago, the most thorough trial to the co-operative system of buying provisions and other necessaries which that system has yet received. The plan was abandoned—but more, Mr. J. Strutt informed me, in consequence of the misconduct of some of the conductors of the society, than from any conviction that the association had been a failure. The managers in question began to attend more to the business of the association than to that of the mill, and more to their own interest than either. Nevertheless, for many years the concern flourished. Goods, edible and wearable, were purchased wholesale and for ready money, and year after year the balance of the sums saved to the contributors was paid over to them in proportions sometimes sufficiently large to defray the greater proportion of their house rents. Suspicions, however, gradually arose, and became more or less confirmed. It was found that secretaries and managers were not always proof to the temptation of a bonus from wholesale dealers, and evils were also believed to result from the people giving up the habit of managing their money wages. At length, therefore, after an existence of more than a dozen years, the Co-operative Society of Belper was voluntarily broken up, and has not since been in any degree revived.

Mr. J. Strutt accompanied me to many of the dwellings of his workpeople. These are almost entirely built of substantial blocks of stone, of which there is abundance in the neighbourhood. The smallest class consisting of two rooms, and generally occupied either by married couples without family, or by widows, are let as low as 15d or 18d. The highest rented class come to 4s per week. In the first house we visited, I found on the ground floor, a large roomy kitchen and living room, and upstairs two good bedrooms. The lower rooms were paved with prettily tesselated brick. There was a back door, ensuring thorough ventilation, and decent back accommodations. To every house, large or small, a garden is attached, and every householder may rent an extra garden for about 3d weekly. The appearance of matters inside denoted decided comfort. There were good cooking utensils, and some mahogany furniture, a sofa and a clock, with ornaments on the chimney piece and books on the window sill. The rent was 2s 5d. In another cottage there were three rooms on the ground floor—a living room, kitchen, and scullery, two bedrooms upstairs, and a garret above them. The garden was about twenty yards long, and half as wide. For this house the rent was 3s 10d. All the upper rooms in all the houses are boarded. In the centre of this pleasant and clean-looking factory village is the boys, girls, and infant school. The children appeared to me to be decidedly cleaner, and under far more perfect control, than is usual in the majority of the schools of the class. The girls were getting a knitting and sewing lesson when I visited them. The fees are 2d per week and 1d for the infant school. The children of widows are received into both schools at the latter rate. I should not omit to add that the factory part of the village of Belper is well lighted, paved, and drained and small flower patches extend before every house, bordered in several of the streets, by carefully-trimmed rows of sycamores.

Leicester

Introduction

The town of Leicester, like its neighbour Derby—and to a still greater degree—boasts of having been in ancient days, a place of note, while it still preserves a considerable commercial importance. A hamlet built where Leicester now stands was a post the possession of which, in the early days of our history, was fiercely contended for by Saxon and Dane. In the time of the Heptarchy, a cathedral stood upon the banks of the Soar; and when Duke William attacked the place, so stoutly was it defended that he won nothing save the ruins of the struggling Saxon town. At this early period it is said that there were in Leicester 322 houses, built of clay, timber, and wattles. The town was speedily rebuilt, and in process of time became a Norman stronghold, and a fair abbey and a stately castle rose over the narrow streets. The spirit of trade was, however, even then beginning to spring up in the cold shade of feudalism, and as early as the days of Henry II, there existed in Leicester guilds of handicraftsmen. Throughout the fourteenth century Leicester throve greatly. Churches, hospitals, gaols, were erected; fairs were established, charters granted. During the next age Parliaments met in the ancient religious houses of the borough, and the Leicesterians won the favour of Edward IV by sending out almost the whole of the male population against the Last of the Barons. In 1485 the burghers of Leicester saw Richard III pass through the town on his way to Bosworth Field, and after a short space, his body was brought back and burned in a small church belonging to the Grey Friars. The remains of another great historical personage rest in Leicester. In November 1530, the once omnipotent Minister of Henry VIII, then "an old man broken with the storms of state" alighted at the Abbey gate, and early in the following month was laid beneath the pavement of "Our Lady's Chapel". In 1563 the still scanty population included no more than 333 families. About a half a century afterwards Leicester was erected into a "staple town for the buying and selling of wools". Its growing industry was however severely checked by the turmoil of the Civil Wars. The Leicesterians were staunch Puritans, forward in insulting the Church and defying the King, so that in 1645 Charles laid seige to the town and stormed it—the stout burgesses fighting from house to house and church to church. The charter of the borough was finally restored by James II.

The eighteenth century saw Leicester rapidly rising to its present position. Many schools, almshouses, and hospitals had already been built, newspapers were established, stage coaches started, and the knitting of woollen stockings by machinery was increasing rapidly. This manufacture had been commenced in Leicester about the time of the Revolution. It was very unpopular at first, and the few artificers were forced to work their frames in secret places, and by night. They hawked their wares round the country, each manufacturer riding his pannier-laden horse. The trade, however, soon outgrew the prejudices by which it had been first kept down. In 1712 it was computed that in Leicester 1,000 persons were employed in sorting, combing, and dyeing; 6,000 in spinning, doubling and throwing; and 6,000 in weaving, seaming, and dressing up the woollen goods. The greatest quantity of these was produced in Leicester—the finest quality in Nottingham. In 1785, the invention of a worsted spinning-machine gave the trade an impetus, and in 1792 there were upwards of 70 hosiers in Leicester, employing no less than 3,000 frames. In 1831 the number had doubled; and in 1845 there were in Leicester and the villages around about 10,000 frames employed in making stockings, shirts, drawers, socks, and caps; about 2,000 in making gloves and mitts, and about 750 machines employed in the production of "fancy hosiery". In this department are included coloured scarfs, shawls, cravats, boots and leggings for children, braces, worsted "polka jackets", and so forth. Many of these articles are knitted by hand in the villages of the Midland Counties; but the greater portion of the fancy hosiery made is wrought by complicated machinery in Leicester. In this department it was calculated that in 1845 between 7,000 and 8,000 persons were employed. There were also used about 500 stocking-frames, ingeniously adapted to this new branch of industry—about 150 warp-looms, those accommodating engines, which produce every fabric, from the most gossamery lace to the coarsest carpeting, and about 100 machines called "grinders", of ingenious and complicated construction. About one-half of the fancy hosiery then produced was destined for the foreign, and one half for the home market. In 1845 there were 52 steam-engines, employed in propelling the machinery used in the town.

The present condition of the woollen hosiery trade in the town and county of Leicester may be gathered from the following information, furnished to me by Mr. Bigg, a late manufacturer, and a gentleman who has paid great attention to the industrial statistics of the district:

"There are in the town and county of Leicester about 20,000 frames, employing a manufacturing population of about 35,000 persons. Of these, upwards of six-tenths are occupied in the production of common woollen hosiery, two-tenths are engaged in the fancy trade, and the remaining two-tenths in the manufacture of cotton or merino fabrics in the villages of Hinckley and Loughborough. Many frames included in the estimate for the fancy trade produce a particular sort of cloth used by the glovers in Worcester and the west of England. Upwards of seven-tenths of the woollen manufactures of Leicester are now consumed within the United Kingdom. The remaining three-tenths are pretty equally divided between the foreign and the Colonial markets. Power is partly applied in the fancy trade, but not in any other department of wool knitting."

As regards a general estimate of wages throughout the various branches of the manufacture, I give the following upon the same authority: "Wages are somewhat naturally higher in the fancy than in other branches, because the work performed requires superior skill for its execution, and because being partly under factory regulations, the labour goes on steadily and continuously. For a man a fair average would be 20s per week; for a woman 10s, and for a child 5s. In the glove trade a superior hand may obtain 25s per week, a middling workman 20s, and an inferior hand 15s per week. In the manufacture of underclothing, the wages range from 20s to a much lower sum, the average may be taken as 12s. In knitting 'straight up and down stockings' on broad frames, the remuneration would range from 10s to 8s to 6s. These rates are, in all cases except the last, upwards of 15 per cent higher than the average of the last seven years." It is Mr. Bigg's decided opinion that the condition of the framework-knitter will not be permanently improved until the machines are gathered into factories and something like factory regularity of work established. "At present," he in effect added, "the men often work very long, but as often very irregular hours; sometimes they are idle, sometimes exhausted. Very many of them do no work on Mondays and not much on Tuesdays." In confirmation of his opinion as to the better wages which might be regularly earned by framework-knitters were the factory instead of the domestic system adopted, Mr. Bigg handed to me the monetary results of an experiment of the sort actually tried. Some years ago the firm of which he is a member collected their glove-frames, or a great portion of them, into several extensive factories of workshops, insisting upon the observance of regular hours of labour. The experiment was persevered in for several months; and from the tables handed to me of wages actually paid, I take at random the individual amounts for three distinct weeks, earned in two of the shops in question. They were as follows:

SHOP No. 1.

Wages earned by	Week ending Feb. 10		Feb. 17		Feb. 24	
	s	d	s	d	s	d
Workman No. 1	20	9	21	8	21	4
,, 2	21	0	24	10	24	5
,, 3	24	5	28	9	25	3
,, 4	15	4	15	9	13	2
,, 5	11	9	16	7	18	9
,, 6	14	7	14	6	16	1
,, 7	16	8	15	9	24	7
,, 8	18	1	20	3	15	2
,, 9	29	1	31	3	22	1
,, 10	11	0	3	8	11	6
,, 11	16	10	18	7	10	3
,, 12	20	1	17	4	18	2
,, 13	20	1	20	6	20	7
,, 14	24	8	13	7	26	0
,, 15	18	10	18	10	24	4

	SHOP No. 1. cont.					
	Week ending Feb. 10		Feb. 17		Feb. 24	
Wages earned by	s	d	s	d	s	d
Workman No. 16	12	2	20	6	13	8
,, 17	23	4	21	10	20	1
,, 18	16	9	18	2	19	1
,, 19	19	4	13	5	18	6
,, 20	17	5	20	1	2	6
,, 21	18	1	18	10	12	10
	SHOP No. II					
	Week ending Feb. 10		Feb. 17		Feb. 24	
Wages earned by	s	d	s	d	s	d
Workman No. 1	14	1	11	7	11	5
,, 2	15	2	17	1	16	1
,, 3	20	9	21	4	17	5
,, 4	11	6	15	7	13	2
,, 5	18	6	17	4	14	5
,, 6	18	6	21	5	15	2
,, 7	21	6	21	6	20	10
,, 8	23	5	21	3	18	6
,, 9	16	9	16	3	14	5
,, 10	24	4	21	6	21	6
,, 11	18	3	19	2	20	5
,, 12	9	4	9	5	9	8
,, 13	16	3	18	6	8	3
,, 14	10	4	9	2	8	7
,, 15	15	6	10	4	14	6
,, 16	19	10	17	6	19	3
,, 17	21	5	21	6	12	2
,, 18	23	6	17	4	16	0
,, 19	20	2	20	1	13	8
,, 20	14	4	17	2	13	4
,, 21	20	7	22	0	16	4
,, 22	22	4	21	6	10	7
,, 23	14	4	17	2	13	4
,, 24	23	2	24	7	17	5
,, 25	15	6	20	7	15	11

The Sanitary Condition of Leicester

The town of Leicester lies in a gentle hollow, sheltered, except towards the east, by the undulations of the Dane and Spinney hills—eminences branching from the ridgy range of Charnwood Forest. The sluggish stream of the Soar winds through the town; and in wet weather the adjacent meadows are swampy and often overflowed. The consequence is, the frequent prevalence of fever in the lowest-lying portions of the town. The population of Leicester in 1831 was 38,904. In 1841, it amounted to 48,167. The number of inhabited houses in 1831 was 8,348—the number in 1841 had increased to 10,046; and in 1848 a local census gave the number of inhabited dwellings as 13,139, and that of the uninhabited as 852, making a total of 13,991 houses. In 1846, there took place in Leicester 587 marriages, in 165 of which the men, and in 273 of which the women, signed with marks. The tables of mortality show that there are annually in Leicester about 36 persons living to one death—a proportion indicating no very satisfactory sanitary state of things. Accordingly, I find the local medical authorities examined before Mr. Ranger, the Inspector of the Board of Health, pointing out considerable districts of the town as being fruitful in "fever cases". In 1846 and 1847, temporary "fever houses" were obliged to be established, and in one district the medical officer connected with the Poor Law administration stated that upwards of one in three of the labouring classes had in 1840 obtained at least one order for medical relief. In 1840, 1841, 1842, the average mortality of Leicester was 3.0 per cent; in 1848 it was 2.65 per cent per annum—the average mortality of England not being above 2.2, and in some great districts not above 2.0 per cent. The mean duration of life in England is 29.11 years. In Leicester it is 25 years, and it is estimated that at least 8,000 of the working classes in the town annually receive medical assistance from the various charities.

The drainage is miserably defective. Out of 242 streets and 3,417 courts, alleys and yards, only 112 are entirely culverted, and about 130 partially so. There are nine outfalls of sewers, all situated in the town, and all pouring their contents into the almost stagnant waters of the Soar. The surface drainage is equally defective. There is seldom sufficient fall to carry away the dirty water, which is sometimes obliged to be "swilled" along the kennels for upwards of a quarter of a mile. The entire length of the roads and streets in this condition is nearly 30 miles, occupying an area of more than 113 acres. At the back of each block of the more ordinary class of houses is a common yard, with privies, cesspools, and ash-pits, for the use of the occupants. From these places there is seldom or never any sub-soil drainage. Slops and liquid refuse are left to evaporate, and send up their noisome effluvia. From one of the Health of Towns Commissioners' Reports I transcribe the following very instructive piece of evidence as bearing on the connection between the mortality and insufficient sewerage in parts of Leicester (see p. 193).

Of the 13,991 houses in Leicester only 120 are supplied with water closets—the average cost of each being £31 10s, a sum equal to half the amount necessary for building a four-roomed house. Many of the cesspools are of great depth; some of them not less than 25 feet; and the consquence is that, in numerous instances, the water which is found still nearer the surface is poisoned by noxious percolations. The present supply of water is derived from wells, a few public pumps, and from the river Soar. In 1848 it was estimated that the number of wells in Leicester, each furnished with a pump, was 2,800, or about one well to every $4^5/_7$ houses. Ther average depth is about eleven yards, and their cost, including the pumps, about £12 10s. There are besides nearly 3,000 cisterns and tanks for collecting and preserving rain water—the average capacity of these receptacles being 700 gallons, and their average cost £9 10s. The water principally used in Leicester for culinary purposes is exceedingly hard, and by no means pleasantly-tasted. Owing, indeed, to the bad quality of the water supply, many dyeing operations require to be sent out of the town for

COMPARATIVE MORTALITY IN THE DRAINED AND UNDRAINED DISTRICTS OF THE TOWN OF LEICESTER

STREETS	1840		1841		1842		Av. Age at Death for three years
	Average Age of Death In Years	Proportion from Epidemics	Average Age of Death In years	Proportion from Epidemics	Av. Age of Death In Years	Proportion from Epidemics	
East District							
Culverted	23½	¼	24	1/12	26½	1/12	24⅔
Partly Culverted	17½	⅓	21	⅛	21½	⅛	20
Not Culverted	13½	½	18	⅙	17½	1/7	16½
West District							
Culverted	20	⅙	30	1/14	29	1/12	26⅓
Partly Culverted	21	⅕	22½	⅛	22	1/11	22
Not Culverted	14½	¼	21	1/7	17½	1/9	17⅔
Culverted	25½	The three yrs. average 21 and rather more	.....	These years were taken because the year 1840 was remarkable for the increase of disease and the number of deaths throughout the town.			
Partly Culverted	21						
Not Culverted	17						

performance to other localities where a purer and softer species of fluid can be obtained. The quantity of soap necessary in washing with Leicester water is most uneconomically great. A waterworks company exists. They are incorporated by Act of Parliament, but a sufficient amount of capital could not be raised, and the scheme remains a dead letter. A large public swimming bath has lately been opened at the charge of 1d per head, the corporation paying £100 per annum to the proprietor. During the first month, 7,026 persons availed themselves of the privileges. There are no parks or gardens in Leicester, nor any space for public recreation, save about four acres used as a cricket ground, and granted for that purpose by the corporation.

Like Derby, and unlike Nottingham, Leicester is rather a widespread and straggling town. There are very few back-to-back tenements, and not one cellar dwelling. Courts with houses on either hand exist, but in no great numbers. The general plan of building adopted in the construction of houses for the labouring classes is to erect them in blocks, each block perforated by a passage leading to a common back yard, in which are situated several privies and ash-pits—generally speaking placed in a cluster. These houses are of two general classes; the better consisting of four rooms, two above and two on the ground floor. The inferior class of dwellings consist of two rooms only, one above the other. For a house of the former class the rent charged is from 2s 3d to 2s 6d per week. For one of the latter it ranges from 1s 6d to 2s, according to situation. There are very few of the dwellings of the working-classes cellared. The ground floors are invariably paved with red-brick; the floors of the upper chambers are plastered with gypsum. When there are two first-floor rooms there is always a fireplace in one of them.

The framework-knitters ply their trade either in shops erected at the back of the middlemen's houses, and frequently forming one side of the common yards above described, or in their own rooms. The shops in question are generally miserable places—mere shells of brick, and rough (yet slight) timber work; the windows clouded with the dust and dirt of weeks; the bare brick walls and sooty joists festooned with cobwebs, the floors unswept—in most cases I suppose since the structure was built—the frames huddled as closely as possible together, and the whole aspect of things squalid, dirty, and slovenly to the last degree. There may be exceptions, but the foregoing is the general rule. If the frame of a workman stands in his own house, it is usually placed beneath a window in the lower room—never, as is the fashion in Nottingham, in the uppermost apartment.

Industry in Leicester

As in Derby, the factories are almost all devoted to the manufacture of silk thread for weaving and knitting—so those at Leicester are occupied in the production of woollen yarns for similar purposes. The fleece in Leicester is sorted, carded, combed, and subjected to all the spinning processes requisite to fit the filaments which it produces for the stocking-frame, the grinder, or the warp-loom. The principal part of the thread thus produced is worked up either in the town or the surrounding district. A few of the factories are introducing the practice of combing wool by power, but the greater part is still combed by hand.

Various kinds of woollen factories—those dealing with the short-stapled wools, as at Huddersfield, and with the long stapled wools as at Halifax—have already been described; and the processes by which yarns fitted for the production of fleecy hosiery are manufactured do not very materially differ from those necessary in preparing the raw material for broad-cloth or merinos. The combing by machinery is, however, a feature of the Leicester trade, and one, as may well be believed, by no means popular amongst the hand-combers. There are as yet, I think, only two establishments into which the combing mechanism has been introduced, but in these it completely supersedes the labour of skilled adults. Boys and young women only are requisite to superintend the machines, which, to a certain degree, feed themselves. The wages thus earned range from 8s to 10s per week. Two girls can manage, if I mistake not, three circular machines and each machine performs—although I believe not quite so delicately—the work of several men. The engines in question are of recent introduction, and not dissimilar in principle to the mechanism used in heckling flax.

Amid the woollen factories of Leicester a large new mill, just opened, is beyond all cavil the most splendid and admirably arranged carding and spinning establishment I have yet seen. The name of the proprietor I withhold at his own request, but it is impossible to describe a factory of this kind without its speedy and accurate local identification. For the first time, I believe, in the history of English textile manufactures, there has been erected a spacious building destined for the labours of the steam-engine, the carding-frame, and the spinning-frame, in which architectural beauty and symmetry have not been wholly forgotten. "You must," said a Manchester gentleman to one of the partners lately, "you must have flung hundreds of pounds away in these ornaments, pediments, and entablatures, which are not of the slightest use." But the feeling of the rearers of this noble industrial structure is, that a fair and due sum expended in securing not only the most perfect ventilation and convenience to the workpeople, but in providing a degree of architectural symmetry and grace unhappily and too long and too systematically despised by our manufacturers, is money expended in a mode which, in due time, will bear both its pecuniary and its moral harvest. It is the opinion of the gentleman in question—one in which I fully concur—that a well-arranged and well-ordered mill has a powerful tendency in producing in turn well-arranged and well-ordered homes. The habit of constantly seeing, throughout working hours, perfect cleanliness and perfect symmetry upon every side, is a powerful adversary to slatternly and filthy practices out of working hours. In the mill in question the lowest portion of the ceilings of the working rooms is eleven feet from the floor, and as these ceilings are uniformly arched, the mean actual height is still greater. Each room is ventilated quite independently of those above or below it. A rush of air either hot or cold, can be directed into each chamber through a separate flue, while the foul air constantly escapes through apertures in the ceiling communicating with the chimney. The consequences of these arrangements are, that the atmosphere, even in the carding rooms, is almost as pleasant as would be desired in the drawing room. The mill is as yet hardly in working order, but when it is, a functionary will be especially appointed to attend to the ventilation. From the pay books I took the following averages of wages, as earned in a Leicester woollen factory:

	s	d	
Wool sorters (men)	about 18	0	per week
Washers (men)	" 16	0	"
Boys (their assistants)	" 2	0	"
Carders (women)	" 7	0	"
Preparers (including drawers and rowers —women)	" 6	10	"
Spinners (women)	" 7	6	"

To give an idea of the working discipline of the mill, I may mention the amount of wages paid for four successive weeks, with the fines deducted from them—it being understood that irregularities of attendance and inattention to work are thus punished:

Wages for one week	£180	Fines 1s 1d
" another	£175	Fines 1s 1½d
" "	£180	Fines 3d
" "	£179 13s	Fines 5d

In laying on these fines, a certain discretionary power is exercised, and a few minutes' absence is excused in a regular hand, but punished in an offender by habit and repute. There is a small library connected with the mill, but the superintendent complains that the girls will hardly read anything save the trash of penny romances.

The wool-combers attached to this establishment work in shops at their own houses. Fully as I have described them in Bradford, there are, however, some peculiarities connected with the combers of the midland counties, which I shall detail as they were recounted to me in the wool-combing establishments which I visited. The first one was a shop prepared on purpose for the work, and well ventilated. There was a "pot of four" glowing in the centre, and the same number of men employed. Their answers to my questions may, I think, be condensed much to the following effect:

"This room we're combing in was intended at first for a kitchen, but as it's an out-house it makes a very good shop. There are few so good in Leicester. Generally the combers work up in the top of the house, but it's very seldom that anyone sleeps in the room. There are no charcoal pots whatever made use of here. If anybody sleeps in the shop room it's usually the children of the family. The new machine for combing, we fear, will make a great difference to us. We haven't half work in Leicester as it is already. If it wasn't for Yorkshire we couldn't make a living. The Leicester trade is generally brisk for only four or at most five months in the year. It begins about the end of August and if it runs on to Christmas then we call it a good trade, and think that we are well off. After Christmas time it is very common for the Leicester wool-combers to go to Yorkshire—to Bradford generally—in search of work, until the Leicester season comes round again. A great number work regularly in Bradford in the winter and spring, and in Leicester in the summer and autumn. Those who can get work from Yorkshire may, perhaps, stay in Leicester all the year round. If the combers have the means they take their wives and families with them to Bradford; but it is not always that they can. The masters provide no proper shops for the combing. To this rule there is but one exception in Leicester. A great grievance which the midland wool-combers have to complain of is that the manufacturers are the proprietors of the combs, and that they make the workmen pay regular rent for them, just as in the framework-knitting trade. The rent is generally 3d per week. If the manufacturer has a pair of combs idle, he will not allow the workmen to labour with their own should they have any. They must use his, and pay rent for them, while their own are lying uselessly by. This is not the case in Yorkshire, and it is not the case in Leicestershire when the men are doing Yorkshire work. In that case, they use whatever combs they please.

"In some instances, I was seriously assured, combs have been given out and paid for, so old and decayed that they were unfit for the work, which was actually executed with other implements—the comber thus paying rent for a double set of tools.

"We work"—I continue the epitome of my conversation with the men—"we work what hours we please, but the shop is open for us from five in the morning until nine at night, upon Fridays until ten, and upon Saturdays up to any hour we choose to stay. The pot is never extinguished from Sunday to Sunday. We are paid money for fuel at the rate of 2d per score. This amounts to about 6d per week. For shop rent we pay 10d per week. We estimate our average earnings when fully employed as from 10s to 12s per week, but wool-combers cannot count on making so much during more than six months in the year."

The second combing shop I visited was situated in a top chamber, approached by a ladder and a trap. The men at work here informed me that in addition to 10d for shop rent, and 3d for comb rent, they paid upwards of 1s weekly for the washing of the wool. In answers to questions as to the original price and actual value of the combs, I was informed that a pair of combs, with four rows of teeth—the implements at present principally in use—might cost about 35s. "When I was a boy," said one of the men, "a pair with three rows cost £2 10s. We have more work to do with the four-rowed combs, and although the price of the article has fallen so much the manufacturers do not reduce one penny of the rent; it is just what it used to be long ago." All the combers whom I questioned agreed in stating that Yorkshire was better than Leicestershire work, being free from several drawbacks incidental to the latter. Still, although they passed one half of their time in the West Riding, they one and all talked of Leicester as their home.

Fancy Work

The fancy branch of the wool-knitting trade is, so far as the altered stocking-frames are employed in it, carried on exclusively in shops and factories. The frame rent system appears more or less to exist in all the branches of the occupation in which the instrument, either in its original or its adapted form, is employed. Indeed, so deeply rooted in the industrial system of the midland counties is the method of making the textile workman pay a fixed charge for the use of his tools, that, as I have just shown, it has found its way into the wool-combing trade. It is gratifying, however, to state that the principal fancy houses in Leicester are building new and improved frames, principally for the manufacture of woollen shirts—machines with which they intend to fill factories of their own, and to employ workmen at fixed rates of remuneration, clear of all frame or standing charges whatever. At present the rent and charges payable for a broad frame, suitable for the fancy trade, may amount to 3s, 3s 6d, and 3s 9d weekly. Of this sum, 6d goes to the "second master or middleman" for standing room, and 9d for winding. The rent paid for the frame varies from 1s 6d to about 2s 6d. As in the plain hosiery trade, the situation of the workman depends in some degree upon the character of the middleman. Occasionally the former may be required to pay a full week's rent when he has received from the second master only a half-week's work; but as a general rule, the machines, being more costly and elaborate than the ordinary stocking-frames, are kept more under the eye of the proprietor, and the men are sometimes provided with work direct, the usual agency being dispensed with. After many conversations with many workmen, I should be inclined to consider the estimate already given of their average earnings as correct. Upon a good job, a good workman may earn as much as £2 per week; upon an inferior one, an inferior hand may receive as little as 10s. One pound is about the average recompense weekly earned by a fancy-work knitter in good work; but taking one month with another, and one person with another, a number of the men warned me against stating a higher average than 15s.

The establishment of Messrs. Harris and Sons, in Leicester, is quite an epitome of the fancy hosiery trade of the town. There machines—of every variety and every combination of varieties, wrought both by power and by hand—are assembled for the production of every species of figured and coloured worsted goods. Many of these machines are exceedingly complicated and ingenious, working, in frequent cases, with the aid of the jacquard. Men are principally employed in tending the machinery at wages ranging from 18s to 25s. Boys are engaged in filling and shifting the bobbins and arranging them upon frames, so as to produce a warp with the requisite diversity of hue, earning at these several occupations from 3s up to 5s, and even 9s per week. The men are paid by the pound weight of the fabric which they produce. In the establishment in question every variety of textile manufacture is carried on—goods are knitted, netted and woven, figured and plain, by hand and by power. I was informed that the quantity of bobbins, in stock and in use, sometimes reached the astounding amount of six or seven millions. A considerable quantity of hand-knitting work is given out by the Messrs. Harris. The labour is performed by the wives and daughters of the cottagers throughout the district, who earn from 1s 6d and 2s to 3s 6d and 5s, according to their ability, and the time which they are able to bestow upon the manufacture.

In the plain woollen hosiery trade of Leicester about one-third of the operatives are women. They work at the narrower kind of frames, and earn very much the same amount of wages as are made by the men who labour at the same species of machines. Many of the Leicester middlemen have upwards of thirty frames. The machines are almost universally placed on the ground-floors of the houses or in shops. The average charges are 1s rent, 6d winding, 8d for standing room, taking-in and preparing—making a total of 2s 2d. If the middleman finds two days' work, he charges half a week or three days' rent. This, two middlemen admitted to me themselves—observing at the same time that others made the framework knitters pay rent whether they got work for them or not. Independent frames are sometimes collected in a single shop to the number of a dozen, the workmen stating that individual private frames are hardly worth the working. The highest price paid for knitting the largest size of woollen hose is 2s 1d per dozen—the smallest price for the most inferior kind, 1s per dozen; but these last articles, my informant added, and I dare say very truly, "are not worth picking up in the street". The prices rise by twopences, according to the different sizes of the articles produced. One penny three farthings of each of these twopences go to the workman—the remaining farthing to the seamer or stitcher. The lowest price paid for seaming is 4½d per dozen, and a good seamstress can manage a dozen and a half a day—for stitching, 3d per dozen, and a skilful hand can turn out about three dozen a day. In the manufacture of ribbed hose, men are almost exclusively employed. The work to a certain extent is of a superior kind, requiring superior hands, and therefore commanding superior prices. The lowest remuneration paid is 1s 6d per dozen, and the highest 3s 6d per dozen. One person makes the legs—the other the feet. The same division of labour, by the way, takes place in the manufacture of some other kinds of plain stockings. In the ribbed stocking-shop which I visited, the person knitting the feet was paid 1s 4d per dozen and he could make two dozen per day. The person knitting the legs was paid 2s 2d per dozen and he could make about fourteen pair per day. The leg-making is by far the most difficult part of the operation. Apprentices are seldom taken nowadays, the trade being so overcrowded—but when they are, they are bound for seven years, during the greater part of which they receive about two-thirds of a journeyman's wages. I ought to add, that from 12s to 14s was the highest sum at which the plain woollen hosiery knitters fixed the average of their earnings.

Be the causes what they may, there can be no doubt of the miserably depressed state of the framework-knitters. They appear to labour without either energy, or hope, or heartiness. Of the different branches of the trade, it appears to me that the Derby silk glove manufacturers are the best off and the most intelligent, and the Nottingham cotton hose makers the worst off, and the most unintelligent. Almost without exception, however, the houses of this class of labourers are squalid and neglected-looking; and in point of personal appearance and decent comfort of attire, the framework knitters must take the very lowest rank in the social scale connected with textile industry. Frame rents have been blamed for this result—the middleman system has been blamed—and the irregular semi-domestic labour, as opposed to the industrial discipline of a factory, has been blamed. As to the door at which the fault really lies, it is not my business to try and arrive at a decision. I have pointed out the peculiar industrial conditions under which framework knitters labour, and I have stated the low social status which, whether it springs from these conditions or not, at all events co-exists with them.

Index

Accidents in mines
  atmospheric causes 8, 41
  causes (1838) 9
  inadequacy of safety lamps 15
  obnoxious gases 8, 14, 25, 41, 43-5, 87
  statistics 8, 21, 40, 41
  underground deaths not always investigated by coroner 40
  vested interests seek to 'hush up' accidents 40
Acklington 4
Aircastle Hill 112
Allotments
  in a colliery village 39
  Stone Waterings, Nottingham 171-2
Amble 4
Amusements
  bowling 63
  Christmas Mummers 63-4
  cricket 128, 194,
  dog and cock fighting 63, 128
  foot racing 63
  gardening 35, 39, 172
  keeping birds (canaries) 40
  quoits 35, 63
  reading 35
  small allotments 39, 171-2
  small furniture making 35
  smoking 35
  swimming 194
Appearance of country around Wolverhampton, Willenhall, and Bilston 85
Apprentices in Potteries 116, 117
Apprenticeship not served
  Midlands knitting frame trade 168
  Nottingham lace trade 154
Arboretum 175
'Arles' 11, 31
Arnold 147
Ascent and descent of mines 9, 12, 13, 20, 20-1, 22, 42, 86
Ashby-de-la-Zouche 161
Ashley, Lord 90, 176, 178

Back-to-back housing
  Derby 175
  Leicester 194
  Nottingham 144
Baller, pottery 116
Bandsman (or bondsman) 89
Banksman 18-19, 90

Bankswoman 85, 90
Barnard Castle 3, 4
Basford 147
Beachburn Colliery 57
Beaver hat trade 137
Beeston 147
Belmont Colliery 59
Belper
  cotton factory, Messrs Strutt 185-6
  education 187
  housing and rents 186-7
  Joseph Strutt 175, 185, 186
  supply of food and necessaries 86
Benefit Societies 77
Biddick North, Colliery 12
Bigge, Mr
  on condition of woollen hosiery trade in town and county of Leicester 189-90
Bilston
  cholera 101, 103
  inhabitants almost exclusively colliers and iron workers 101
  markets 91-2
  numbers attending and not attending church and chapel 101
  population 101
  rents 103
  town 84, 112
  water supply 103
Binding
  annual 'binding' money increased 11
  'Arles' 11, 31
  contract with miners 9
  general features of 'binding' or 'bond' 31-2
Biscuit firing, Potteries 118
Bishop Middleham 4
Blackboy Colliery 59
Black Prince Colliery 60
Blast furnaces 103
Blast furnacemen 103, 104
Bleaching 154
Bloxwich 83
Blythe 4
Board and pillar method of mining 8, 24, 25, 27
Bobbin fillers 152, 153
Bobbin net or twist method of lacemaking *see* Nottingham Lace Trade
Bobbin net machinists 153-4
Bootlaces, manufacture of, in Derby 174
Borderlings 149, 151
Bouden, Mr (lace factory, Derby) 182

201

Boundaries
  Northumberland and Durham coalfield 3
  South Staffordshire coalfield 83
Bowling see Amusements
Boys' occupations
  mining
    attending to horses underground 90
    duties above ground 90
    loading refuse in iron-stone mines 87
    trappers 28, 33
    under-aged boys regularly employed in S. Staffs. collieries 90
  potteries
    assistant
      dipper 118
      dish and plate maker 117
      turner 117
    making 'stilts', 'triangles', 'cockspurs' 121
  textiles
    lace
      bleaching 154
      power weaving 182
      threading 152, 183
      warp machine assistant 149
      winders 151
    silk
      at spinning frames 177
      cleaning 181
    silk, sewing
      'twisting' boys 177-9
    wool and woolknitting
      bobbin filling and shifting (fancy branch) 199
      woolwashers' assistant 196
Brakesmen 78
Branding Junction Railway 13
Branspeth Colliery 57
Bridgett, Thomas and Co. (silk throwing and weaving establishment), Derby, 176, 180
Bridgewater Canal 112
Brindley, J. 112
Broomside Collier 58
Buckland, Professor 4, 5
Buckworth Colliery 57
Building Societies 126
'Builtass' 93 see also Fines
Buddle, Mr 6
Burnishers 120
Burslem 112, 113, 125, 128
Butty
  butty system 88, 93, 127
  character 88
  hires and pays all underground workers 88
  provides beer for underground workers 92
  tommy shops 105, 106

Canaries see Amusements
Callerton 4
'Callsman' 34
Carding and spinning factory, Leicester 195-6
Carrington 142
Cassop Colliery 49, 58
Castle Eden Colliery 47, 58
'Cavil' 77
Cemeteries
  Derby 175
  Nottingham 143
Census, hosiery industry (1844) 158, 160
Chalan Colliery 59
Chapels and churches see Religion
Charges
  Midland textile and hosiery industry frame and glove trade in Nottinghamshire district 166-7
  frame rents 149, 163, 164, 165, 166, 167, 181, 182, 184, 198, 199
  legality questioned under 'Truck Acts' 164
  proposals to remove frame rent system 165-6
  Sir Henry Halford's Bill 165
  lighting (candle or gas) 150, 153, 168, 182, 184
  mending 153
  needles 168, 182
  rents, shop 184, 197
  'standing room' 163, 164, 166, 181, 198
  'taking in' 163, 164, 166
  winding 163, 164, 166, 182, 198
  mining, Northumberland Durham coalfield
    candles (paid by hewer) 32
    gunpowder 32
    purchase of picks 32
    sharpening of picks 32
  woolcombing
    woolwashing 197
Charnwood Forest 191
'Chenening' 170
Chesterfield 161
Chester-le-Street 7
Cheque system and truck ironmaster 105
Chilton, Little, Collier 59
'Choke damp' 14
Cholera
  Bilston 91, 101, 103
  Cosely 101
  Hanley 125, 126
  Nottingham 142-3
  Wednesbury 91
  Wolverhampton 99-100
Cholera and diet of collier 101
Christmas Mummers 63-4
Clanny lamp 44

INDEX 203

Clanny, Dr Reid 44
Cleaning in silk factory 177
Clerk, weighing room 19
Coal
  district of Auckland, Teesdale, and Weardale 61
  exports, Tyne and Wear 11
  mines
    accidents 8, 9, 14-15, 21, 25, 40, 41, 43-5, 87
    depth of 3, 4
    duration of supplies 5, 6
    temperature in 7
    ventilation 6, 15, 23-4, 45, 46-51, 51-2, 94
    water in 7, 12
  mining
    occupations
      bandsman (bondsman) 89
      banksman 18-19
      boys 90
      'callsman' 34
      clerk in counting and weighing room 19
      deputies 33-4
      'doggie' 86
      driver of horse and tubs 36
      engineman 88
      hewers 28
      'holers' 88
      'hooker-on' 90
      'kecker' 53
      overmen 33-4
      putters 27, 28
      sinkers 22
      stablemen 30
      trapper 28, 33
      trimmers
        furnace 30
        lamps 27
    organisation
      'butty' system 88, 127
      lease of mines 9
      owners of royalties and mines 9, 88, 127
    technology 8, 11, 13, 18, 21-3, 24, 25, 26, 27, 28, 30, 32, 33, 42, 44, 78, 85, 86, 87-8, 93
Coal pickers 93
Coal pits, Potteries 113, 127-8
Coal trade
  effects of Civil War 119
  duty on coal exports imposed by town of Newcastle 10
  keels
    description of 78-9
    improvements in build and rig 13
    railways and the keel trade 79
    'staiths' 78

Newcastle
  number of ships (1515) 10
  shipping and tonnage, Newcastle and Sunderland (1829) 10
  seamen, numbers (early 17th century) 10
Tyne shipping
  coast trade (1764) 10
  estimates of coal shipping (1676) 10
  number of ships
    required for carrying coal to London (early 18th century) 10
    carrying coal (1772) 10
  See also Geological structure; Northumberland and Durham coalfield; South Staffordshire coalfield
Cockfighting 63, 128
Colliers and ironworkers, South Staffs. coalfield, relations between 83
Collieries
  Beachburn 57
  Belmont 59
  Biddick North 12
  Blackboy 59
  Black Prince 60
  Branspeth 57
  Broomside 58
  Buckworth 57
  Cassop 49, 58
  Castle Eden 47, 58
  Chalan 59
  Chilton, Little 59
  Cowpen 57
  Coxhoe 58
  Cramlington, West 58
  Croppy Crooks 59
  Crow Trees 48
  Danton 59
  Derwent 59
  Durham, New 58
  Edmondsley 59
  Eldon 60
  Elmore and Appleton 58
  Elswick 59
  Fatfield 12
  Gosforth 27, 32
  Grange 58
  Haswell 58
  Hartley 59
  Hatherton 59
  Hebburn 59
  Hetton, Great 58
  Hetton, North 46, 58
  Hetton, South 59
  Heugh Hall 58
  Holywell, West 57
  Huntwick 59
  Kibblesworth 59
  Ludworth 51, 59

204   LABOUR AND THE POOR IN ENGLAND AND WALES

Marley Hill 58
Mickley 60
Orclose 48
Ouston 51
Pittington 58
Rainton 58
Roddy Mark 59
Seaton Burn 51, 57
Seaton Delaval 57
Shelburn Hill 58
Shincliffe 58
Shotton 59
Tanfield Lee 59
Trimden Grange 50
Trimdon 58
Usworth 42
Walker 59
Wall's End 57
Washington 47, 58
Wingate Grange 49, 58
Wingate Grange South 59
Woodfield 57
Woodhouse Close 59
Collieries, Staffordshire
  at night 94-5
Collieries, Tyne Valley
  numbers 11
  numbers employed in 12
Consumers Cooperative at Belper, trial of 186
Cornwall, Duchy of
  owners of royalty, coal pits, Potteries 127
Courts (housing) 144, 194
Cowpen Colliery 58
Coxhoe Colliery 58
Cramlington, West, Colliery 58
Cricket 128, 194
Crime
  mining district of Northumberland and Durham 60
  Staffordshire 83-4
Croppy Crooks Colliery 59
Crow Trees Colliery 59
'Cut-ups', hosiery trade 162
'Cut-ups' and grievances of framework knitters 162

Danton Colliery 59
Darlaston
  strike against 'truck' 106
  'tommy' prices and ordinary prices 106, 107
Davy, Sir Humphrey 44
Davy lamps 8, 11, 27, 28, 32, 42, 44
Depth of pits 3, 4
Deputation to Professor Phillips 45
Deputies, mining 33, 34

Derby
  industry
    textiles
      lace
        domestic work and middlemen 183
        factory (Messrs Morley and Bouden) 174, 182, 183, 184
        hours worked 182, 183
        wages 185
      silk
        broad weaving
          domestic work 184
          few Irish weavers 184
          Messrs Stone and Kemp 185
          quality of labour and product 184
          general modernity of mills and machinery 186
      gloves and hosiery
        domestic work and the middleman's workshop 181
        middleman system 181
        Messrs Bridgett and Co (throwing and weaving mill)
          ribbon weaving 179
          'throwing' process 176
          sewing silk manufacture 177
          'twisting' and 'twisting' boys 178-9
          wages 177, 178, 179, 180, 182, 184, 185
          charges 181-2, 184
          contract 176, 184
    iron
      iron founding 174
  social
    Arboretum 175
    cemeteries 175
    education 176, 180, 187
    housing 175
    population 174
    religion 175-6
    rents 175, 186-7
    rise and progress of Derby 173-4
    River Derwent 173, 175
    sanitation 174, 176
    Strutt, Joseph 175
    water supply 175
Derwent, River 59
Dish and plate making, Potteries 117
Dipping, Potteries 118, 119
Dogfighting 63, 128
'Doggies' 88, 93
Domestic economy
  absence of
    cellar dwellings, Leicester 194
    gardens, South Staffs. colliery dists. 84, 97
    personal cleanliness, South Staffs. collieries 91

INDEX

water closets in colliery villages, Northumberland and Durham coalfield 192
alleged improvidence
　of South Staffs. iron workers 104
　of pottery workmen 128
allotments
　colliery villages 39
　Nottingham 171-2
coal pickers 93
dress of miners, South Staffs. collieries 91
food and drink 29, 35, 36, 77, 91, 92, 126, 128, 164
fuel 39, 92
furniture and furnishings 39, 40, 96, 122, 123-5, 127, 144
gardens 39, 83
level of living 91, 161
personal cleanliness 35, 36, 91, 113
social security 77, 104, 126
women, role of 40, 77, 169, 170, 171
see also Housing, Rents, Wages
Domestic work 128-9, 149-50, 155, 156, 157, 168, 169, 170, 171, 183, 184, 194, 199
Doubling 148, 149
Drainage 37
Dress, miners 21, 36, 91
Dress, pieces, silk 174
Drink 84, 92, 128, 164
Drivers, horse and tub (mining) 26
Dryers, pottery 116
Dudley 83
Duty, export of coal 10
Durham, Earl of 9, 61
Durham, New, Colliery 58
Dyers, silk factory 177
Dykes
　'dykes' 6
　Great Dyke 6, 7
　Hemerth Dyke 7

Edmondsley Colliery 59
Education
　adult education 101, 102
　dame schools 57, 60
　education census, Earl of Durham's pits 61
　education of children, pitmen's attitudes towards 61
　education and morality, Nottingham 146
　factory schools 180, 187
　level of education, mining districts 60
　libraries and reading rooms 57-9
　Londonderry, Marquess of, contribution towards education in his pits 60
　mechanics' institutes 128
　numbers attending and not attending 'cheap public schools' 84
　number, nature of schools, news rooms and libraries connected with each pit in the Northumberland and Durham coalfield 57-60
　quality of teachers 60
　Sunday schools 62, 84, 101, 176
　Tremenheere's report on education in the mining districts 60
Eldon Colliery 60
Ellmore and Appleton Colliery 58
Elswick Colliery 59
Emigration *see* Potters' Joint Stock Emigration Society and Savings Bank
Enamel firing, pottery 120
Engine house (mining) 18
Engineman 88
Embroidery work, lace ('rubbishing', fancy lace) 183
Etruria 123-5
Evictions in a colliery village
　Charlaw Colliery 74-5
　Kepier Grange 70-4
　worsened relationships between employer and employed 70
Explosions, South Hilda pit 14

Factories
　cotton: Messrs Strutt at Belper 185-7
　doubling 148
　fancy hosiery: Messrs Harris and Sons, Leicester 198, 199
　lace: Messrs Morley and Bouden, Derby 149, 150, 151, 174, 182-4
　silk throwing and weaving: Messrs Thomas Bridgett and Co., Derby 176, 179
　woollen, Leicester 196, 198
Family in the mining districts
　contribution of children to family income 63
　family ties unbroken until marriage of children 62
　marriage and the pitman 63
　security for widows, disabled, and aged 63
'Fashioned' hosiery 162
Fatfield Colliery 12
'Faults' (geological) 6
Felkin, Mr *see also* Census, hosiery industry
Fenton 113
Fever houses, Leicester 192
Fines
　'builtass' 93
　'set out and laid out' 53, 77
　Tremenheere's report on the amount lost in fines (1846) 54
　views of miners on 'set out and laid out' 53, 54-5
　views of proprietors and viewers 55-6

Finisher, hat trade 138
Fire damp 8, 14, 25, 41, 43-5, 87
'Fire ribs' 87 *see also* Board and pillar
Flaxman 122
Food and drink
 cotton workers, Belper 186
 miners 28, 35, 36, 77, 91, 92, 101
 potters 126
Foot racing 63
Forging mills and forgeman 103, 104
Fox, Mr Douglas
 evidence before parliamentary committee on health of silk twist boys 178
Foudrinier, Mr 42
Frame rents *see* Charges
Friars Goose Colliery 7
Fuel, household, mining districts 39, 92
Furnace, ventilation 23-4
Furnacemen, Potteries
 biscuit firing 118
 glossing oven 119
 slack baking 115
Furniture and furnishings, household 39-40, 96, 122, 123-5, 127, 144

Gardens and gardening 35, 39, 171-2
'Gassing', lace industry 154
General description
 coal country, Northumberland and Durham 17-18
 South Staffordshire 83-5
 Pottery district 111-13
Geological structure
 Northumberland and Durham coalfield
  classification and location of coal 5
  eight distinct beds of coal 4
  Great Dyke 6, 7
  Hemerth Dyke 7
  irregularities in lie of strata 6, 27
  layers of coal broken and scattered 5
  principal beds of coal, High Main, Low Main, Bensham, Coalyard 4
  quality of coal 5
  strata of varying thickness 3-4
 South Staffordshire coalfield
  subsidence 85
  ten yard seam and narrow seams 85
Glazing, pottery 119
'Goaf', mining, Northumberland and Durham 25
Gosforth Colliery 7, 27, 32
Grange Colliery 58
Granville, Earl of, lessee of mines 9
Gunpowder, underground blasting 13, 28

Halford, Sir Henry 165
Hanley 111, 112, 113

cholera 125, 126
 rents 125
 water supply 126
Hartley Colliery 59
Hartlepool 4
Haswell Colliery 7, 58
Haulage, mining
 horses underground 13, 26, 30, 89
 improvements in coal haulage 12
 introduction of underground inclined planes 13
 ironways after 1780 13·
 locomotives and the conveyance of coal from pit to staith 13
 'skips' 88
 square tubs intead of corves 13
Hawksley, Mr 141, 142
'Headways', mining 24
Health
 fever in Leicester 191, 192
 health of silk-twist boys 178
 ill-effects of pottery 'dipping' 119
 pollution of Bilston Brook 103
 poor law and sanitary authorities, Stoke 125
 public swimming bath 194
 see also Cholera, Drainage, Sanitation
Hebburn Colliery 59
Heddon-Ovingham 4
Hetton Great Colliery 58
Hetton North Colliery 46, 58
Hetton South Colliery 59
Heugh Hall Colliery 58
Hewers, mining 13, 28-9, 30, 32
Heyleyfield 4
'Hitches' 6
Holers, mining 88, 89, 91
Holywell, West, Colliery 57
'Hooker-on' mining 90
Hosiery 147, 158-70, 189-91, 194, 195-6
Hostmen 10
Hours of work
 hat trade 138
 hosiery trade 160, 164
 iron works 103, 104
 lace industry 34-5, 89, 127
 silk trade and 'ten hours system' 176
Housing
 Belper 186-7
 Derby 175
 Leicester 192, 194
 Mining districts
  Northumberland and Durham
   allocation of housing 38, 39
   classification of housing 37, 38
   construction and lay-out 36, 37, 40
   gardens 39
   Marquess of Londonderry and housing 76

INDEX 207

Marchioness of Londonderry and improvements in housing 76
overcrowding 39
part of wage contract 38
South Staffordshire
absence of gardens 84, 97
construction of houses 95-6
few differences in grades of housing 75-6
in Bilston 103
inferior to ordinary standards of industrial districts 84
ownership of houses 95
pitmen's housing 95
pitmen's complaints about housing 40
Nottingham
general plan of construction 144-5
built in courts and back to back 144
Potteries
Burslem 125
Etruria 123-5
Hanley 125
Longton (Lane End) 123
ownership of houses 126
Shelton 125
Stoke 125
Huntwick Colliery 59

Improvidence
ironworkers 104
pottery workers 128
Intemperance *see* Drink
Irish
Derby 184
Newcastle-under-Lyme 137
Iron mining 87, 89
Ironworks
Derby ironfounding 174
South Staffordshire
forging mills 103
forgemen 104
ironworks and the 'tommy' shop 106
relations between ironworkers and colliers 83, 101
'truck' ironmasters and the cheque system 105
Ison-Green 142

Jacquards 147, 184, 185
Jarrow Pit 7
'Jud' 25

'Kecker' 53
Keelmen and Keels *see* Coal trade
Kibblesworth Colliery 59

'Laid out and set out' *see* 'set out and laid out' and Fines
Land tenure, Nottingham
effect on the development of the town 142
Leases, mine
Earl of Granville, lessee working mines 9
Northumberland and Durham 9
Ledgley 84
Lee, William 158
Leicester
industry
wages
average
fancy work 198
framework knitters in factories 190-1
handknitting 199
machine minders 199
warp preparers 199
woolcombing factory 195
charges
fancy branch 198
plain woollens 199
rents for combs 197
woolcarding and spinning
new carding and spinning factory 189-91
woolcombing, hand
cost of handcombs 198
irregularity of hours of work 197
mobility of woolcombers 197
seasonal character of hand woolcombing 197
shop work 196
woolcombers' fear of machinery 196
woolcombing factory
feature of Leicester trade
woollen hosiery
domestic work
middlemen 194, 198
framework knitters 194
fancy branch
carried on in factories and shops 198
manufacture of woollen shirts 198
Messrs Harris and Son 198
handwork given out 199
plain branch
mainly women working narrow frames 199
social
amusements 194
education 196
health 191, 192
historical background 188-9
housing 192, 194
population 192, 193
public parks and gardens, absence of 194

rents 194
sanitation 192
Soar, River 191, 192
water supply 192, 194
Lenton 147
Lewis, Mr (Managing Partner, Thomas Bridgett and Co.) 176, 178, 180
Libraries 57, 58 see also Education
Lighting
  factories 150, 153, 168, 182, 184
  mines 8, 11, 22, 27, 28, 32, 33, 42, 44
Lisle (spun thread gloves) 162
Literature, religious 40, 62 see also Religion
Level of living 63, 91, 161 see also Domestic economy, housing, rents, wages
Local preachers 16, 62, 77-8
Lombe, John 173-4
Londonderry, Marquess of 9, 76
Londonderry, Marchioness of 76
Longton (Lane End) 113
'Long wall' method of mining
  coal 8, 87
  ironstone 87
'Long reckoning' system of wage payment 105
'Long reckoning' system and truckmasters 105
Ludworth 51, 59

Machine minders, fancy work (Messrs Harris and Son) 199
Magnesian limestone 4
Making small furniture 35
Making 'stilts', 'triangles', 'cockspurs', potteries 121
Manufacture of boys' marbles
  domestic work in Burslem and Shelton 128
  earnings 129
  manufacturing process 129
Markets
  Bilston 91-2
  Newcastle 77
Market Harborough 161
Marley Hill Colliery 58
Marriage and the pitmen 63
'Mending' lace 153, 156, 157, 183
Methodism see Religion
Mickley 4
Mickley Colliery 60
Middlemen and middlewomen
  coal
    'butty system'
      coal mining, Potteries 127
      South Staffordshire coalfield 88
  textiles 162, 163, 193, 194, 199
    middlewomen ('missuses') 156, 158, 169

lace manufacture 183
tambour work 156
Midlands hosiery industry
  charges 161, 163, 164, 165-6, 167
  domestic economy 161, 164
  geographical boundaries 161-2
  hours of work 160, 164
  industrial staple of Midlands 141
  location 158-61
  materials used 158
  organisation 162, 163, 164, 168
  rise and progress 158, 159, 160
  'truck' 168
  wages 159
Midlands iron districts
  exhibit some of the worst phases of manufacturing life 83
Miller and milling, Potteries 114, 115
Millmen, ironworks 104
Mines, coal see Coal mines
Mining, iron see Iron mining
Modeller, pottery 122
Modelling, pottery
  French superiority 122-3
Monkwearmouth 3
Monopoly
  hostmen 10
  origins of modern form 13
  of sale of coal in London 10
Monthly system of employment, Northumberland and Durham coalfield introduced after 1844 strike 31
Morley and Bouden, lace manufacturers, Derby 174, 182-3
Morpeth 4
Mosely, Mr (Government Inspector of Schools) 91, 92, 97
Moulding and moulders, Potteries 118
Movement of hatters from Newcastle-under-Lyme 137
Muggeridge, Mr, on causes of low wages in Midland hosiery industry 159

Needles, hosiery trade 132, 168
Newark 161
Newcastle 4, 9, 10, 11, 12, 40, 53, 79
Newcastle-under-Lyme
  industry, hat trade
    decline of hat trade 136
    hours of work 138
    manufacture,
      caps 136, 137
      stuff hats 137
    wages 137, 138
  town
    cholera 126
    general description 136
    influx of Irish 137

mobility of hatters 137
population 136
the Lyme 136
Newlands 4
North Staffordshire Railway 111
North Staffordshire Waterworks Co. 126
Northumberland and Durham
  coalfield
    boundaries and shape 3, 4
    geological structure 3-4, 5, 6, 7, 27
    legislation affecting coalfield 15
    parliamentary committees 13-14
    population 61
    railways 13
    rise and progress 9, 10, 11, 12-14
    rivers
      Coquet 3, 4
      Tees 3, 12, 17
      Tyne 3, 4, 7, 10, 11, 12, 17
      Wear 3, 4, 5, 10, 11, 12
    salt works 7
    towns 3, 4, 7, 9, 10, 11, 12, 13, 14, 40, 44, 53, 78, 79
  coal districts
    collieries 11, 12, 27, 32, 42, 46, 47, 48, 49, 50, 51, 57-9, 60
    crime 60
    education 57-60, 61
    family 63
    religion 16, 36, 40, 60, 61, 62, 77-8
  coal mines
    occupations
      above ground 18, 19, 34, 53, 78
      below ground 21, 22, 26, 27, 28-9, 30, 32, 33, 34, 36, 37
    technology 8, 11, 13, 18, 21, 22-3, 24, 25, 26, 27, 28, 30, 32, 33, 42, 44, 78
    wages
      above ground 66-8, 78
      below ground 23, 26, 28, 29
    wages contract
      hours of work 26, 29, 34-5
      fines and charges 32, 53, 54, 55-6
      regulation of output by pitmen 66, 67, 68, 69
  coal mining villages
    a pit row 36
    absence of underground drainage 37
    amusements 35, 40, 63
    domestic economy 29, 35, 36, 39, 40, 64, 77
    education 57-60, 61
    general idea of a colliery village 39
    housing 36, 37, 38, 39, 40, 75-6
    housing grievances 70-5
    patois of the miners 64
    pitmen and politics 62
    religion 16, 36, 40, 60, 61, 62, 77-8

  sanitation 38
  shops 36
  streets 37
  superstitions of miners 30, 35, 65-6
  coal trade
    a keel 78-9
    keelmen 78, 79
    keel trade and the railway 79
    'paydee' 79
    seamen manning coal brigs 79
    wages 79
    trade unionism and strikes 9, 11, 15-17, 52, 53
Nottingham
  industry
    lace
      hours of work
        causes of loss of time in twist factories 153
        doubling mills and Ten Hours Bill 148
      domestic work
        mending 157
        running 157
      mending (warehouse) 157
      relay system, twist factories 152-3
      stretching rooms 155
      warp factories 150
    middleman, warp domestic organisation 149
    middlewomen ('Missuses') 156, 158
    tambour work
    origins of lace industry 146
    warp and twist (bobbin-net)
      branches 146
    technology
      finishing processes
        domestic work
          mending 156
          running 157
          tambour work 155-6
        factories
          bleaching 154
          dressing 154
          gassing 154
          mending 156
          stretching 154
      manufacturing processes
        doubling
          mills 148
          necessity for 'doubling' 148
          yarns made from cotton or silk thread and delivered in 'cops' 148
        twist (bobbin net)
          preparation of weft
            bobbin filling 152
            threading 152
            winding 151

twist factories, size of 151
twist machines
  cost 150, 151
  origins 147
  steam power 151
wages
  domestic work
    mending 157
    running 157
    tambour work 156
  factories
    doubling mills
      journeyman's scale and
        independent worker's
        scale 149
    twist factories
      bobbin fillers and threaders
        151, 152
      bobbin net machinists 153
      workers in 'fancy goods' 153
      warp factories
        bleaching 154
        dressing 155
        gassing 154
        stretching 155
        warp frame workers 150
        winders 150, 151
  wages, charges
    candles 150
    deductions for middlewoman 156
    frame rents 149
    gaslight 150
    mending 153
hosiery
  domestic work
    manufacture
      chenening 170
      decline in numbers employed
        147
      middlewomen 169
      seamers (fashion) 169
      stitchers (cut ups) 169
      workshop 168
    wages
      seamers 169
      stitchers 169
Social
  allotments 171-2
  cemeteries 143
  cholera 142-3
  domestic economy
    cheneners 170-1
    seamers 170
    seamer and stitcher 171
    stitcher 169-70
  education and morality 146
  furniture 145
  housing 141, 144, 145
  land tenure and its effect on the town of

Nottingham 142
  population 143-4, 145
  rents 142, 145
  rise and progress of Nottingham 141-4
  sanitation 141, 142
  Trent, River 141, 142
  water supply 143, 145, 146
Nottinghamshire, towns and villages
  Arnold 147
  Basford 147
  Beeston 147
  Carrington 142
  Ison-Green 142
  Lenton 147
  Sneinton 147

Occupations
  coal mining
    bandsman 89
    banksman 18-19, 90
    bankswoman 90
    boys 28, 33, 90
    callsman 34
    clerk in counting room 19
    deputies 33-4
    doggie 86
    driver of horse and tubs 26
    engineman 88
    hewers 28
    holers 88
    hooker-on 90
    kecker 53
    overman 33-4
    putters 27, 28
    sinkers 22
    stableman 30
    trimmers
      furnace 30
      lamp 27
    trapper 28, 33
  coal trade
    brakesman 78
    keelmen 78, 79
    off-putter 78
    paydee 79
    seamen 79
    trimmers 78
  hatmaking
    bodymaker 137
    finisher 138
    fougher 137
  hosiery
    framework knitters 158, 159, 160, 182
    seamers 169
    stitchers 169
  ironworks
    blast-furnacemen 104
    forgemen 104

millmen 104
underhands 104
women employed about furnaces and coke ovens 104
lace
  bleachers 154
  bobbin fillers 152, 182
  bobbin-net machinists 153-4
  doublers 148
  dressers 158
  gassers 154
  menders 157
  runners 157
  stretchers 155
  tambour workers 156
  threaders 151, 152, 182
pottery
  apprentices 116, 117
  baller 116
  burnishers 120
  dipper 118
  dish and plate maker 117
  furnacemen
    biscuit firing 118
    glossing ovens 119
    slack-baking 115
  makers of stilts, triangles, cockspurs 121
  miller 114
  modeller 122
  ornamental worker 121
  painters 199
  printer 120
  thrower 116
  turner 117
silk
  boys in cleaning and spinning rooms 181
  doublers 181
  dyers 177
  finishers 177
  reelers 181
  spinners (throwers) 177
  twisters 177
  weavers, power loom 179
  wheelmen 177, 179
  winders 177, 181
wool
  combing 196, 197, 198
  yarn
    carders 196
    preparers 196
    spinners 196
    washers 196
    wool sorters 196
Occupational disease, Potteries 119
Occupational disease, textiles 156, 157
'Offputter' 78
Orclose Colliery 48
Ornamentation, pottery 121, 128
Ouston Colliery 51

Overcrowding 39, 141
Overmen 33-4
Owen Reverend, Vicar of Bilston
  adult education 102
  housing in mining villages 95
Ownership of houses
  Potteries 126
  South Staff. coalfield 95
  see also Building Societies

Painting and painters, Potteries 119-20
Parker, Mr (Chillington Iron Works) 89
Parliamentary Inquiries into Coal Trade 13, 14, 15
Patois, miners' 64
Pawn shops 104
'Paydee' 79
'Pearlings' *see* 'Borderlings'
Personal cleanliness
  of pitmen 35, 36, 91
  of the population in Potteries 113
Phillips, Professor, inquiry into accidents in mines 45
'Pickers', silk ribbon weaving 178
Pillar and board method of working mine *see* Board and pillar
Pit, coal, description above ground 18
Pit heap 18
Pit row 36
Pit shafts, single and double 23
'Pitches and Troubles' 27
Pitmen's Union
  foundation (1826) 11
  politics 62
Pittington Colliery 58
Plain woollen hosiery 199-200
Population
  Bilston 101
  Leicester 191
  Newcastle-under-Lyme 136
  Nottingham and surrounding districts 147
  Pottery towns 123
  vitality and mortality 61, 84, 113, 136, 143-4, 174, 192, 193
  Walsall 84
  West Bromwich 84
  Wolverhampton 84
Potteries
  industry
    coal mining
      butty system 127
      coal pits 113, 127-8
      Duchy of Cornwall, owner of royalty 127
      Earl Granville, lessee of pits 127
      hours worked 127
      outward appearance of coal pit workers 113

'tommying' 127
  wages 127
pottery
  domestic
    a small amount of ornaments only 128
    manufacture of boys' marbles
      Burslem and Shelton 128
      earnings 129
      manufacturing process 129
  hours worked
    furnacemen 118
    millers 115
  manufacturing process
    biscuit firing 118
    dipping 118
    dish and plate making 117
    drying 116
    enamel firing 120
    glossing 119
    making 'stilts', 'triangles', 'cockspurs' 121
    milling 114
    modelling 122-3
    moulding 118
    ornamentation 121
    painting 119-20
    pressing 115
    'saggars' 118, 121
    'slackbaking' 115
    spout and handle making 117
    statuary 121-2
    throwing 116
    turning 116-7
  output 113
  raw materials 112, 114
  wages
    apprentices 116, 117
    baller 116
    burnisher 120
    dipper 119
    dish and plate maker 117
    furnacemen
      biscuit firing 118
      glossing oven 119
      slack-baking 115
    makers of 'stilts', 'triangles', 'cockspurs' 121
    miller and labourer assisting 114
    moulders 118
    ornamental worker 121
    painters 120
    presser and boy assisting 115-16
    printer and printer's assistant 121
    spout and handle maker 117
    statuary worker 121
    thrower 116
    turner 117

  social
    amusements 128
    domestic economy 122-7
    education 128
    general description of Potteries 111-13
    health 119, 125, 126
    housing 123-6
    population 123
    Potters' Joint Stock Emigration and Savings Fund 129-35
      local clubs associated with main body 134
      membership 134
      payment of treasurer and committee 134
      Potters' Examiner 134
      Pottersville 130, 131, 133
      rules, progress, and condition of Fund 129-33
    railways 111
    religion 112, 113
    rents 124, 125
    rivers and canals 111, 112
    sanitation 125
    social security 128
    trade unions 134
    water supply 126
  towns and villages
    Bilston 84, 91, 92, 101-3
    Burslem 112, 113
    Etruria
      housing 123-5
      location 123
      property of Messrs Wedgwood 123
      rents 124
    Fenton 113
    Hanley 111, 112, 113
    Longton (Lane End) 113
    Shelton, 113, 134
    Stoke upon Trent 113
    Tunstall 113
    uniform character 112
    Willenhall 84, 112
Pressing, pottery 115-16
Prestwich 4

Quality of coal, Northumberland and Durham coalfield 5
Quality of teachers, mining districts 60
Quillings *see* Borderlings
Quoit playing 35, 63

Railways
  Branding Junction Railway 13
  early forms of railway 10
  North Staffordshire Railway 111

INDEX 213

Stanhope and Tyne Railway 13
Stockton to Whitton Park Colliery (1825) 13
Rainton 58
Ranters *see* Religion
Raw materials, pottery industry, 112, 114
Reading *see* Amusements
Redburn 4
Regulation of output by pitmen 66-70, 89
Relay system 150, 152-6 *see also* Shift work, Hours of work
Religion
  churches and chapels (other than Methodist) 16, 92, 175, 176
  local preachers, Northumberland and Durham coalfield 16, 62, 77-8
  Methodism 61, 62, 113
  Methodist chapels 36, 62, 112, 113, 176
  Old Testament names 113
  Ranters 16, 62
  religious literature 40
  see also Education, Sunday Schools
Rents
  housing
    Belper 186-7
    Bilston 103
    Derby 175
    Etruria 124
    Hanley 125
    Leicester 194
    Nottingham 145
    South Staffordshire collieries 95, 100
  industrial *see* Charges
Ribbons and trimmings, silk
  one of the principal branches of textile industry, Derby, 174
Rise and progress of
  frame knitting trade, Midlands 158-9
  industry, Derby 173-4
  lace industry, Nottingham 147-8
  Northumberland and Durham coalfield 9-15, 20-1, 42, 55
  woollen hosiery, Leicester 188-90
Roddy Mark Colliery 59
Rolley ways 13, 23, 87
Rougher, hat trade 137
Royal Commissions
  Women and children in mines 1842 15
Royalties, mining
  Duchy of Cornwall 127
  proprietors and payment of wages 88
  royalties and ownership of engines and machinery 88
'Running', lace trade 157, 183

Safety lamps *see* Clanny lamp, Davy lamp
'Saggars', pottery 118, 121

Salt water in collieries 7
Salt works 7
Sanitation
  Derby 174, 176
  Leicester 191, 192, 194
  Northumberland and Durham coalfield 38
  Nottingham 141, 142, 143
  Potteries 125
  South Staffordshire coalfield 101-2
  see also Cholera, Health
Screening, coal 10
Seamen, coal trade 79
'Seamers', hosiery 169
Seaton Burn Colliery 51, 57
Seaton Delaval Colliery 57
Sedgwick, Professor 4
'Set out and laid out' *see* Fines
Shafts, mine 23, 87-8
Shelburne Hill Colliery 58
Shelton 113, 128, 134
Shetland ponies 13, 26, 30, 89
Shields 4, 13, 14, 78, 79
Shift work
  coal mining 34-5
  iron works 103-4
  see also Relay system, Hours of work
Shincliffe Colliery 58
Shotton Colliery 59
Silk industry 174-85
Sinkers, mining 22-3
Skips, mining 88, 89
Slack baking process, potteries 117
Sneinton 147
Social security 63, 77, 104, 126, 128
South Shields Committee 14-15
South Staffordshire coalfield
  general
    boundaries 83
    coal and iron basin 83
    collieries at night 94-5
    country around Wolverhampton, Willenhall, and Bilston 85
    general landscape of dust, mud, and refuse 85
  industry
    economic interdependence of ironworkers and colliers 83
    mining
      coal
        accidents in mines 21, 87
        occupations
          bandsman (bondsman) 89, 91
          banksmen and bankswomen 90
          boys employed above ground 90
          doggie 88
          engineman 88
          holers 88
          hooker-on 90

organisation
  butty system 88
  proprietors 88
technology
  ascent and descent 86, 87-8
  engineering 85, 86, 93
  haulage 89
  subsidence of soil 85
  system of working seams 87
  trade unions and strikes 89, 101
  ventilation 94
  wages 88, 89, 90
iron
  occupations
    putters 89
    haulers (boys) 87
  system of working
    longwall method 87
iron works
  broad classification, smelting furnaces and forging mills 103
  hours of work
    day and night shifts 103
    Sunday work 103-4
    number employed per blast furnace 103
  wages
    blast furnacemen 104
    forgeman 104
    millman 104
    underhands 104
    women employed about furnaces and coke ovens 104
  wages system, long reckoning 105
tommy and truck in the coal and iron trades
  tommy shops
    allegations against some magistrates 105
    butties and tommy shops 105, 106
    comparison of ordinary and tommy prices
      Darlaston 107
      Wolverhampton 106
    kept by great ironmasters 105
    usually on premises of iron works 106
    system of operation between tommy shopkeeper and employer 106
  truck
    habitual violation of Truck Acts 105
    strike against truck, Darlaston 106
    truckmasters and the long reckoning system 105
    truckmasters and the cheque system 105
    views on tommy and truck 108-10

social
  cholera 91, 99-100, 101, 103
  coal pickers 93
  crime in Staffordshire 84
  domestic economy 91, 92, 95, 96, 97
  drink 84, 92, 104
  education 84, 101
  food 91, 92
  furniture 96
  housing 84, 85, 87, 95-6, 97-9
  level of living 91
  population 84, 101
  rents 95
  social consequences of butty system 100-1
towns
  Bilston 84, 91-2, 101, 103, 112
  Bloxwich 83
  Darlaston 106
  Dudley 83
  Ledgley 84
  Tipton 83
  Walsall 83
  Wednesbury 83, 84
  Willenhall 84
  Wolverhampton 83, 84
  West Bromwich 84
Spout and handlemaking, pottery 117
Stableman, mining 30
Staiths 10, 78
Staffordshire collieries at night 94-5
'Standing for alteration', lace industry 153

Tables
  accidents in mines 8. 9
  charges paid by framework knitters 163, 166
  comparative mortality in the drained and undrained districts of the town of Leicester 1840-1841, 1842, 193
  numbers employed in the Northumberland and Durham coalfield 1829, 14
  population of the Potteries (seven towns), 1841, 123
  prices paid for framework knitting in the Midlands 1844, 160
  truckmaster's prices compared with those of the grocer, ironmonger and draper 107
  wages
    Derby silk mill 181
    framework knitters, gloves 190-1
    in and around Derby, silk weavers 185
    in a Leicester woollen factory 196
Tactics of the Times 60
'Taking in' *see* Charges
Tambour work 155-6, 183
Tanfield Lee Colliery 59

INDEX 215

Tattins *see* Borderlings
Taylor, Hugh 6
Technology
  mining
    coal
      ascent and descent 9, 12, 13, 19, 20, 22, 42, 86
      bandsman 89, 91
      banksman 18-19
      bankswoman 90
      callsman 34
      clerk, weighing room 19
      deputies 34
      haulage 13, 26, 30, 78, 79, 89
      hewers 13, 25, 28-9, 30, 32
      hewer's cavil 77
      holers 88, 91
      kecker 53
      lighting 8, 11, 22, 27, 28, 32, 33, 42, 44
      mining engineering 8, 93
      mining technique dependent on thickness of seam 87
        longwall method 87
        pillar and board 8, 24
      overman 34
      passage ways, underground 13, 23, 24, 87
      putters 29, 33, 89
      sinking 22-3
      stablemen 30
      trappers 28, 33
      trimmers, furnace 30
      trimmers, lamp 27
    iron
      haulage 87
      longwall method 87
      putters 89
  potteries
    biscuit firing 118
    dipping 118
    dish and plate making 117
    drying 116
    enamel firing 120
    glazing 119
    making 'stilts', 'triangles', 'cockspurs' 121
    milling 114
    modelling 122, 123
    moulding 118
    ornamentation 121
    painting 119-20
    pressing 115
    printing 120-1
    'saggars' 118, 121
    slack-baking 115
    spout and handle making 117
    statuary 121-2
    throwing 116
    turning 116-17
  textiles
    lace
      bleaching 154
      'catching-up' 155, 157
      cotton and silk yarns 148
      dressing 154
      gassing 154
      mending 155, 156-7
      stretching 155
      tambour work 155-6
      twist (bobbin net) 151-3
      warp making, domestic and factory 149-50, 174, 182, 183
    silk
      'cleaning' 177
      finishing 177
      glove and hose 181-2
      sewing silk 177-8
      throwing 177
      weaving
        broad 184
        ribbon 179-80
      winding 177
    wool
      hosiery
        fancy
          handknitting 199
          machine knitting 199
        plain
          narrow frames 199
          seaming and stitching 162, 199-200
      woolcombing, hand and machinery 196-7
      yarn preparation 195
Temperature of mines 7, 8
Ten hours system and silk trade, *see* Hours of work
Ten yard seam, mining 87
Theory of coal strata 4
Throwing, pottery 116
Throwing, silk 174, 176, 177 *see* Derby, silk industry
Tipton 83
Tommy and truck, *see* South Staffordshire coalfield
Trade unions and strikes
  1832 strike and influx of rural labour 11
  1844 strike on northern coalfield 15-17, 52-3
  dissolution of Potters' Trade Union 134
  effects of 1844 strike on Miners' Union 9, 11
  extinction of coal miners' union, South Staffordshire 89
  labour surplus, northern coalfield and regulation of output 69-70
  miners' views on regulation of output by

pitmen 66, 66-7
strike against 'truck', Darlaston 106
Trappers, mining 28, 33
Tremenheere, Mr 54, 60, 90
Trimdon Colliery 58
Trimmers
   coal trade 78
   furnace 30
   lamp 27
'Troubles' 6, 27
Tunstall 113
Turning, pottery 115-17
Twist, lace 147, 150, 151, 152, 183
Twist, silk 177, 178, 179
Tynemouth 3

Underhands, iron works 104
Uniformity of pottery towns 112
Upcast and downcast shafts, pit 23-4
Usworth Colliery 42

Vend, limitation of 66
Ventilation, mines 6, 11-12, 15, 23-4, 94
Village, colliery see Northumberland and Durham coal mining villages

Wages
   coalmining 11, 12, 13, 23, 26, 28, 29, 34, 66-8, 88, 89, 90, 92, 93, 127
   coal trade 10, 12, 78, 79
   hatmaking 137, 138
   hosiery 159, 160, 182, 190-1, 196, 198, 199-200
   ironworks 104
   lace 149, 150, 151, 152, 153, 154, 155, 156, 157, 183
   pottery 114, 115, 116, 117, 118, 119, 120, 121
   silk 177, 178, 179, 180, 181, 182, 184, 185
   woolcombing 195, 198
   wool yarn 196
Wages
   contract 9, 31, 31-2, 38, 39, 79, 105, 127
   fines and charges
      coalmining 32, 53, 54-5, 55-6, 93, 105
      hosiery 162, 163, 164, 165, 166, 167, 168, 181-2, 196, 198, 199
      lace 110, 149, 153, 156
      woolcombing 197
   hours of work
      coal mining 26, 29, 34-5, 89, 127
      hatmaking 138
      hosiery 160, 164
      ironworks 103-4
      lace 148, 150, 142-3, 155, 157, 182, 183
   pottery 115, 118
   silk 176, 184
   woolcombing 187
   tommy and truck 105, 106, 107, 108-10, 168
Walker Colliery 59
Wall's End Colliery 57
Walsall 83
Warp 147, 149-50, 151, 199
Washington Colliery 45, 58
Water in mines 7, 12
Water supply 103, 126, 143, 145, 146, 175, 192, 194
Watt, James 12
Weaving
   lace 182
   silk, broad 179, 184, 185
   silk, ribbon 179, 180
Wedgwood, Messrs 123
   see also Etruria, Potteries
Wednesbury 83, 84, 91
Weighing of hewn coals 19
Wesley, J. 113, 122 see also Religion
West Bromwich 84
Westerton Colliery 46, 59
Willenhall 84, 112
Winding charges see Charges
Wingate Grange Colliery 49, 58
Wingate South Colliery 50
Wolsingham 4
Wolverhampton 83, 84, 99-100
Women and girls
   coal 12, 15, 77, 85, 90, 93
   hosiery 169
   iron works 104
   lace 148, 149, 150, 151, 152, 154, 155, 156, 157
   marbles 128
   pottery 116, 117, 119, 120, 121
   silk 177, 180, 181, 183, 184, 185
   wool 196, 199
Woodfield Colliery 57
Woodhouse Close Colliery 59
Woolcombing
   hand
      cost of combs 198
      domestic woolcombers 198
      irregular hours of work 197
      mobility of woolcombers 197
      seasonal character of woolcombing 197
      woolcombing shop 196
   machine 195, 198
Wool washing charges see Charges
Woollen hosiery, state of trade 189-91
Woollen shirt manufacture 198
Woollen yarn 195
Workshops 156, 163, 164, 168, 181, 183, 184, 196, 197, 198, 199

For Product Safety Concerns and Information please contact our EU representative GPSR@taylorandfrancis.com
Taylor & Francis Verlag GmbH, Kaufingerstraße 24, 80331 München, Germany

www.ingramcontent.com/pod-product-compliance
Lightning Source LLC
Chambersburg PA
CBHW070249230426
43664CB00014B/2456